W9-CGQ-635

TWENTY - SIX

Minnesota
Writers

T W E N T Y - S I X

Minnesota
Writers

Edited by Monica & Emilio DeGrazia

NODIN PRESS
Minneapolis

Copyright © 1995 Nodin Press

All rights reserved. No part of this book may be reproduced
in any form without the permission of Nodin Press except
for review purposes.

ISBN 0-931714-67-2

NODIN PRESS

a division of Micawber's Inc.
525 North Third Street
Minneapolis, MN 55401

Contents

Acknowledgments

Nodin Press gratefully acknowledges the publishers of the following works:

Paul Michel Baepler. "Travel." *Weber Studies,* 10.2, 1993.

David Bengtson. "Revival Meeting" and "The Cows Nearly Make It" from *The Best of Northlight,* 1990. "Her Eyes" and "Limited Supply" from *Biggy's Candy Store,* 1992. "Spiritual Fallout" from *New England Review,* 14.4, 1992.

Jack El-Hai. "All-America Grocery." Excerpt published in *Night Talk,* The Loft, 1991.

Jean Ervin. "Second Growth." First published in the *1990 Roberts Writing Awards Annual* © 1991 M. G. Roberts Foundation, Inc. Reprinted by permission of Jean Ervin.

Jon Hassler. Chapter from *Rookery Blues.* Park Rapids *Enterprise,* 10-30-93.

Dan Huntsperger. "Pandemonium, Bird Song, and the Great Unknown." Excerpt in *Loonfeather,* Spring, 1985.

Peter Leschak. "Viridian Gate." From *Seeing the Raven,* University of Minnesota Press, 1994.

Marianne Luban. "A Romance Language." *The Green Mountain Review.* Fall/Winter 1994.

Melanie Richards. "Blue Aluminum." *Shenandoah.* Winter/Spring, 1995.

Gerald Vizenor. "Ice Trickster." From *Landfill Meditations,* Wesleyan University Press, 1993.

Preface

This book is the result of a serendipitous encounter with Norton Stillman while we were browsing in a bookstore. We tried to remember how long ago his Nodin Press had published the creative prose anthology *Twenty-five Minnesota Writers.* About fifteen years ago, he said. We asked him if it was time for a second volume and if we could edit it. He said yes.

Since 1965 Nodin Press has published forty-five books, most of them by Minnesotans. The first volume of *Twenty-five Minnesota Poets* appeared in 1974, followed by a second volume in 1977 and by *Twenty-five Minnesota Writers* in 1980, all three edited by Seymour Yesner. These anthologies, often adopted by schools, showcased writers from all over Minnesota. Some of the contributors, such as Frederick Manfred and Robert Bly, were already well known, and others, such as Jon Hassler and Patricia Hampl, had yet to gain national reputations.

For this second volume of *Twenty-six Minnesota Writers* we received almost two hundred submissions of fiction and creative nonfiction. We agreed at once about accepting some manuscripts and discussed others at great length, testing our literary values. Inevitably, in selecting only twenty-six, we had to reject many excellent works. For this anthology we tried to provide variety and solid examples of the high quality of Minnesota's diverse writers. Authors include a few from the first volume, several who have made their marks during the last two decades, and others just starting out.

And we are very pleased to have Randall Scholes design and illustrate this edition. He began illustrating books with *Twenty-five Minnesota Poets.* This volume of *Twenty-six Minnesota Writers* is the one-hundredth book of his career.

Monica and Emilio DeGrazia

GERALD VIZENOR

Ice Tricksters

UNCLE CLEMENT TOLD me last night that he knows *almost* everything. Almost, that's his nickname and favorite word in stories, lives with me and my mother in a narrow house on the Leech Lake Chippewa Indian Reservation in Northern Minnesota.

Last night, just before dark, we drove into town to meet my cousin at the bus depot and to buy rainbow ice cream in thick brown cones. Almost sat in the back seat of our old car and started his stories the minute we were on the dirt road around the north side of the lake on our way to town. The wheels bounced and raised thick clouds of dust and the car doors shuddered. He told me about the time he almost started an ice cream store when he came back from the army. My mother laughed and turned to the side. The car rattled on the washboard road. She shouted, "I heard that one before!"

"Almost!" he shouted back.

"What almost happened?" I asked. My voice bounced with the car.

"Well, it was winter then," he said. Fine brown dust settled on his head and the shoulders of his overcoat. "Too cold for ice cream in the woods, but the idea came to mind in the summer, almost."

"Almost, you know almost everything about nothing," my mother shouted and then laughed, "or almost nothing about almost everything."

"Pincher, we're almost to the ice cream," he said and brushed me on the head with his right hand. He did that to ignore what my mother said about what he knows. Clouds of dust covered the trees behind us on both sides of the road.

Almost is my great-uncle, and he decides on our nicknames, even the nicknames for my cousins who live in the cities and visit the reservation in the summer. Pincher, the name he gave me, was natural because I pinched my way through childhood. I learned about the world between two fingers. I pinched everything, or *almost* everything, as my uncle would say. I pinched animals, insects, leaves, water, fish, ice cream, the moist air, winter breath, snow, and even words. I pinched the words and learned how to speak sooner than my cousins. Pinched words are easy to remember. Some words, like government and grammar, are unnatural, never seen and never pinched. Who could pinch a word like grammar?

Almost named me last winter when my grandmother was sick with pneumonia and died on the way to the public health hospital. She had no teeth and covered her mouth when she smiled, almost a child. I sat in the back seat of the car and held her thin brown hand. Even her veins were hidden, it was so cold that night. On the road we pinched summer words over the hard snow and ice. She smiled and said, *papakine, papakine,* over and over. That means cricket or grasshopper in our tribal language and we pinched that word together. We pinched *papakine* in the back seat of our cold car on the way to the hospital. Later she whispered *bisanagami sibi,* the river is still, and then she died. My mother straightened her fingers, but later, at the wake in our house, my grandmother pinched a summer word and we could see that. She was buried in the cold earth with a warm word between her fingers. That's when my uncle gave me my nickname.

Almost never told lies, but he used the word almost to stretch the truth like a tribal trickster, my mother told me. The trickster is a character in stories, an animal, or person, even a tree at times, who pretends the world can be stopped with words, and he frees the world in stories. Almost said the trickster is almost a man and almost a woman, and almost a child, a clown who laughs and plays games with words in stories. He brushed my head with his hand and said, "The almost world is a better world, a sweeter dream than the world we are taught to understand in school."

"I understand, almost," I told my uncle.

"People are almost stories, and stories tell almost the whole truth," Almost told me last winter when he gave me my nickname. "Pincher is your nickname and names are stories too, *gega*." The word *gega* means *almost* in the Anishinaabe or Chippewa language.

"Pincher *gega*," I said and then tried to pinch a tribal word I could not yet see clear enough to hold between my fingers. I could almost see no *gega*.

Almost, no matter the season, wore a long overcoat. He bounced when he walked, and the thick bottom of the overcoat hit the ground. The sleeves were too short but he never minded that because he could eat and deal cards with no problems. So there he was in line for a rainbow ice cream cone, dressed for winter, or almost winter he would say. My mother wonders if he wears that overcoat for the attention.

"*Gega, gega*," an old woman called from the end of the line. "You spending some claims money on ice cream or a new coat?" No one ignored his overcoat.

"What's that?" answered Almost. He cupped his ear to listen because he knew the old woman wanted to move closer, ahead in the line. The claims money she mentioned is a measure of everything on the reservation. The federal government promised to settle a treaty over land with tribal people. Almost and thousands of others have been waiting for more than a century to be paid for land that was taken from them. There were rumors at least once a week that federal checks were in the mail, final payment for the broken treaties. When white people talk about a rain dance, tribal people remember the claims dancers who promised a federal check in every mailbox.

"Claims money," she whispered in the front of the line.

"Almost got a check this week," Almost said and smiled.

"Almost is as good as nothing," she said back.

"Pincher gets a bicycle when the claims money comes."

"My husband died waiting for the claims settlement," my mother said. She looked at me and then turned toward the ice cream counter to order. I held back my excitement about a new bicycle because the claims money might never come; no one was ever sure. Almost believed in rumors, and he waited one morning for a check to appear in his mailbox on the reservation. Finally, my mother scolded him for wasting his time on promises made by the government. "You grow old too fast on government promises," she said. "Anyway, the government has nothing to do with bicycles." He smiled at me and we ate our rainbow ice cream cones at the bus depot. That was a joke because the depot is nothing more than a park bench in front of a restaurant. On the back of the bench was a sign that announced an ice sculpture contest to be held in the town park on July Fourth.

"Ice cube sculpture?" asked my mother.

"No blocks big enough around here in summer," I said, thinking about the ice sold to tourists, cubes and small blocks for camp coolers.

"Pig Foot, he cuts ice from the lake in winter and stores it in a cave, buried in straw," my uncle whispered. He looked around, concerned that someone might hear about the ice cave. "Secret *mikwam*, huge blocks, enough for a great sculpture." The word *mikwam* means ice.

"Never mind," my mother said as she licked the ice cream on

her fingers. The rainbow turned pink when it melted. The pink ran over her hand and under her rings.

❈ ❈ ❈

Black Ice was late, but that never bothered her because she liked to ride in the back of buses at night. She sat in the dark and pretended that she could see the people who lived under the distant lights. She lived in a dark apartment building in Saint Paul with her mother and older brother and made the world come alive with light more than with sound or taste. She was on the reservation for more than a month last summer, and we thought her nickname would be Light or Candle or something like that, even though she wore black clothes. Not so. Almost avoided one obvious name and chose another when she attended our grandmother's funeral. Black Ice had never been on the reservation in winter. She slipped and fell seven times on black ice near the church and so she got that as a nickname.

Black Ice was the last person to leave the bus. She held back behind the darkened windows as long as she could. Yes, she was shy, worried about being embarrassed in public. I might be that way too, if we lived in an apartment in the cities, but the only public on the reservation are summer tourists. She was happier when we bought her a rainbow ice cream cone. She was dressed in black, black everything, even black canvas shoes, no, almost black. The latest television style in the cities. Little did my uncle know that her reservation would describe a modern style of clothes. We sat in the back seat on the way back to our house. We could smell the dust in the dark, in the tunnel of light through the trees. The moon was new that night.

"Almost said he would buy me my first bicycle when he gets his claims money," I told Black Ice. She brushed her clothes; there was too much dust.

"I should've brought my mountain bike," she said. "I don't

use it much though. Too much traffic and you have to worry about it being stolen."

"Should we go canoeing? We have a canoe."

"Did you get television yet?" asked Black Ice.

"Yes," I boasted. "My mother won a big screen with a dish and everything at a bingo game on the reservation." We never watched much television though.

"Really?"

"Yes, we can get more than a hundred channels."

"On the reservation?"

"Yes, and bingo too."

"Well, here we are, paradise at the end of a dust cloud," my mother announced as she turned down the trail to our house on the lake. The headlights held the eyes of a raccoon, and we could smell a skunk in the distance. Low branches brushed the side of the car; we were home. We sat in the car for a few minutes and listened to the night. The dogs were panting. Mosquitoes, so big we called them the state bird, landed on our arms, bare knuckles, and warm shoulders. The water was calm and seemed to hold back a secret dark blue light from the bottom of the lake. One loon called and another answered. One thin wave rippled over the stones on the shore. We ducked mosquitoes and went in to the house. We were tired, and too tired in the morning to appreciate the plan to carve a trickster from a block of ice.

Pig Foot lived alone on an island. He came down the wooden dock to meet us in the morning. We were out on the lake before dawn, my uncle at the back of the canoe in his overcoat. We paddled and he steered us around the point of the island where bald eagles nested.

"Pig Foot?" questioned Black Ice.

"Almost gave him that nickname," I whispered to my cousin as we came closer to the dock. "Watch his little feet; he prances like a pig when he talks. The people in town swear his feet are hard and cloven."

"Are they?"

"No," I whispered as the canoe touched the dock.

"Almost," shouted Pig Foot.

"Almost," said Almost. "Pincher, you know him from the funeral, and this lady is from the city. We named her Black Ice."

"*Makate Mikwam,*" said Pig Foot. "Black ice comes with the white man and roads. No black ice on this island." He tied the canoe to the dock and patted his thighs with his open hands. The words *makate mikwam* mean black ice.

Black Ice looked down at Pig Foot's feet when she stepped out of the canoe. He wore black overshoes, the toes turned out. She watched him prance on the rough wooden dock when he talked about the weather and mosquitoes. The black flies and mosquitoes on the island, special breeds, were more vicious than anywhere else on the reservation. Pig Foot was pleased that no one camped on the island because of the black flies. Some people accused him of raising mean flies to keep the tourists away. "Not a bad idea, now that I think about it," said Pig Foot. He had a small bunch of black hair on his chin. He pulled the hair when he was nervous and revealed a row of short, stained teeth. Black Ice turned toward the sunrise and held her laughter.

"We come to see the ice cave," said Almost. "We need a large block to win the ice sculpture contest in four days."

"What ice cave is that?" asked Pig Foot.

"The almost secret one!" shouted Almost.

"That one, sure enough," said Pig Foot. He mocked my uncle and touched the lapel of his overcoat. "I was wondering about that contest. What does ice have to do with July Fourth?" He walked ahead as he talked, and then every eight steps he would stop and turn to wait for us. But if you were too close you would bump into him when he stopped. Black Ice counted his steps, and when we were near the entrance to the ice cave she imitated his prance, toes turned outward. She pranced seven steps and then waited for him to turn on the eighth.

Pig Foot stopped in silence on the shore where the bank was higher and where several trees leaned over the water. There, in the vines and boulders, we could feel the cool air. A cool breath on the shore.

Pig Foot told us we could never reveal the location of the ice cave, but he said we could tell stories about ice and the great spirit of winter in summer. He said this because most tribal stories should be told in winter, not in summer when evil spirits could be about to listen and do harm and names. We agreed to the conditions and followed him over the boulders into the wide cold cave. We could hear our breath, even a heartbeat. Whispers were too loud in the cave.

"Almost the scent of winter on July Fourth," whispered Almost. "In winter we overturn the ice in shallow creeks to smell the rich blue earth, and then in summer we taste the winter in the ice cave, almost."

"Almost, you're a poet, sure enough, but that's straw, not the smell of winter," said Pig Foot. He was hunched over where the cave narrowed at the back. Beneath the mounds of straw were huge blocks of ice, lake ice, blue and silent in the cave. Was that thunder, or the crack of winter ice on the lake? "Just me, dropped a block over the side." In winter, he sawed blocks of ice in the bay where it was the thickest and towed the blocks into the cave on an aluminum slide. Pig Foot used the ice to cool his cabin in summer, but Almost warned us that there were other reasons. Pig Foot believes that the world is becoming colder and colder, the ice thicker and thicker. Too much summer in the blood would weaken his, so he rests on a block of ice in the cave several hours a week to stay in condition for the coming of the ice age on the reservation.

"Black Ice, come over here," said Almost. Then he told us what he had in mind. A trickster, he wanted us to carve a tribal trickster to enter in the ice sculpture contest.

"What does a trickster look like?" I asked. Trickster was a

word I could not see, there was nothing to pinch. How could I know a trickster between my fingers?

"Almost like a person," he said and brushed the straw from a block as large as me. "Almost in there, we have three days to find the trickster in the ice."

Early the next morning we paddled across the lake to the ice cave to begin our work on the ice trickster. We were dressed for winter. I don't think my mother believed us when we told her about the ice cave. "Almost," she said with a smile, "finally found the right place to wear his overcoat in the summer."

Pig Foot was perched on a block of ice when we arrived. We slid the block that held the trickster to the center of the cave and set to work with an ax and chisels. We rounded out a huge head, moved down the shoulders, and on the second day we freed the nose, ears, and hands of the trickster. I could see him in the dark blue ice; the trickster was almost free. I could almost pinch the word trickster.

Almost directed as we carved the ice on the first and second days, but on the third and final day he surprised us. We were in the cave dressed in winter coats and hats, ready to work, when he told us to make the final touches on our own, to liberate the face of the trickster. Almost and Pig Foot leaned back on a block of ice; we were in charge of who the trickster would become in ice.

Black Ice wanted the trickster to look like a woman. I wanted the ice sculpture to look like a man. The trickster, we decided, would be both, one side a man and the other side a woman. The true trickster, almost a man and almost a woman. In the end the ice trickster had features that looked like our uncle, our grandmother, and other members of our families. The trickster had small feet turned outward, he wore an overcoat, and she pinched her fingers on one hand. He was ready for the contest, she was the ice trickster on July Fourth.

That night we tied sheets around the ice trickster and towed her behind the canoe to the park on the other side of the lake. The ice floated and the trickster melted slower in the water. We rounded the south end of the island and headed to the park near the town, slow and measured like traders on a distant sea. The park lights reflected on the calm water. We tied the ice trickster to the end of the town dock and beached our canoe. We were very excited, but soon we were tired and slept on the grass in the park near the dock. The trickster was a liberator; she would win on Independence Day. Almost, anyway.

"The trickster melted," shouted Almost. He stood on the end of the dock, a sad uncle in his overcoat, holding the rope and empty sheets. At first we thought he had tricked us, we thought the whole thing was a joke, so we laughed. We rolled around on the grass and laughed. Almost was not amused at first. He turned toward the lake to hide his face, but then he broke into wild laughter. He laughed so hard he almost lost his balance in the heavy overcoat. He almost fell into the lake.

"The ice trickster won at last," said Black Ice.

"No, wait, she almost won. No ice trickster would melt that fast in the lake," he said and ordered us to launch the canoe for a search. Overnight the trickster had slipped from the sheets and floated free from the dock, somewhere out on the lake. The ice trickster was free on July Fourth.

We paddled the canoe in circles and searched for hours and hours but we could not find the ice trickster. Later, my mother rented a motorboat and we searched in two circles.

Almost was worried that the registration would close, so he abandoned the search and appealed to the people who organized the ice sculpture competition. They agreed to extend the time and they even invited other contestants to search for the ice trickster. The lake was crowded with motorboats.

"There she floats," a woman shouted from a fishing boat. We paddled out and towed the trickster back to the dock. Then we hauled her up the bank to the park and a pedestal. We circled the pedestal and admired the ice trickster.

"Almost a trickster," said Almost. We looked over the other entries. There were more birds than animals, more heads than hips or hands, and the other ice sculptures were much smaller. Dwarfs next to the ice trickster. She had melted some overnight in the lake, but he was still head and shoulders above the other entries. The competition was about to close when we learned that there was a height restriction. Almost never read the rules. No entries over three feet and six inches in any direction. The other entries were much smaller. No one found large blocks of ice in town, so they were all within the restrictions. Our trickster was four feet tall, or at least she was that tall when we started out in the ice cave.

"No trickster that started out almost he or she can be too much of either," said Almost. We nodded in agreement, but we were not certain what he meant.

"What now?" asked Black Ice.

"Get a saw," my mother ordered. "We can cut that trickster down a notch or two on the bottom." She held her hand about four inches from the base to see what a shorter trickster would look like.

"Almost short enough," said Almost. "He melted some, she needs to lose four more inches by my calculations. We should have left her in the lake for another hour."

Pig Foot turned the trickster on his side, but when we measured four inches from the bottom he protested. "Not the feet, not my feet, those are my feet on the trickster."

"Not my ear either."

"Not the hands," I pleaded.

"The shins," shouted Black Ice. No one had claimed the shins on the ice trickster, so we measured and sawed four inches from his shins and then carved the knees to fit the little pig feet.

"Almost whole," announced Almost.

"What's a trickster?" asked the three judges who hurried down the line of pedestals before the ice sculptures melted beyond recognition.

"Almost a person," said Black Ice.

"What person?"

"My grandmother," I told the judges. "See how she pinched her fingers. She was a trickster; she pinched a cricket there." Pig Foot was nervous; he pranced around the pedestal.

The judges prowled back and forth, whispered here and there between two pedestals, and then they decided that there would be two winners because they could not decide on one. "The winners are the Boy and His Dog, and that ice trickster, Almost a Person," the judges announced.

The ice trickster won a bicycle, a large camp cooler, a dictionary, and twelve double rainbow cones. The other ice sculptors gave me the bicycle because I had never owned one before, and because the claims payment might be a bad promise. We divided the cones as best we could among five people, Almost, Pig Foot, Black Ice, me, and my mother.

Later, we packed what remained of the ice trickster, including the shin part, and took him back to the ice cave, where she lasted for more than a year. She stood in the back of the cave without straw and melted down to the last drop of a trickster. She was almost a whole trickster, almost.

Gerald Vizenor. I imagine the landscapes of Minnesota in everything I write, in both fiction and critical studies. Many of my stories open with a reference to nature. For instance, in "Oshkiwinag," I began, "Lake Namaran never hides the natural reason of our seasons. The wind hardens snow to the bone, cements over the cedar ruins, and hushed currents weaken the ice under the wild reaches of winter."

Manifest Manners, *a collection of essays, and* Shadow Distance:

A Gerald Vizenor Reader, *are my most recent books.* Gerald: An American Monkey King in China *won the American Book Award. I teach Native American literature at the University of California, Berkeley, and I am a crossblood member of the Minnesota Chippewa Tribe.*

Note:

It is appropriate to begin with Gerald Vizenor because Gerald was the original publisher of Nodin Press, purchased in 1967 by Norton Stillman. In the Anishinaabe language Nodin means "Wind."

JEAN ERVIN

Second Growth

Time is like a river made up of the events which happen, and its current is
strong; no sooner does anything appear than it is swept away, and another
comes in its place, and will be swept away too.

—*Marcus Aurelius Antoninus*

UNLIKE OTHER SIGHTS that I have admired and then
ceased to look at, I have never been able to ignore the
Mississippi River and its bluffs as it cuts a seven-mile
gorge through the cities of Minneapolis and St. Paul. In fine
weather when I stand on the east side of the river watching a
grain-filled barge mosey downstream and half listen to the lonely
bark of a dog from across the water, it seems impossible that a city
hides just behind those heavily wooded banks on the opposite
shore. I am smack dab in the middle of a metropolitan area of two
million people, but it is singularly blessed with a continuous park
through the gorge area with fine paths for walkers, skaters, bicy-
clists, and runners. Like so many Americans I retain a nostalgia
for a rural past while being aware that I thoroughly enjoy the con-
veniences of an urban area. The truth is that I want it both ways,
one foot in the past, but the other tentatively edging towards a
new, uncharted, and possibly dangerous precipice.

It is here at the top of the one-hundred-foot-deep river gorge that I can see the Mississippi encountered by the early explorers, and, later, nineteenth-century painters such as George Catlin and Seth Eastman. Not so very long afterward came the tourists including that prototypical Victorian Englishman, Anthony Trollope, who found the scenery of the Upper Mississippi more impressive than that of the Rhine. The bluffs, he said, were "like strange unwieldy castles . . . a succession of hills which group themselves forever without monotony."

Each season I have a new Mississippi: during spring and summer a succession of wildflowers bloom, the delicate pink rue anemone, yellow bellwort, wild geranium, and the gentle pussy willow in spring, later, thistles, goldenrod and yellow daisies. In autumn my reward as a river watcher is not just the flamboyant maples and oaks. In late afternoon, when the sun punches the water with migraine-like concentration, the quiet tenacity of still-green bushes vies with the flaming of the staghorn and skunkbush sumac, and the extravagant gold coins of the aspen tempt those greedy for adventure to make the perilous descent to the river.

But it is the bleak winter river that tantalizes. All during cold weather the ubiquitous crows caw in their hunt for food, some years congregating in mobs, an invading force of Hitchcockian fiends. One day in March this past year, snow-covered ice floes floated on black water, creating a gigantic, brutal version of a Monet water lily painting. Yet the Mississippi displays its most delicate beauty during this season when it is frozen into motionless white waves by killer winds, when no foliage impedes the panoramic views, and when the oaks lining the banks wave their bare arms in a frantic call for help—then the majesty of this heartland river is borne in on me. I am gripped with a feeling of unbearable loneliness and I think of those young soldiers stationed nearby at Fort Snelling in the early nineteeth century. This is their Mississippi.

Or is it? I never have to look far for condoms and Michelob

cans, and if I hang around for a bit I'll see a house and garden burgher cross the river road and glance around furtively before dumping last fall's leaves and less appetizing matter down the steep bank.

In the 1830's, one Pig's Eye Parrant set up a thriving business selling illegal hooch to Indians and soldiers a few miles downstream from here, one of the disreputable ancestors we all love to talk about provided they are far enough removed in time to have acquired a scrim of nostalgia. Even today, more than a century after Pig's Eye and Huck Finn knew the darker currents of life on the Mississippi, tragedy stalks this riverine world. Along one stretch of beach my family and I used to picnic and watch a beaver emerge from his lodge, but now it has become a pick-up beach: in August of 1991 a man was murdered and another badly injured. One idyllic summer morning my husband and I walked in Hidden Falls Park, wondering why Ramsey County police boats were incessantly dragging the water. The next day's newspaper told the story, a river party, a reveller missing.

And the many bridges, majestic to mundane, that span the river as it snakes through the two cities, are too often an invitation to suicides. The Washington Avenue Bridge in Minneapolis entered literary history when poet John Berryman leapt to his death in January of 1972. A sampling of newspaper headlines from the past few years shows that the bridges continue to tempt the desperate. "Man dies in jump from Minneapolis bridge; identity probed." "Minneapolis man, 80, jumps to death from Third Avenue Bridge." "Man, 24, leaps to death off the High Bridge." "Mississippi River dragged after man jumps from Wabasha Bridge." "53 year-old man dies in jump from Washington Avenue Bridge."

Some years ago the Lake Street-Marshall Avenue Bridge joining Minneapolis and St. Paul was declared the most dangerous in the state, but remained in use. For a time busses decanted passengers into a parking lot on either side of the river where a van drove them—slowly—across the rickety thing, so that they could continue their journey in another bus on the other side. We breathed a sigh of relief when at last a new bridge was begun parallel to the old one, but the great river still serves to concentrate the mind powerfully. On a beautiful spring evening cracking noises were heard hours after concrete was poured for new arches. One arch collapsed, killing a worker and narrowly missing a barge passing underneath. For months the ruined wooden mold stood like a toy snapped in two by an angry child. A testament to hubris?

But when you cross a bridge there is always the possibility of some magical change for the better. On even the smallest, one has momentarily left the earth. To poets a bridge has been the metaphor for a transitional state of being, for a mystical experience, or a journey to an ideal land. Is it any wonder that bridges are photographed and described so lovingly in travel books? The George Washington Bridge in New York, San Francisco's Golden Gate, London's myriad bridges, the seductive spans across the Seine, the Charles bridge in Prague—all have inspired visual and verbal artists. In the old mill district of Minneapolis, the handsome nineteenth-century stone arch railroad bridge known as "Jim Hill's folly" strides like a Roman aqueduct across the Mississippi, its catenary arches formed from riverbank limestone. Most beautiful of all is the Hennepin Avenue suspension bridge in Minneapolis whose cables form reverse arches, seeming to float over the Mississippi, its high towers beckoning you forward, like the gates to a medieval city.

❀ ❀ ❀

The birds are going crazy this April day as I gaze at the sand flats far below. There yellowing second-growth trees resemble the frosted hairdos that were so popular in the Sixties, an attempt, I suppose, to foster the illusion that one might extend youth a little longer. Are those trees nature's capricious way of tantalizing us, of saying come on, keep going, there's still another act? This is, after all, a "youthful" gorge in geological time, a postglacial formation cut as the St. Anthony Falls moved upstream through the Platteville limestone and St. Peter sandstone within the last seven thousand years. Before the trees are in full leaf is the best time to observe the phyllo pastry layering of grey limestone pressing on the soft sandstone. But picturesque as they look from here, I know how dangerous it is to climb down one of these steep banks to the river's edge. Ragged shards have come loose and lie scattered on walls of limestone like gravestones overturned in an abandoned cemetery.

From these heights I am as apt to look down as up at birds. On a sand spit which he could have reached only by wading through a small stretch of the icy water, someone flies a kite which at first I see as a herring gull floating on an updraft. What lures someone to climb down a steep riverbank to indulge in this somewhat childish pastime? Hope that at the end of the kite string he can recapture a childhood belief in his own invulnerability and immortality before too many people remind him that all kites are tethered? But I too like looking at the kite today, perhaps because it suggests something utterly useless and playful after the serious business of surviving a winter here. It looks a bit tentative in the April wind, but it seems to have some staying power. And though the kite is tied it also transcends the flatland and need never resign itself to being completely earthbound.

I don't need to breathe deeply to catch the fishy stench of decay drifting up from the river as I stand on the east bank watching the opposite shore, where red and blue jackets move in and out of a sandstone cave. I reflect that imagination need not climb into one of those yellow caves at some particular age, turning its back on the reaches of its youth.

In low-water years the river is a sluggish stream, one that hardly fits its portentous father-of-waters image. Then the bluffs are too grand for this aging dodderer, and I wonder if the Mississippi will make it through the current season. New islands appear every few days, the shoreline widens ominously, and towboats are called out to break up the debris jamming the river. It is hard to recall the fast-flowing, strong brown god of heavy rains and snow melt.

But how quickly I forget that discouraging old party when, in a year of plentiful snow and rain, the great river becomes a high stepper, nearly filling the bottom of the gorge. In April when at last the ice is gone I hope to spot a barge chugging upstream. Why do I romanticize these ungainly invaders? Carrying coal and oil upriver and grain downstream, they require a nine-foot channel to navigate; wildlife sanctuaries are damaged when the sand and mud plucked up by dredgers cause sterilization of the rich backwaters. After a winter of low water the dredgers hum incessantly all spring and, knowing that they are up to no good, I nevertheless delight in watching the old-fashioned grab and dip digger, as if storybook Mike Mulligan and his steamshovel had come to rescue the barges. Harmful though they may be, the barges remind me of our recent past, that Minneapolis and St. Paul were built here because the river was our first highway. They suggest Mark Twain's wry tales of learning to pilot a steamboat up the Mississippi, when he had to "get up a warm personal relationship with every old snag and one-limbed cottonwood and obscure woodpile that ornaments the banks of this river for twelve hundred miles." Perhaps it's just sentiment that holds me, for the unhurried barge seems a nineteenth-century leftover, one that has defied the odds, and as a nation of optimists we can never resist the ones who beat the odds. But I have to remind myself that the barge is a survivor of a once-thriving river commerce that has nearly disappeared, and that today I am as apt to see a lean and lovely racing shell slice through the early morning river or a powerboat headed for the passage through Lock and Dam #1 at the Ford Bridge.

On the west bank stands a patch of virgin prairie. "Do go and see it!" a local enthusiast urged me. "Virgin prairie, right here, in the city!" When I found prosiac mouse-brown grass, dutifully I reminded myself that this is after all *virgin* prairie. But why must we get so excited about a virgin forest, a virgin prairie? What is wrong with second growth? To me a Minnesota woodland is one highlighted with delicate birches, a sure sign of second growth. To listen to the environmentalists nothing but a pristine forest will do, and I should not even allow myself to enjoy some of the latecomers. But hasn't our capacity for new growth been one of our strengths?

Not far from here on the East River Road in Minneapolis lived Jeannette Piccard, the first woman to enter the stratosphere. In 1934 with her husband, Jean, Piccard piloted a balloon in an historic ascent of nearly eleven miles, a flight that is considered the beginning of space travel. When the Piccards made their voyage from Dearborn, Michigan, to Cadiz, Ohio, disapproving balloon pilots referred to it as "Mrs. Piccard's folly," and sponsors strongly objected to allowing a woman, who was also the mother of three children, to undertake the voyage. As a consequence of their pioneer flight, the College of Engineering invited the Piccards to the University of Minnesota, but it was Jean Piccard who received the professorial appointment, with Jeannette as his unpaid aide, a familiar story. Eventually she became a consultant to NASA and in 1971 received the Gilruth Award for contributions to manned space flight.

Arrogant, humorous, handsome Jeannette Piccard refused to be bound by the mundane routine expected of a faculty wife at a time when it took more than ordinary courage to rebel. With degrees in philosophy and chemistry, Piccard went on to earn her Ph.D. in education, but she was told that she could not take practice teaching courses in order to qualify as a teacher because she was "too old for a career" in the 1960s.

The intrepid pilot refused to be grounded and, working against an establishment that may have been even more formidable than the stratosphere, Piccard decided in the late 1960's to pursue her lifelong dream of becoming an Episcopal priest. In 1971 she was made a deacon and then, with the kind of viscera that few of us will ever display, Piccard entered theological school in her seventies, pitting her scholastic abilities against those of much younger students. She passed the ordination examination, but the notion of admitting women to the priesthood caused a furor within the Episcopalian church. With ten other women, Jeannette Piccard became known as one of the "outlaw" priests when she was ordained in 1974 at the age of seventy-nine.

In summer the Piccards often walked across the River Road and made their way down the steep banks of brush and limestone to swim in the river, an easy descent for two who had flown so high.

❊ ❊ ❊

When I walk on the River Road I occasionally meet a man whose name I have never learned, and usually we fall to talking. How middlewestern to chat in this small-town manner with someone I know only casually, although we are in the center of a large urban complex. (Actually I met him at Pete LeBak's barbershop, another small town institution.) He seems to have read everything ever written by Ambrose Bierce, the consummate nineteenth-century American—Civil War hero, adventurer, a man with virtually no education who became literary dictator of the West Coast, and, ultimately, revolutionary. Both of us have read *The Old Gringo*, Carlos Fuentes' fictional account of Bierce's final years. Though Bierce had become soured with his life in the States, I suspect that he carried with him south of the border that ragbag of hometruths from which we still select solace, even now in a far less adventurous era. There's always a second chance, it's never too late, you're only as old as you feel. Today Bierce would be told that he was having a mid-life crisis, though I'm sure he never heard the term. And this particular crisis came a little late. Bierce was seventy-one when he went to Mexico to join the revolution in 1913. There he disappeared. But what a dramatic way to bow out of the play.

Alas, in spite of his rich material, Fuentes succeeded in making the Old Gringo into something of a bore, possibly by stretching short-story material into a novel. But I wonder, too, is this a danger of the much vaunted mid-life or mid-career changes? Like other faddists the new-direction-seekers seem all too often to tread a much-rutted road, leaving wife, husband, children, job, simply because all the other guys are doing it, believing that, like the Old Gringo, they are joining the revolution, albeit a private one of self-realization. Anyhow, can it be a revolution if practically everyone has joined it?

And to be truthful, few of us will ascend to Jeannette Piccard's heights, or like Bierce, ride off into our personal sunset with Pancho Villa. The danger of enthusiasm for such giants is that it leads me to believe that, like the barge, with enough grit and determination I too can go on forever, on my own steam. But I had momentarily forgotten that the barge itself is being propelled from behind by the tough little towboat. It never was on its own. Without the tow it would meander all over the river, getting caught up in those shifting sandbars and hidden channels that Twain had to anticipate almost intuitively.

Though common sense warns me away from too much kite flying, still I'm charmed by the aspirations of some of my fellow elders. My barber shop-river walk acquaintance, the Bierce specialist, tells me that he is reading each issue of *The New York Review of Books* and *The New Yorker* from cover to cover in order to improve his writing style. Surely he is pushing sixty (and given the implacable length of their articles I wonder that he has any time left for writing!). Is this belief in the endless possibilities for self-improvement peculiarly American, like beating the odds? In an interview with Patricia Hampl in *The Ivory Tower* in 1966 Jeannette Piccard said, "When you fly a balloon you don't file a flight plan; you go where the wind goes. You feel like part of the air, you almost feel like part of eternity and you just float along." Here in the far Middle West we are perhaps particularly subject to the notion of new beginnings, ones with no flight plans. With untamed parks and woodland claiming parts of our spread-out cities, it sometimes seems that time is limitless too as we watch the giant Canada geese going north along the Mississippi flyway, as we fly kites and explore caves along the river bank in the middle of a metropolitan area. Less than a four-minute drive from downtown St. Paul some five hundred acres of the Crosby Nature Preserve lie along the river. Once the Crosby family farm, today this is a wilderness of swamp and second-growth woodland. In here white-tailed deer roam and gigantic yellow daisies reach for sunlight as the forest grows dark and menacing with enormous vines that entwine birch and poplar in a deathly stranglehold all summer. Walking through a swamp on raised wooden paths, I stop at a pond where magnolia water lilies will offer their tropical voluptuousness in July. Here too the great blue heron will pose in magnificent hauteur looking as if it had stepped out of a Japanese kakemono. In these woods it is possible to believe that for me time is endless too.

But then I listen. Up on Shepherd Road traffic vrooms toward downtown St. Paul and I realize that I too am moving somewhat faster than I would like to think toward my own inevitable end.

Never mind. I've squirreled away a couple of secret notions of my own. I know it's too late to learn to play the violin, but if a Jeannette Piccard can spend a lifetime soaring to new heights, perhaps I too can levitate a few more times. I'd love to learn the Charleston, and though my novel has not quite jelled, like all mothers of late-born children I know it has a bright future. My husband and I are always planning not only this year's trip, but next year's and those far down the road, the easy ones, the journeys we are saving for our "old age." (I am sixty-eight now. How American to consider that old age is not quite here yet!)

But wait. This morning, in this corridor of runners, walkers, natureniks, I hear a saxophone. And then I spot him; part way down the bank he stands on a limestone ledge playing notes that I'd last heard at Eddie Condon's half a lifetime ago. Now a tenor saxophone is a peculiar instrument to hear where you might expect the vernal flute or recorder. A sexy sounding thing, a sax belongs in rooms filled with lung-destroying air and talk that has little truck with the great blue heron and scenic wonders. The informality of its very name—sax—speaks of speakeasies, Billie Holiday, the mucky side of life.

Maybe the sax is a fitting herald of the barge, explorers climbing in and out of caves, and condoms and beer cans tossed into a sylvan world. Far better than the melodies of the delicate reedy panpipes, its suggestive tunes tell us what spring is really all about: the stink of the great river and the rest of the world unfreezing, opening itself up once again, mixing memory and desire. Standing on that limestone ledge, the latter-day Coleman Hawkins suggests the precariousness of it all. As his lusty flights and laments float downriver to Pig's Eye's old haunts, I move my feet in what just might be the rudiments of the Charleston.

Jean Ervin. I was raised in the Connecticut River Valley of Massachusetts. After graduating from Smith College I went to New York where I worked as a librarian and remedial speech teacher for five years. When my husband and I moved to Minnesota in 1957 I regarded it as a temporary exile from civilization, but here I am almost forty years later, extoling the virtues of living near the great river in an urban and urbane space. While my five sons were growing up I at-

tended graduate school and taught at the University of Minnesota, receiving my Ph.D. in 1970, and since then I have been teacher, publisher, editor, writer.

The theme of an essay or a story always seems to come at me obliquely. Walking along the Mississippi River, eavesdropping as I ride the city buses, recalling a journey—anything can trigger a new story or essay. The finished products that I like most have led to self-knowledge, but getting there is often as difficult as walking on the perilous, wooded paths that lead down to the river.

I have written two books on the Twin Cities, and I compiled and edited The Minnesota Experience, *an anthology of prose. My essays and stories have appeared in a number of publications, including* Nimrod, Iowa Woman, North Dakota Quarterly, Great River Review *and* New Mexico Humanities Review. *My essay, "Afterthoughts," was selected by Joseph Epstein for* Best American Essays 1993.

Jean Ervin

Photo by Ellen Benavides

JACK EL-HAI

All-America Grocery

I 'M HERE," called a voice in English at the front of the All-America Grocery. "Has anyone asked for me yet?"

Mei, the only worker in the store, glanced up from the banana buds she had been stacking. The tall Caucasian man staring at her over the sacks of preserved prunes looked unfamiliar. She wiped her hands on her apron and walked from the produce aisle in the rear of the store to the cash register.

The man's eyes followed her. A folded newspaper stuck out from his armpit, and he wore a soiled broad-brimmed hat. He moved toward her, striding slowly like a stork, and held out the newspaper. "You're confused," he said. "Read this. It explains everything."

Mei was the best reader of English in her family. A small advertisement was circled in green:

FINNY
is back in Minneapolis.
Hopes to see old friends at
All-America Grocery, 1615 Portland Ave.
on Tuesday the 17th.

The man smiled a mouthful of yellow and the blood rushed to his forehead. He pointed to the locked glass case that held the ginseng products—small brown bottles of extract capped with eyedroppers, straw-colored tea bags, bricks wrapped in red foil, and whole roots. "Right there used to be the barrel of grape leaves. Mr. Dovalcik would grab a pair of big wooden tongs and fish the leaves out of the brine for the Greek ladies. You still carry grape leaves?"

"I have never heard of them," Mei said.

"But the mark of the barrel is still on the floor."

Mei looked down at the worn hardwood. A quarter-moon of black was faintly visible in front of the ginseng case. Never before had it caught her attention. She looked away—her uncle, if he ever noticed it, would want her to scrub it until it faded.

The man laughed. "You show your bewilderment easily, my girl," he said. "It comes from being an immigrant. I know. Where are you from?"

Mei clenched her hands behind the counter. The banana buds would attract flies if they were not refrigerated promptly. She tossed her head and felt her thick braid thump her spine. "Vietnam. My family owns this store."

"I'm from Finland, originally. That's why people call me Finny. But my earliest memory is here in Minneapolis, at Minnehaha Falls—a hot day like today, with the waterfall a trickle. My father was holding me high in the air." He examined Mei's face. "Has anyone asked for me?"

"Nobody." Mei could not understand why this man had advertised for people to meet him in her uncle's grocery store. She watched him turn away from her and roam the aisles of food.

Finny bobbed up and down between the rows of food, stopping at items that caught his attention—packages of green dragon noodles, cans of jackfruit and lime leaves, bags of dried lily flowers, the open plastic bins containing live shrimp and orange squid. He suspiciously eyed the tray of apple pie slices that Mei had made in her pastry class at the community college. After taking a sniff, he made a bad face.

Mei remained at the cash register, feeling like a guard. "Any plantains?" Finny called out.

Mei shook her head. She had never heard of plantains. She winced: After a year spent at the community college learning the foods and cooking methods of this country, in comes a man talking about all kinds of food about which her teachers have taught her nothing.

Mei waited. Uncle Neng would be coming in at 10:00, just before she had to leave for class, and he would remove the man if he hadn't left by then.

"This shelf was heaven to me when I was a kid," Finny said. "You'll never guess what Mr. Dovalcik kept on it."

"Who is Mr. Dovalcik?"

"Shoe leather. That's what he called it, anyway. It was dried apricots, pressed into a sheet thin as paper. We'd tear some off, buy it five cents a foot. I think that's why I bought the store next door for my business—to be nearer to the shoe leather."

The shop next door, Mei knew, was a beauty salon owned by an Iranian woman. Mei's mother went there monthly for a tint and pedicure. She always tried to convince Mei to go there, too, but Mei didn't want her hair cut. As for getting a pedicure, nobody ever looked at her feet.

"After I went into business, Mr. Dovalcik bought my rubber stamps for years. Dozens—he didn't need so many, but he kept buying them. He had me make one for him that said 'Thank you' in big 72-point caps. He'd stamp it all over everything—customer's receipts, envelopes he'd mail, the little white butcher's cap he wore. You'd unwrap a package of herring and it would say 'Thank you' underneath all the fishies."

Finny rolled up the newspaper and swatted his knee. "He

owned this grocery thirty years, at the least. Until I walked through the door just now, I thought he'd be here forever. Your father bought it from him, I guess."

"Uncle. My father is dead." Mei said it without intending it. For a second she stared at Finny with a shocked expression. Then she walked back to the refrigerated bin and resumed stacking the banana buds.

Living with Uncle Neng had conditioned her not to talk about her father. Whenever the topic of her father arose in the house, Neng stopped what he was doing to take a position on the first step of the staircase, face Mei and her mother and deliver a furious speech. "That man called himself a husband and a father," Neng would shout, "but he was stupid and he deserved to die. Who else but a stupid man would purposely anger the black marketeers?"

In the back room of a Saigon poultry shop, the black marketeers had stabbed Mei's father behind the ear when he changed his mind about selling them his wife's old pocket watch. With his palm pressed against the side of his head and the blood streaking his forearm, he had stumbled the few blocks home and died in their only upholstered chair. Mei remembered seeing the round wound, its surface still dusted with wisps of duck feathers.

Mei did not look up from the banana buds for several minutes. Flies buzzed her ears. She heard Finny roaming the shop, pushing jars and poking plastic bags. She could not look at him.

The telephone rang. The old man stood straight and extended his neck like a turtle. Mei ran to the phone at the front counter, and Finny followed her. She placed her hand on the telephone, but before lifting it she looked over her shoulder. He was right behind her, breathing shallowly, his lips parted.

A woman was on the line. Her voice sounded accented and hoarse. "Is Finny there?"

Mei slowly lowered the receiver to her throat. Finny's cheeks had turned yellow. "It is for you," she said.

A squawk came from the phone. "No, no!" the woman said. "I don't want to *talk* to him! Why would I want to talk to him? Miss, are you there?"

"Yes," said Mei.

"I don't want to talk to him. I don't even want to think about him. So he's really there—the jerk! I just wanted to check." The woman hung up.

Mei reset the phone and stood silently. Finny had walked to the front window and looked out into the street. His sleeve slipped up his arm as he scratched the back of his neck, revealing a dry, cracked wrist. The cuffs of his pants were dirty, and a loop of torn fabric hung over the back of his shoe.

The door flew open, and the Bao family entered: Mr. Bao, round, sweaty, clad in tight pants: his wife, small and long-nosed, her hair tightly permed; and two food-stained toddlers. Finny fell back to the rear of the store. Mei looked back at him a few times, but he seemed to have disappeared among the fruits and vegetables.

The Baos bought a 20-pound sack of rice flour, frozen shrimp, milk, a carton of oatmeal, almonds, cans of mung beans and curry paste, and rose-water suckers for the kids. After they had paid for it all, Mrs. Bao set a package of dried file fish on the counter. "How do you make this?" she asked in Vietnamese.

Everyone in the neighborhood knew that Mei was a cooking student. "They only teach us American food preparation in school," she said. "But I have seen Uncle Neng make dried fish. He soaks it overnight in salt water with garlic. In the morning he pounds it with the side of his hand to make the fish tender." For a second Mei saw her uncle's hands flattened and raised to his temples, as they often were when he complained and shouted at her mother about the burden her family placed upon him—"A girl in cooking school! Her *mother* should teach her, to spare the expense of strangers doing the teaching!'"

Mei continued. "Then he bakes the fish in the oven until it's nearly burnt. He serves it with sesame oil, mustard greens and tomatoes."

Mrs. Bao left the package on the counter. "Sounds too hard," she said. The children tugged her sleeves. They left the store, followed by Mr. Bao, who cradled the sack of flour in his arms like a baby. He looked at Mei. "Don't let Uncle Neng burn you," he said. The door rattled shut.

Mei closed the cash register and leaned against the drawer for a few seconds. The store was completely silent. A panic grew in her chest. She slipped out from behind the counter, knocking over a pile of cans of adzuki beans, but did not pause to restack them. Back by the produce bin, Finny was sprawled on his stomach on the wooden floor, a heavy marking pen in his hand. Slowly, almost imperceptibly, he drew the letter "g" on a white piece of cardboard, the kind that Uncle Neng used for labeling the vegetables in their bins. Finny had already written out most of the other letters in "red cabbage."

"One moment," he breathed. After the words were completed, he held up the cardboard for Mei to see. Mei had never before seen hand-lettering like it—it was almost typographically perfect. Without a false move, each letter leaned toward the next, and each word had a beautiful shape. By comparison, Uncle Neng's signs looked like hurried scratchings.

"I hand-carved the matrix boards for some of my rubber stamps," Finny said. "Even if a stamp just says 'Received' or 'Payment Overdue,' it can still look pretty. Lots of people see your signs—they should look nice." He pulled the signs with Uncle Neng's lettering off the produce case. "This one—I can't even read it. What does it say?"

"Plum," Mei answered.

"Now it will really say what it means to." He placed the tip of his marking pen to the fresh white surface of a new card. A smooth line of black flowed out. "I sold my shop and left Minneapolis twenty-two years ago. Can you guess where I went?"

"St. Paul," Mei offered.

"Panama. One of my customers, Enno the barber, 1712 Port-land Avenue, had a pile of travel magazines in his shop. I was waiting to get my hair cut and the magazine I was holding fell open. There in my lap I saw a picture of the port of Cristobal—a yellow sky, purple sea and creamy sand. Colors like that do not exist in Minneapolis. The taste of salt does not exist. You know what I mean."

Mei liked the taste of salt, but even more she longed for a big room, a long corridor like the one at the community college, a stretch of grass, a king-sized bed. What did the color matter? "How could you leave America?" she said.

"I had saved money. I had a trade that I could practice any-place. I was born in a foreign country, I thought, so why should I consider this city—any city—my home? Before a week was over I paid my month's rent, closed the shop, and took the Silver Streak to L.A. I boarded the *S.S. Smart* in San Pedro Harbor and stepped onto the pier in Cristobal, not knowing anyone, 53 hours later."

Finny's "Plum" was fat-lettered and cheerful. Uncle Neng wouldn't like it. "I'll tape up the sign," Mei said.

"These potatoes are next," Finny said. "How was I to know that rubber stamps were considered ridiculous extravagances in Panama? I went from shop to shop demonstrating my wares: "Correo aéreo" on envelopes, "Gracias" on bills and receipts. The shopkeepers laughed at me. They could write out those words in a second, they said, if they ever wanted to. Women stared into the windows of my tiny storefront, shook their heads, and walked on. My business starved. I took another job, delivering corn chips. You sell corn chips here?"

"Curry flavored."

The bell rang as a woman hobbled into the shop. Mei moved halfway to the register. The woman appeared to be holding her breath, and her hand clutched several small colored pictures. She glanced once at the rear of the shop and marched up to Mei.

"Where is a scale?" she asked. Her neck quivered with tension.

Mei pointed to a scale next to the meat counter. The woman turned and tossed her packet of picture cards onto it. She squinted to read the weight, making her eyes black slits. "Barely two ounces," she declared loudly. "Two ounces in 22 years. Less weight than a—" She looked around the store, swung her short arms and grabbed a piece of purple meat on the meat counter. She threw the meat onto the scale. "—than a pig's liver."

Blood from the liver had splattered the floor. Mei bent over and wiped the spots with her apron. She recognized the woman's voice.

The woman continued: "Lying on the floor—think I don't see you back there? What did you come back for?"

Finny rose to his feet. He blinked like a man emerging from a cave. "Gloria," he said.

"Who else would see your crazy ad and show up here? The rest are all dead. You thought you'd find Boris Dovalcik behind the counter in this shop, selling his phyllo and piroshkis? He's gone. He retired years ago to Bullhead City, Arizona, and then he died. He said he got a couple postcards from you, same as me."

Finny rubbed his yellow hands together. "Gloria, you look fine."

"Liar." She turned to Mei. "How's your English? Can you talk?"

Mei felt her adrenaline rising. "You heard me speak on the telephone. What do you want?" Uncle Neng, if he were around, would already be apologizing for the tone of her voice.

"I want you to explain to me how a grown man can all of a sudden pack his suitcase for a foreign country, leave his junky possessions with all his friends—I've still got his Studebaker in my garage!—and board the first train out of town without even a look backwards." Gloria's mouth shrank. "A couple postcards. That's the best he could do."

Both women looked at Finny. He still held the black marking

pen in his hand, delicately, as if it were a fine cigarette. He bit his lip and smiled like a naughty boy. "She's Hungarian—*that's* why she's excitable," he said.

"I'm looking at a fool—that's why I'm excitable." Gloria turned to Mei. "Is he, or is he not, a foolish old man?"

Mei had never written to her relatives remaining in Vietnam. She didn't even like to think about them. Uncle Neng said it was their own fault that they had missed the final boats able to leave safely for Hong Kong. "They talked too much about the beautiful trees and people of Vietnam. Too much talk," he said. "Now they have all the trees and people they want. And the centipedes." Mei feared that if she wrote, her cousins and aunts and uncles would respond with detailed descriptions of her father's shallow grave at the foot of the orange tree.

"It's too complicated," Mei said to Gloria.

"That's right," Finny piped. "You don't know everything. You think I was on vacation, that I had leisure time to write postcards? I was struggling—an immigrant all over again. I had to bribe the damned postman with corn chips just to get him to *deliver* my mail."

A rustle of paper interrupted Finny. Uncle Neng, wearing his sunglasses and holding the brown paper sack that contained his daily hardboiled egg and bottle of tomato juice, stood inside the front door. As usual, he had sneaked in quietly.

He coldly surveyed them, rolled up the sleeves on his shirt and twitched a corner of his mouth. Without a word he walked through the store to the refrigerator in the back room.

Finny shifted his feet uneasily, and Gloria stared straight down at the floor and sealed her lips over her protruding teeth. Finny suddenly picked up a handful of banana buds and carried them to the counter. "You worked so hard on them," he said to Mei.

Mei rang the transaction and took Finny's money. "I have to go to class," she said. She reached behind the front counter and grabbed her day pack. In four strides she made it to the front door and looked back. Finny and Gloria were frozen in place. In the rear of the store stood Neng with his arms folded around his chest, staring at the new fruit and vegetable signs.

Mei pushed open the door and walked to the bus stop right outside. She let a bus go by without rising from the bench. Finally, Finny and Gloria came out of the grocery store.

Finny fanned his face with his hat. "It's like this all year in Panama," he said.

Mei looked straight into the street.

"You think I should feel sorry for you?" Gloria responded.

"It wouldn't kill you."

Gloria laughed, a rumble that ended abruptly. "Still slick. Still a phony."

"Aren't you glad to see me?"

"I'm not sure. And don't push those little bananas at me. I don't want them."

Without noticeably turning her head, Mei peered back at the storefront of the All-America Grocery. Finny and Gloria bowed their heads at each other in combat. Behind them, behind the thick glass and the stacked display of ribbon noodles and black pickled eggs, Neng's face, without sunglasses and flat as cheese, watched. He blinked slowly. Finally, with a flick of his gaze, he looked at Mei, and his eyes narrowed.

A bus came, and even though it was the wrong bus, Mei bounded aboard. The driver rounded the corner sharply, whirling away Uncle Neng's face and spilling a young man's lunch bag into the aisle. Food tumbled out: a tuna salad sandwich, an apple and a bag of pretzels. Mei picked up the food for the man and marveled at the feel of each item. For a moment she wanted to write to her relatives in Vietnam and claim this food as her own.

Jack El-Hai. *My grandfather Abraham ended 69 years of smoking by suddenly quitting at the age of 84. During his remaining 15 years* *he needed some other way to keep his mouth busy, so he told stories. He told them compulsively, just as he had puffed cigarettes. His tales were about people whose vanity proved their undoing, animals that tried to upset God's natural order, and old ways of doing things that were much better than today's. Some of his stories were true; the rest he made up and said were true.*

As I grew up in Los Angeles, I'd listen to him, struggling to follow his meandering plots. I didn't aspire to become a storyteller. But I did want to have a view of the world, as he did, that allowed me to understand everybody's motivations and to authoritatively state whether they would fail or succeed in their endeavors. That's how I started writing stories. I'd begin at the end with a character's situation, then try to figure out how he or she could possibly end up that way.

Now, a Minnesotan since around 1980, I make my living writing non-fiction, but I find fiction much harder to produce. In a good year, I write two or three short stories. My fiction has appeared in Sunday Magazine *of the Minneapolis* Star Tribune, Twin Cities Magazine *and* Northern Lit Quarterly, *among other publications. I've also won a Loft-McKnight Award, the Loft's Mentor Series and Creative Non-Fiction competitions, and the Great Lakes Regional Writers Competition.*

Photo by William Reichard

ELIZABETH MISCHE

Berlin

M Y NEIGHBOR IS leaving her husband. I hear her going away from him, night after night through walls too-thin between houses. She says he doesn't try to make anything of himself. Tonight there's an ice storm pelting down. Our living room windows face south, where the street lamps' shadows reflect up from the glassy sidewalks as tenants skid toward home.

The Berlin Wall has been coming down for days now. Five thousand miles away, I am interested in this. I spent my childhood watching television documentaries on the vagaries of the old united Germany. Every Sunday at six my father tuned in "The Twentieth Century." He'd light yet another cigarette, there where he lay on the floor in front of the television, burning holes in the rag rug my mother'd hooked from old coats. Through wisps of smoke good Germans goose-stepped across the screen; bad ones huddled together outside communal showers, or lay stacked in intricate heaps, like so much cordwood.

"Lies," he would say at the station break, clearing his throat and sitting up to light a new smoke and to rub his ears. "It was war. Everyone was starving."

My neighbor is telling her husband that she's done everything she can, that now it's up to him. He can't just dream away his afternoons. A real man, she says, would take any job. He says something indistinct. I hear her say "Hah!" in her high-pitched accent. She is *ein Auslander;* she is, truly, a Berliner. Her husband is a dreamer—romance is the province of men, after all.

My father was a young man when I was born, and never aged in the linear way the parents of my classmates did. When I was thirteen, Nancy Kneeland told me my father was "sexy." I thought he was just fat, and wore too much grey.

Other women still tell me my father's good-looking. People still tell me I look like him, and I often catch a yellow glint from his speckled green eyes glancing back from my mirror. There are times, in a pique of anger at my children, say, or when I have to suffer some fool, when the teeth clench in my mouth and I feel what I think must be his roar swelling up in my throat, when I could swear I have not become separate from him.

This past week a friend of mine called from Wurzburg where she works for the Department of Defense. She's a school psychologist and tells me things. The IQ scores of American servicefolk stationed overseas are classified information, not merely confidential as they are stateside. She is going to Berlin for the weekend, she told me, to chip at The Wall. She plans to give each of her friends a piece of The Wall in our Easter baskets. She says it twice. I call out across the Atlantic, where have you been so far? She has been in Germany since summer, and worries out loud what her father will say if he ever meets her new boyfriend. The boyfriend is an Egyptian, which is almost African. He is supposed to be a diplomat for some extinguished government. The telephone connection is always bad, as though dolphins are nosing at the cable. Or the satellite is preoccupied with messages from a more interesting planet.

"Where have you been so far?" I shout a second time. Perhaps she didn't hear; I thought she whispered back to me, "Auschwitz."

My neighbor's husband is African-*American,* a professional

drummer, often unemployed. He is an extraordinarily cheerful man, and shovels the common sidewalk to our doors all winter, even when it's my turn. My neighbor herself is blonde, a type my father calls *echt Deutch*. She isn't very tall, but she is nicely proportioned. Their nine-year-old son Burton plays with my nine-year-old daughter Kateri.

I think of Burton's family as a sort of talisman, a touchstone of sanity in a divided world, my creative neighbor courageous and her husband and son proof of her wholeheartedness. I hope, therefore, that she changes her mind and doesn't leave—it would break Kateri's heart.

❊ ❊ ❊

The big non-surprise, of course, as the planet revolves through our seasons, is that the breach in the wall has evoked in the East Germans an interest in merchandise. This is the big evening news, how each East German is given Deutschmarks by the West German Bundesbank, and they run right out and buy VCRs and toasters and compact disc players and stuff: a case of canned pears or a pint of Eau de Freiheit. Then they go back home to the East, most of them, and then—and that's the thing: then nobody knows what. But the news is stuff; I don't know what they know about the West except for stuff. But they've plenty of experience reconstituting rubble. They're selling bits of the despised wall, one *avant* earring at a time, to believing Americans.

It just goes to show, my father says. That this is the Destiny of The Nation, he means. When I was little, even before "The Twentieth Century," he used to sing *"Mein Hut der hat drei Ecken,"* and he taught me important German words for conversation: *Kase, Brot, Aschenbacher.* He likes sentimental German songs, about Lorelei and Roslein *auf der Heide,* and *muss i' denn* to the City go, and you, *mein Schatz,* stay here. No one ever seems to be married in these songs full of Lieblein and Maries and darling Marlena. He even dances in German, with elaborate polka steps and Southern waltzing.

❊ ❊ ❊

My friend in Wurzburg calls and tells me she may transfer to Korea. She's afraid the Department of Defense may have seen its day in Europe, and there are already so few children. She says something about the rending of the Iron Curtain. "Don't," she says, "buy any Piece-of-The Wall paperweights." She'll bring home plenty for all.

My daughters aren't home tonight; they go every other weekend to their father's house in a small prairie town. Marcellus is a sweet man, thin and dark and muscular, who never voluntarily reads. He's a pretty good mechanic and keeps his jars of nuts and bolts and washers sorted to the least milli-millimeter. Inexplicably, my parents—who normally distrust strangers—loved him on first sight, my father only mildly disappointed that Sal is of Polish extraction. Dad is careful not to mention a somewhat weak chin, and insists he has a Teutonic forehead. When I left Prairie du Nord and divorced Sal, I could make no adequate explanation to anyone (it sounded silly to say the Kenny Rogers tapes were killing me). When I married him, of course, no explanation was expected.

The men since Sal have been mainly unsatisfactory. One had a fine sense of humour, yet was too broad in the hips. Another with a trim physique was stingy in small things. Another wore beautiful shirts, but I couldn't ignore a tendency to pun and read the fiction of Borges and Céline. None of them has been as good a kisser as Sal.

For the past year I don't seem to fall in love at all, except with gay men. My current crush is Alexei, a film scholar with a Bart Simpson haircut and long legs, who teaches parttime at the University in Minneapolis. He shares with me all the details of his love affairs, all longing and disappointment. He once told me (thinking a brassist would understand) that orality is a more significant theme in gay semiotics than the heterosex's phallicism. I ventured to suggest that orality might have been given short shrift in heterosexual typology. We've said no more on that subject.

Alexei loves to sleep until late morning. After the kids have gone to school and I have spent a couple of hours reading scores, and before I can decently practice my French horn (the walls being thin, and it always being simplest to avoid complaints) I sometimes wake him. We schmooze a while about the state of the planet and the latest show Uptown. Alexei will interrupt some small silence with a question about groceries. He is an adventuresome chef, and several times a week cooks at my house, where the light is better, he says. Also, his housemate sometimes brings home a date for cocktails. And you know what that means.

I wonder. Why it is that I always anticipate disaster and mayhem within my field of vision? Why do I anticipate the leaden lining to each silvery cloud? The Wall, for instance. I worry: while everybody's dancing in the streets, history is realigning itself, dialectics moving aside for new adventures. My sense is that opportunity, like melody, is liable to endless permutations. Who, for instance, would have imagined I'd marry Sal, the son of a farmer (well, the son of a sod farmer) and give birth to three exquisite girlchildren, redhaired and browneyed and cheerful.

They never stop talking. Becky loves facts, and will inform a person of the major exports of any country in the Western Hemisphere at a moment's notice. Josie is a social commentator, interpreting the ebbs and tides of popular culture. "Did you know," she said last week, "that pegged pants are on the way out? It's due to nostalgia for the mini-skirt." She cast a critical eye on my circa 1970 jeans, the last bellbottoms extant in North America.

Kateri is even more aesthetically severe. She can't believe, for instance, that musicians are real artists. Her friend Burton's mother, my neighbor, is a painter, and real artists, Kateri tells me, keep interesting arrangements of pods and cones and photographs on real wood shelves, and they burn jasmine incense and cook with cumin.

If I tried to cook with cumin they'd beg for Burger King. And incense makes me wheezy, not the thing for a horn player at all. Kateri plans to be a real artist when she grows up, like Burton's mother. I certainly hope so.

Alexei cooks two meals whenever the girls are home, one fragrant with lemon grass or sumak or cilantro for him and me, slivers of turkey breast or roughy in a thin delicious sauce and some amazing pilaf or kasha, and for the girls something he calls porcupines, hamburger-and-rice balls in mushroom soup gravy, and baked custard and sometimes a dense chocolate cake without eggs, red from a spoonful of vinegar. He mixes up pie crust for them, just to sprinkle with sugar and cinnamon, encourages them to eat the flakey mess in front of the television while he and I sip espresso in the kitchen, sucking spoonsful of raspberry mousse. Last Christmas he gave me a garlic press and a demitasse set with tiny forget-me-nots on the saucers. "They're just old," he claimed, "not antiques, just old." Old light shines under the glaze, and the crazed little blue flowers glow.

I sometimes make Alexei out to be a bit precious. He has other interests besides food and film. For one thing, he plays softball. Whenever he can. He found a class at the University where he could play a couple of innings. The class was filled with housewives getting their B.A., girls trying to meet guys, a really pussycat class, he said. "You should sign up," he said, encouraging me to exercise.

Then last week, during my quintet's rehearsal of a Handel cantata, he phoned from the hospital. One of the pussycats threw him out at second; disbelieving, he'd turned and caught the ball on his nose. The blood, he said, was amazing.

The emergency room nurses told me he'd made such a fuss

about disfigurement that they'd given him a tranquilizer. While we waited for the last X-rays he stopped passersby to discuss pain and baseball. Every few minutes he patted my knee and socked my shoulder. I thought, we should go home and take a nap—then caught myself in the impropriety of this. He smelt of blood and his bitter aftershave, something green and metropolitan.

I telephoned the girls and told Becky to put clean sheets on her bed, we'd be having a guest. Josie said she'd run to the corner store for a box of popsicles, comforting for a patient with a throat full of blood. Was Lexei ugly now? Kateri wanted to know.

He hid out at my place, only going home to check his phone messages and pick up a bottle of olive oil ("You people would starve around here. Don't you know where they keep the grocery stores?") He was fixing clams in white sauce when my father came to the door.

※ ※ ※

When The Wall first began to come down he called me late one night, happy as a clam or child, exulting that it was inevitable, you can't keep a good German down. Well, I said, at least now they can send home all those Turkish guestworkers; the West Germans could take more satisfaction in an underclass of their own complexion.

"It's natural to be happy for people of the same culture and language," my father responded. "This is just what we need to revitalize Europe."

Then, the last evening Alexei stayed with us, my neighbor called to ask if Burton could spend the night at our place; she and her husband had been having a tough time and needed a few hours alone, I probably know how it is. Throughout the early evening there was a steady murmur through the walls, punctuated by a door slamming, twice. After Alexei was asleep I popped corn for the kids and turned off the television when they'd fallen asleep. About midnight, as I was reading a Dorothy Sayers mystery in bed, I was relieved to hear cheerful rhythmic thumping on the wall behind me. I hummed a bit of Vivaldi to their beat.

So the next day at noon the living room was still wall-to-wall sleeping bags and the house reeked of garlic and I was practicing a passage from Britten's Horn Sonata in F Minor, a lament, when Dad rang the doorbell again and Burton answered our door. Kateri later told me what Dad said, "Oh, I'm sorry, I'm looking for my daughter. I must have the wrong house."

Burton must have noticed the family resemblance, because, Kateri told me, he hollered, "Some one of your relatives is here, Katerinky." I was at the adagio about this time, a doleful bit of melody.

Alexei said my father was smiling and looking for escape when he followed Kateri to the door, a dishtowel tied around his waist. "Oh," my father said, staring at the bandage taped over a metal splint on Alexei's nose. "Oh, I'm looking for my daughter." Kateri hugged Dad's hand and said, "You're in time for lunch, Grandpa. Lexei's making clam linguini. Ycch."

By the time I put down my horn and followed the garlic to the kitchen Alexei had already poured my father a Tom Collins. They were discussing farm markets they had known and loved. My father specializes in buying in quantity, squashes and eggplant and string bags full of onions from the oddly androgynous square farmwives of Yarrow County. Alexei favors the small bundles of greens and herbs the leathery Hmong gardeners sell in the outdoor market in Saint Paul, where we walk on summer Saturdays to buy spring rolls and bagels for breakfast.

They were lamenting Minnesota's climate, that makes year-round produce marketing unfeasible, as I got myself a bottle of water from the fridge and added a dollop of gin. There was a half-bottle of Piesporter to go down with the clam sauce, another attempt at anesthesia.

"How 'bout a hug for your old man?" Dad fixed me a conspiratorial gaze, daring and imploring me not to decline this formulaic show of affection. I acquiesced, caught Alexei's raised eyebrow over my father's shoulder. I patted Dad's back three times, a signal to let go. Alexei handed me a knife to slice the hothouse tomatoes.

"So, Alex, how'd you wreck your nose? Car accident?" Alexei doesn't drive. He flexed the scant muscles beneath his jersey. "Playing ball. Stupid stunt."

My father, who shops but does not cook, decided he liked Alexei, and having decided, he did the masculine thing. "Where'd you find a ball game this time of year?" He thinks sport silly, but I half-expected him to spit tobacco into the dust beneath the kitchen table.

"Oh, it's just an indoor thing at the U's palaestra. I try to keep in shape, so I scrimmage a little in the off season." No mention of "pussycats, housewives."

"Grandpa," Kateri interrupted, "I've got a joke. What's the difference between an elephant and a porkchop?"

Dad doesn't like jokes, either, unless he's the one telling them. If he hadn't decided Alexei was all right, he'd have taken the opportunity to explain to Kateri the difference between a riddle and a joke. But, feeling sporting (Alexei had mixed him another Tom Collins) he replied appropriately, "I don't know. What *is* the difference between an elephant and a pork chop?" He groped for his cigarettes.

"Well, Grandpa, if you don't know the difference between an elephant and a porkchop, I'm sure glad you're not cooking dinner tonight."

Alexei and I groaned through Kateri's giggling. And Dad laughed behind a little grimace.

Josie and Becky had set the table with the good forks and the everyday dishes, and Josie knew to put out cloth napkins for her grandfather. Becky agreed to eat the linguini, buttered; Kateri accepted the mousy-cheese sandwich Alexei grilled for her, and two—small—slices of tomato. "What's for dessert?" Burton asked.

"Surprise," Alexei told him.

"Ycch."

My father said, "Pass the bread, please."

"Grandpa," Becky asked, "do you know how many East Berliners have applied to live permanently in West Germany?"

For a moment I was afraid this was another riddle, but I had the sense to keep quiet. By the time Dad had had two platesful of linguini and begun on the Treaty of Versailles, Kateri and Burton had lost interest and asked to be excused.

While the Big Girls and my father considered the state of the world, I made coffee. Alexei said he'd forgotten to bring cream— was there milk?

"Damn," I said. "I'll run next door and borrow a cup."

Just then Josie interrupted Dad to ask, "But Grandpa, did the Poles *want* to be part of Germany?"

She had him. "Let me do that for you," my father suggested, quite out of character. He took the pitcher from my hand and asked, "Neighbor on the left or neighbor on the right?" I directed him to Burton's mother, hoping she was out of bed.

"What's making you so uptight?" Alexei asked me. "Don't pour more gin. It won't help your twitchiness."

"He makes me crazy," I sputtered, though actually my father had been pretty well-behaved so far. "Everybody else in America is glad the Allies won the Second World War, but Dad still hasn't forgiven Woodrow Wilson for his Fourteen Points."

"How does Grandpa know so much about history, Mom?" Becky was asking a genuine question, but I was fraught with history of my own.

"He makes it up as he goes along," I answered, disloyal to father and daughter both. We'd already loaded the dishwasher by the time Dad came back with his little pitcher of milk.

"What an intelligent person your neighbor is," he said. "You

didn't tell me she was Deutch. Tina's her name? A lovely woman."
While he drank his coffee he expanded upon Tina's intelligence.
"Did you know she's from Berlin? People tell me things, you
know; they can see I'm interested in their origins." I didn't suppose, then, that he'd met Tina's brown husband.

"She said that Helmut Schmidt was nothing more than the
colonial governor of Germany for the United States—Americans
don't understand, and even a lot of Germans don't realize that.
She's sharp, that woman, Tina." Dad must not have gotten
around to her traitorous naturalized U.S. citizenship. "She speaks
classical Hoch Deutsch. You can see that she's got a European education. And the true German coloring and physique."

My Dad's actually about fifth generation, depending which
side you count, his forebearers farmers and skilled steel mill
workers with enough cash to hire Irish maids. He's a certified
welder, but has read Tacitus and Neitzsche (he boasts of never
having read a novel). "You know," he says to Alexei, "when
Catherine the Great of Russia wanted to improve the quality of
life in her empire, she imported German craftsmen and engineers
and intellectuals." No mention of the later pogroms against Teutonic corruption.

Alexei said was that so, he'd had a meagre historical education.
He asked whether any of the Germans in Russia married into that
population. My father said yes, but the children weren't well accepted by their German relatives.

We took our coffee into the living room, where Alexei had
neatly folded his sheets and blankets and stacked them on the
couch. Dad sat next to the pile of bedding, then hopped halfway
to his feet when he noticed an object beneath his thigh. A brooch,
a small enamel affair, crushed pink paper varigated and creased
under a clear glaze, the three borders gold. A pretty piece of work,
seemingly too pretty for politics. Alexei's premium for donating
to an AIDS hotline.

"You should teach the girls to be more careful with their

things," my father admonished, turning the bit of jewelry in his hand. He tested its heft, palm upward, open. "Girls and their jewelry. I've never been able to figure it out, fashion. Why, during the Reich a pink triangle would have been a warning that the wearer was a homosexual."

Kateri and Burton galumphed in and Kateri asked, "Lexei, if you're spending the night again could we bake meringues?"

My father cleared his throat, the momentary intimacy suddenly too close. He avoided looking in my direction and, looking for some socially redeeming DNA to link Alexei to the Fatherland, asked, "Alec, are your family by any chance Russian?"

"No," Alexei said, grinning a charming, dangerous smile around his bandage. "They're Serbian. My father was born just outside Sarajevo."

Dad finished two of the popsicles Alexei served for dessert and discussed the flaws in the Federal Reserve System with him before sighing that he'd better start his drive back to Prairie du Nord. I suggested, insincerely, that he spend the night. He avoided looking at Alexei. "No, I sleep better in my own bed. And you know how your mother worries." She doesn't.

Kateri stood on the tops of his shoes as he walked to the door. As he buttoned his overcoat he asked her, "What do you get when you add three apples and three oranges?"

"Six," Kateri said with some contempt. "That's cinchy, Grandpa. You get six."

"No, Miss Smartypants. You can't add apples and oranges."

Kateri and Burton each rolled their dark eyes. Just then Tina came to our door looking thoroughly refreshed.

"Thanks so much" she unblushingly told me, as though there were yards of stone between the noisy pleasures of her bedroom and mine. "I can't tell you how we appreciate the break. Burton, we're going to McDonald's for lunch. *Willst du mitkommen?*" She smiled at my father, a little flirtatiously, and he tipped his feathered cap at her. They exchanged *"wiedersehens"* and she took Burton's cocoa-colored hand and strolled next door.

"Lovely woman," Dad said. "So graceful. And kind—how nice of her to take your little friend to McDonald's, Katerina." He rolled the r.

"She'd better take him," Kateri said. "She's his mother."

❊ ❊ ❊

After Dad left Alexei poured me another cup of coffee and broke out a box of Godiva chocolates. This was extravagant, especially in mid-day, but they were a gift from the woman who broke his nose. I felt my mood lift as I swallowed a praline truffle while Becky and Josie pinched the caramels and mint creams and Kateri snatched a gold-wrapped brick of dark chocolate. They went away.

"Honestly," I heard myself whine. "I don't believe the way he still goes on. I can't stand it. I always feel like I should start whistling the Swiss national anthem. But he certainly liked you. What was that about?"

Alexei stretched out the muscles in his neck and shoulders, bent his elbow 'til his small biceps bulged. "He thinks I'm your lover." He made his baritone voice bass, and growled, "Real Men play ball."

"My father despises anything remotely resembling play. He's never forgiven me for becoming a musician rather than a laboratory technician."

"Maybe, but any guy with a schnoz like this obviously possesses great physical courage. A man's man." He laughed, snorked, winced behind his bandage.

I handed him the pink brooch. "Could you believe it? I mean, that schtick with the triangle? 'During the Reich—heh heh—this would have warned the normals . . . ' And then that old strategy of his, like the Pope, inviting all people of goodwill to agree with him—Real Men, like he thinks the two of you are."

"Well, he's afraid."

I'm disappointed to have him take my father's side, and shamed by his generosity.

"I must say," my voice went on, "that you're pretty kind, considering. All those nineteenth century racial theories. The phrenology of the Faggot. The alchemy of culture and nation. I thought you'd think he's a jerk."

"I do think he's a jerk. Why do you think he got popsicles and I saved the chocolates 'til he'd gone? Ice on a stick is just what I'd like to give guys like him." He mimed cudgeling, kicked with one foot, and seemed satisfied to have accomplished his revenge with one utilitarian dessert. "It's really just theory to him. You're a little harsh toward him, you know."

"If you think he's a jerk, why are you scolding me?" My protest is thunder in my ears, but a squeak as it dribbles off my tongue.

"Because he's your father. It's different for you. You've got to let it be different for you."

Male bonding is bizarrely subtle. I may not forgive Alexei. "You never told me you were a Serb. You always say your family came from East Anglia."

"Well, they did. Those who got out."

"From Sarajevo? Come on."

"Well, let's say we were good enough for the camps everywhere, but aren't good enough for Israel."

"But you let him think. . . . "

Alexei just shrugged.

❀ ❀ ❀

Then today I had a note from my father, written in pencil on my mother's best stationary. "I hope Alexander's nose is healing. I enjoyed our visit, though there's never been a remarriage in our family. In any case, I don't know that it's wise for him to spend the night—you'll understand my meaning—when the girls are home. I hope everything will turn out for Tina and her son. The skies are clearing. We're in for a cold spell."

I am not too harsh with him; I understand every word he says: I want Tina and her husband to go back to living happily ever after; there, Dad expects ashes.

I have never been there, but I have seen the maps, with Berlin a hostage island in the midst of an inaccessible Eastern terrain. The city divided into chambered regions possessed by various national imaginaries. An organ with a lumpish function, something like a human heart, murmuring the patterns of separation, never quite having a life of its own; an existence defined by the accident of place, booming the recirculation of infected history, disappointment and anemic hope in a dreary minor key.

In time for the ten o'clock news I turn on the television, and there are more pictures, handsome blonde men kissing pretty blonde women. One curly-headed fellow pours wine into a buxom girl's mouth, buries his head in her breasts. Her mouth stays open, swallowing or laughing or ecstatic.

On this other continent the icy rain's percussive whisper continues against my walls and windows. And lying here on the rug, above the din of accordion bands and cheering, I get it; what I bet Alexei already knows: that these are the pictures my father watched for, all those years ago.

There is something Early Baroque in the repetitions I hear, a prefigured dance Dad watches for small missed steps which he imagines might be amended. Yet each altered note alters the next measure. I suppose my father is watching these same pictures tonight, though they tell us different stories. And then, with a pang of what can only be fear, I know that he, too, wishes to be good. Tear down that wall, one part of me calls out; don't touch that wall, another threatens.

They go on and on on the screen. One brick, one chunk of aggregate falls, and then another follows.

What happens when we start mining the mortar in a wall? Is the other side where we've been, or the place we start out from? Nobody knows what comes next, not the goose-stepping Waffen, or the crouching dark people; not my clever friend in Berlin or Wurzburg; nor my angry blonde neighbor who can't know what her husband might become should he cease to be a dreamer.

And where are Alexei and Burton and I in my father's frightened daydreams? He does not see us dreading him in a corner; he sees us only making his pathway smooth, and impassable, like whoever it is that showers the sleet outside down onto the pavement. I turn down the sound on the television; even without the music and the sounds of laughter, it could be the biggest party ever. Or the end of the world.

By morning the ice will have made the city shiny with danger; it will look very beautiful in the sun.

Elizabeth Mische. I love books and stories, I think, because of a Catholic girlhood preoccupied with stories of the grand scale and variations thereon. The susceptibility of truth to point of view has given me an affection for the unreliable narrator, the very rock to which mercy clings when justice fails us. After a prolix adolescence I stopped writing things down for more than a decade, instead engaged by rearing three splendid daughters and listening to what might turn into writing, the dialogue in my mind's ear between what I lived and what I read. In my thirties I began to write on the page, moved to the City, allowed cats into my life and completed the master's degree in Creative Writing at the University of Minnesota. I've most recently made my living teaching writing and literature at the University and in the community, and I've published about 50 poems and several stories in numerous magazines. I received a Loft-McKnight Award for Fiction in 1993, and I'm at work on a dissertation on representations in North

American fiction of working class women who read too much or are educated beyond their sphere, as well as two long manuscripts of fiction that may be novels. Writing is one way for me to figure out what it means to be a good person; I think it's the truth of the matter rather than the facts that count, in life and in fiction.

Photo by Malcolm MacFarlane

MELANIE RICHARDS

Blue Aluminum

WITHOUT MY GLASSES, the myopic world blurs pleasantly, giving everything a diffuse quality that suits my temperment. When I'm really concentrating, I like to lower my eyelids and gaze through my lashes because I find that when objects lose their focus, I see to the heart of things. It may be just a compensatory survival skill kicking in: as I move closer to blindness, my gut reaction sharpens.

But today the glasses come off at the psychologist's request. Prim in her navy suit, Patricia's a behaviorist who's outraged by Rorschach blots, though she did let me know that she nevertheless got an "A" in that class. I smile as her blurry but proper left hand appears to be squeezing toothpaste onto her right index finger and imagine her on a camping trip brushing her teeth with her finger, having forgotten a toothbrush. But no, the blob is transparent and looks and feels a lot like K-Y Jelly as she daubs it on my temples.

"I need to use this where I attach the electrodes," she explains. I lean back in the reclining chair, looking across at the orange light of the computer; after a moment's hesitation, I opt to put my glasses back on so I can watch the zig-zag that travels from my head down the leads and onto the screen. I'm trying biofeedback for my headaches. She says we're taking a ninety second baseline first. Sometimes I feel so erratic, I'm surprised to think I might indeed have a baseline.

Now she wants me to relax. Naturally, I relax best when I am not trying. I've never conceived of it as a state produced by will, but I don't want to be one of those whiny people who can only do things when they are "in the mood." I decide to free associate and keep scanning the computer to see what type of imagery seems to lower my tension level without rendering me a flatliner. A sucker for the forbidden, my mind turns immediately to Rorschach blots. The first one looks like a blob of ink slammed between the pages of a book; it is symmetrical, doubled perfectly. I think of a pair of mating bats or a set of androgynous angels making love. As I run through a short parade of images, I check the screen and see that these are not doing much in the way of lowering my orange line; instead, the little peaks are actually higher than when I started. Maybe I should try the black hole method: sink further and further back into a murky semi-conscious state. I think of memory and abbreviation, of how the part stands for the whole: the gull overhead for the beach beneath it, the broken chandelier of one specific childhood evening for the whole year I was eleven, and the green pick-up truck for the man who drives it. I take off the glasses again, thinking it might help. The therapist has by now turned off the overhead lights and is sitting at her desk, rifling through her Rolodex and rustling papers. I have a hard time incorporating these rather mundane noises into my fantasy life; I can't dissolve them into the shadowy place where I am trying to recede.

I decide rhythm might help, catatonic rocking maybe, but the reclining chair is something of an impediment. While looking for some lulling kind of repetitive movement, I repeat a line of Philip Levine's over and over: "To be human and to love is to feel this pain." I've always been lulled by incantation. When I was a child, I used to try and induce a trance state by repeating the phrase "blue aluminum, blue aluminum" over and over until the words blurred into each other and it would just become a pattern of sound, like a series of identical waves, like a musical refrain, something I could count on. Now I am breathing slowly, just as I do on nights when I am trying to figure something out without thinking. Then I lie on the floor in a darkened room and put my feet up on the couch; maybe the blood flow to my brain does something for me. This works especially well if I lie down at twilight and face a window. The natural transition of day to dark seems to sweep my mind gradually along with it. I try to approximate these conditions in Patricia's reclining chair. When I am finally approaching a reverie, the overhead lights suddenly flash on. I sit up and put on my glasses so I can see the orange line, which looks a lot more like the prairies of Kansas now than the Rocky Mountains, except for a last steep rise in response to the lights. As I stare at the screen, I let my thoughts wander to a man whose hands, I imagine, could do serious damage to my peace of mind; the line makes a pretty impressive peak.

Just this morning I was walking into work from the parking lot with a friend when this man materialized suddenly from his green truck as though appearing fully realized from my imagination. I could still carry on a conversation with Helen, but now I had a sense of time suspended, of one possible future hovering just beyond my reach. With his long legs, he was gaining on us, staring at me with those serious animal eyes, green and quiet and deep. I asked him if he wanted to see the newspaper I was carrying, although it was unquestionably clear that the morning's news was beside the point; still he stood for a moment reading the headlines over my shoulder, breathing lightly in my hair, before he went on.

"Did you see how he was staring at us?" Helen asked. "Do you suppose he was ravished by our collective beauty?"

"I don't think anything short of a mountain lion could ravish that man," I told her. Helen continued chattering as we walked into work and I nodded but was lost to her. I could still feel him, like an afterimage, standing behind my left shoulder.

❈ ❈ ❈

"What happened just then?" Patricia says. "Did the lights surprise you?"

"I guess I got distracted," I tell her.

She removes the electrodes and gives me a Kleenex to wipe off the goo. Then she flips through a few screens on the computer to compare my enforced period of relaxation with my baseline. Patricia indicates that I'm supposed to move to the couch for an interlude of talk. I don't know what you say to a behaviorist though I did have a rat in a Skinner box as an undergraduate. I was startled by his zest as he learned the signals that rewarded him with a single bland-appearing pellet. I admit my rat was something of a virtuoso, pressing the release bar with a precisely modulated response that convinced me I could have taught him a simple musical refrain if the course had lasted longer. As it was, the second semester explored the physiologic aspects of psychology and I was instructed to kill and dissect the very rat I'd spent all fall tutoring, cajoling and admiring. It was out of the question so instead I dropped the course, having learned long ago that whenever you can't rescue the situation, you at least have the option to run.

Unfortunately, that same semester I had a modern humanities professor named Hans Randolph who spent the first two lectures talking about World War II in what seemed to be a self-congratulatory German accent and showing slides of dead bodies, victims of the Nazi death camps. Somehow the piles of broken bodies and the rat now reduced to ligaments and sinew under someone's scalpel fused into one message for me: I dropped out of college that spring.

❋ ❋ ❋

The litany of questions begins.

"Did you get carsick as a child?"

"Yes, actually I was something of a Dramamine queen; the back seat of the car was anathema to any sense of well being."

"Are the headaches always on the same side?"

I work at a clinic and I know this is the brain tumor rule-out question. "Almost always on the left side but not inevitably."

"Do you have an aura?"

Here I barely resist the impulse to tell her, "Of course I do—people generally say it's lavender," but I know she means an aura that announces an impending headache, something theatrical like flashing lights.

"No, but I usually know beforehand when a headache is coming on. They build slowly and worsen towards nightfall, which makes me feel slightly vampirish. When I have a really bad one, I can't sleep all night." An off-Broadway production, I think: The Wedding of Hemicrania and Insomnia. The headaches start either around my left eye or at the base of my neck, then they spread in a now predictable route. The sensation becomes so distinct I could trace the pattern in ink, circling my left eye, down through my neck and into my left arm. At these times, I am a woman divided, my left side an occupied country whose primitive army carries spears and runs from my left eye to the fingers of my left hand. If I look in the mirror, what I see out of my left eye is blurry, and in the middle of the night I tentatively reach my right index finger toward my reflection, trying to trace the lines of pain, like an ancient cartographer mapping out the savage landscape of the new world.

Patricia asks what medications I have tried and scribbles down some notes while I talk. I've used ergots; you're supposed to let them dissolve under your tongue, the theory being that they get into the bloodstream quicker, and speed is essential in blocking migraines. I don't know if it's impulsiveness or basic irreverence for following directions, but about two-thirds of the time I swallow the pill before I remember I was supposed to put it under my tongue.

"If you can't abort the headache with ergots, what other meds have you tried?"

"Tylenol with Codeine and Fiorinal. Sometimes they help; sometimes nothing helps."

I was fifteen when I was first introduced to Fiorinal, long before I started having migraines. My stepfather was a drug rep for Sandoz in the seventies, shortly after Sandoz had become famous for inventing LSD. He had a company car, a yellow Impala that I had to bathe every weekend except during the Watts riots when it was declared too dangerous for me to go outside, so, fifteen years old, I sat inside reading *The Idiot* while Los Angeles burned and the yellow Impala collected dust. I knew that the trunk of the Impala was filled with samples of drugs that he would present to doctors he was trying to woo to Sandoz products. I don't know how, drunk that he was, he ever got the job. Perhaps his Great Santini person buffaloed them. I never would have trusted him with a trunk full of drugs, but then I had witnessed him smashing a hole in the bedroom wall with his fist and shattering the chandelier with a two by four. Something happened eventually, as I knew it would, and he was unemployed again. My brother and I, stationed in the bathroom one night until two or three in the morning, were crushing tablets of Mellaril and Fiorinal and washing the white and blue powder down the sink, under orders from Santini. We never did know why. Somewhere there were amphibians in the sewer systems of L.A. who were probably drowning, convinced they were aerial creatures and forgetting to run shivers of water through their gills. There was a cloud of hallucination washing into the waterways, not the first damage my stepfather had perpetrated. Every closet shelf in the house had been stacked to the ceiling with samples of barbiturates; we watched them dissolve in a haze, like a fading black and blue mark. Many years later, and again not so serendipitously, Fiorinal had entered my life when the migraines began.

Patricia tells me to relax while she reads the neurologist's report. I work with Dr. Witek and have often joked with him about his Tolstoyan consults, approaching *War and Peace* in their scope and sheer duration. Until the headaches started, I had never imagined myself the subject of one of these manifestos but I know his style well. He speaks fast, in convoluted sentences, and has that kind of comprehensive intelligence that seems most at ease summarizing, conjecturing and stepping back to view the complexities of the cosmos before coming to a conclusion. As I sat in the exam room, what bothered me most wasn't the array of tiny flashlights and little hammers that I knew were part of the routine. It was simpler than that: he was just too handsome for that kind of disinterested body contact. I knew it was just a regular part of his job but it wasn't a routine experience for me and I now thought of him as a person, not a doctor. This possibly incorrect impression was abetted by the fact that he never wore a white lab coat but instead often opted for purple shirts which struck me as distinctly unclinical. Even if I'd deluded myself about being calm, I'd had to face my physiologic agitation when his nurse took my pulse and it clocked in at 104 rather than its usual 65.

I felt a lot better when the exam actually started, reassured that I could handle it after all. My legs kicked out appropriately when my knees were hammered; he shined the flashlight in my myopic eyes, explaining that the optic nerves are the two direct routes to the brain. So there I was, pulse racing, on an exam table, letting John Witek look right into my brain. Apparently what he saw wasn't too alarming.

We talked for a while and he told me it sounded like I had classic migraines. I liked the sound of this—I've always been drawn to pure forms.

He paused to reflect and added, "I hate, at this point, to throw another drug into the fray."

I couldn't help being amused by his word choice: "Into the fray? As though I'd flung my gauntlet down?"

"Sometimes I forget that I talk like that. I must say most of my best lines in a fugue state," he responded, laughing. Then he asked about my stress level.

"Pretty high, I guess. I think too many things happened to me all at once and I'm having a hard time pulling myself back together. Have you ever had a tarot reading? There's a card with three swords through a heart. Someone drew that card for me seven years ago when I was in grad school and now it has come true. Now I know what the three swords are."

"What happened exactly? I know you got divorced."

"The next year I lost my teaching job. The department had voted me at the top of the untenured list but at the eleventh hour the dean refused to sign my contract. She was an ex-nun who was dating the head of our department. Single women never fared well under her; she always seemed to exercise a sort of executive branch veto and never even had to give any reasons. That's when I came to work at the clinic. At least I had a large vocabulary and could type. And I bought a house in a semirural area so I could keep my nine dogs; I'd been breeding and showing them. Then the little town rewrote their dog laws and took me to court, refusing to give me a grandfather clause and forcing me to find homes for seven dogs in ten days or euthanize them. They didn't even give me the option to sell the house and move. The judge said he didn't care which dogs I put to sleep. There's still a permanent restraining order on file at the county court house. Whenever there's a knock at the door, I still think it's the police. They were coming several times a week, saying the neighbors called because the dogs were barking, but it was always quiet when they arrived. Finally, I had the dogs surgically debarked; then the officer told me, 'Your neighbors know and they don't like that either.'"

"That's a lot of losses in a short period of time. And a lot of major changes. That certainly could affect the frequency and severity of your headaches."

"I often wonder if I'll ever be the same person again. It's all presented a major threat to my idealism."

"Oh no, an idealist! You can't cure idealists of headaches."

The memory of the visit makes me smile but I'm pretty sure his final words aren't included in the consult. Patricia finishes reading and asks how much free time I have.

"Well, that's a problem," I answer. "I'm working and going to school and sometimes it's very hectic."

"How many classes are you taking?" she asks.

"Just one this quarter, a literature class. It's been a challenge to how I view the world, or at least how I want to view it. In one class, the man teaching announced to us that 'up until a certain age, men just view women as a collection of body parts.' I asked him when that stopped. Later in the course, we were discussing a story and he told us, 'This is a love story that could never have happened in real life,' and I told him I was still hoping it could.

"How do you feel about what he said?" she asks.

"Before I was divorced, I would have dismissed it as cynicism but now I'm not so sure. I was driving on the freeway last week and I had a sort of epiphany—I realized it was time to either face reality or pray."

"And what did you decide?"

"To pray," I answer, allowing myself to think again of the man with long fingers, the man who drives a green pick-up truck. And I wonder if this is just part of my weakness for men in all-terrain vehicles. Is it just the accompanying flannel shirts that trigger my tactile sense, or the notion that with four-wheel drives and the requisite hiking boots, they might have the perseverance and agility to forge ahead into the depths of my heart, that darker un-charted terrain that both fears and invites invasion? I am not a woman of manicured lawns, siliconed breasts and balanced checkbook, and my life has not proceeded in a steady and linear fashion. When I was fourteen, I learned the word "vicissitudes" from reading Thomas Hardy's novels. Now at forty-one, I have lived that word, and yet I am amazed to find myself in a psychologist's office on a winter afternoon still veering toward hope, thinking to myself, "This man could be a real near-death experience." I have become acutely attuned to green trucks since this particular man has come to occupy a prominent place in my imagination. I find myself abruptly glancing over at every green truck I see, as though I really expected him to one day just drive right into my life. But it's not so simple, really. I fear a certain canine faithfulness in myself, and I worry about anyone who might trigger that, so half my brain is wishing and half is dreading, no doubt the left half.

Patricia consults her date book to come up with a second appointment for me. I actually look forward to the faux K-Y. I'm drawn to the machine whose orange line is the faithful testament to my inner world; I like to think of that orange fire flaring up when I feel desire or anger or fear. Now I will go home and lie on the floor in a darkened room practicing, as Patricia has urged me to, repeating "blue aluminum, blue aluminum" as dusk falls.

Melanie Richards. *I was born in Milwaukee, moved to Los Angeles just before my thirteenth birthday, attended Reed College, U.C.L.A. (Academy of American Poets Prize), Goddard and the University of Minnesota. Two degrees, no very tangible job skills. I've been writing poetry about twenty years (poems in* Yankee, Wisconsin Review, Aspen Anthology, Milkweed Chronicle, *and elsewhere).*

Four years ago, I attempted to write prose and it was a struggle since I had never even written narrative poetry. The length seemed overwhelming; I felt like I needed psychic trail mix. After about a year and a half, I finished my first prose piece, which Phillip Lopate selected as one of the winners of the 1992 Loft Creative Nonfiction

Awards. During the Lopate workshop, I wrote the first draft of "Blue Aluminum," and a few months later it was accepted.

I have some genre confusion with prose and when Shenandoah *published this piece as fiction, I began to realize the borders were pretty blurry. I've now come to accept that prose is on a spectrum from nonfiction to fiction and what's important is the imaginative shaping of the material, a process not unlike what memory and perception naturally do to our experience.*

I am working to find a prose structure that is more circular than linear and that works to unite intuition and emotion, experience and imagination. Why do I write? A story I recently finished, "The Childhood of an Insomniac," ends with this sentence: "I did it to calm me down, to help me remember, to make something finally that would last."

Photo by Greg Helgeson

C. W. TRUESDALE

Arabian Nights

1. Bruno

BRUNO, THE TERROR of Oxford Place in his sleek, near-blind Volvo, Bruno, out for his morning constitutional. He is old now, maybe 79 or 80, red-faced, always smiling.

Nights, you can see him sitting upstairs in his window across the street. His eyes are mirrors only, glimmering in reflected light, but he sees everything. I'm sure he saw her many times, so often he asked after her, a faint glint of wildness in his old eyes.

Days—come late spring and summer—he keeps the best and most productive garden on the street. Mostly fruits and vegetables and flowering shrubs, all groomed and cared for like the best thoroughbred. There are more spectacular gardens along Victory Boulevard—pyrotechnic ones with shooting red flowers and trumpeting vines like Mr. Panzianni's—but none are as warm and friendly, as productive and well-designed as Bruno's. His vine-ripened tomatoes, picked just a little too early, are as luscious in my kitchen window as any midwestern ones, and his pears are as succulent and juicy as any from California.

Bruno is the oldest living resident of Oxford Place. He and his brother built many of the rough sturdy old three-storey houses there. And still, warm days you can see Bruno scampering up around there in the wind. He is the smiling history of that street. A dreadful gossip. But not its conscience. Events move through his eyes but do not move him, his word a wry sort of kindness, his smile a blessing—perhaps because he's done it all: the wildness, the women, the hoosegow, and every single bar on Staten Island.

"How do you feel, Bruno?"

"Oh, I feel just fine, Bill. Just fine. It was all just a dream."

And he shoved it all away from him with his hands, like a wheelbarrow full of weeds or the booze he couldn't take any more. One day the ambulance came to take him away. He was gone for weeks and weeks. A prostate operation, and it almost did him in. For awhile after he came back he was just a grim harvest of himself. "It was all just a dream, Bill."

I know what you mean, Bruno. I know what you mean.

2. Schirra

I was walking with Rhoda down along an escarpment stretching far out to sea (like Shovel Point on Lake Superior with its long rust-colored cliff sloping down into the water). She was clinging to me like a big monkey, out of fear, though normally she wasn't afraid of the heights I took her to. (O—those incredible heights!) There were dangerous cliffs all around and the surf was pounding wildly. When we had gotten very close to the water, we realized we would have to climb down through the icy surf to reach the tiny gold island just beyond, with its Greekish pavilions and Victorian summer houses and its arrangement of Bonsai trees. I knew that I would have to carry her and that this would make me feel very strong and proud, as she always did, even after we stopped seeing one another. And I knew that she would enjoy this too, as she did everything.

On the western slope of the island was a hidden ashram-type building with lots of American Buddhists sitting around, not doing much of anything, but listening to the strange music that tugged at the curtains a little and ruffled their beards. Allen Ginsberg was there. And Buff Bradley, my old student. And Armand Schwerner, the poet. And I think that my former therapist, Betty Kronsky, was there too, because I remember the many times she urged me to try Buddhism, as a way perhaps of containing or even countering my dangerous obsession with Rhoda, the Scheharazade of this story, my Lady of a Thousand Nights. And Peter Mathiessen was there too, a little stoned, holding a miniature snow leopard by a golden chain. Armand looked painful enough as usual—he was holding his Pain like a baby and rocking or nursing it—at which point in this dream I heard Schirra (which means "song" in Hebrew), a real baby, in Rhoda's room singing and singing pieces of an inscrutable melody, from no culture I know of—lovely but unpatterned.

It seemed so real: the girl-child singing in her crib in the dark side of the room, and Rhoda breathing quietly. We were almost a family and Schirra was almost our song.

3. Armand

I had one of those long talks with Armand yesterday in the seedy bar down the street from Mr. Panzianni's garden. It was the first time I'd seen him since I got back from Minnesota and had to face the particular hell Rhoda had prepared for me. I was feeling very low when I went down to meet him (it being Sunday—"our day" after all, when her ex-husband Phil took her kids). But I came away feeling very different and wondering whether Armand did, as some friends claim, possess special powers. It wasn't anything specific—to the point or the story—that he said or I said, just something that happened, the way a dull piece of writing will sometimes just take off for no apparent reason and there are birds everywhere, chattering along the furrows.

Armand, his funny body, big chest, small hips, short legs—

Armand reminds me exactly of the Goat God Pan, even to the straggly beard and the always strange intensity of his eyes. Hypnotic. Like a cobra's. More than any of the friends I've talked with over these past difficult weeks, Armand was very philosophical towards me (as a priest might be, if I were inclined that way). He kept pushing me through Rhoda to the universals, through his Tantric Buddhist texts, always from the specific to the general, from Rhoda to Woman to Women to the universality of Pain. I came away feeling light as a bird or a feather in the winds of chance.

That night I had what I took to be an excessively lovely and romantic dream, though Armand—either from discomfort over his role in the experience or his guttural dislike of Rhoda—suggested, later, there might be just a wisp of sentimentality here, wishful thinking or dreaming, which distracted me from what he defined as my Task.

In the dream, I am walking in a slow stately procession along a clean white road in Arabia. It is a wedding procession. The bride is Rhoda, is Scheharazade, the captive Jewish Princess. The husband-to-be is the Dreamer. The Three Wise Men gaily surround the couple. They are called the Great Persuaders. The procession is led by the Magician dressed conventionally in a starry blue toga (all strewn with stars and comets and constellations) and a tall blue cone-shaped hat with a long flowing gold tassel. Rhoda is wearing loose-fitting white pantaloons. She is barefoot and pigeon-toed and there are low-pitched sacred bells around her ankles. Her blouse is delicately embroidered and almost transparent, revealing her large, heavy breasts. She is wearing many necklaces and rings of exquisite workmanship and color—reds, purples, rich browns, and yellows. Roses are stitched into her hair and she is smiling with the fragrance of flowers and fruits and spices.

The First Wise Man is a dealer in rare and exotic herbs and ointments that have the power to expunge the past and illuminate the future.

The Second Wise Man is a purveyor of oriental rugs and maybe flying carpets.

The Third Wise Man is the English poet Charles Tomlinson who is chanting translations of Persian and Sufi love songs.

The Magician is not Prospero or Merlin or Rumpelstiltskin. He is goat-bearded, Pan-like Armand Schwerner, and he is reciting over and over this saying of the Tantric Buddhists: "The only two things are the Certainty of Death and the Reality of Energy."

The procession vanishes into nothing as quickly as it had appeared.

4. Party Time

Bliem and I came up through the basement of the Chrysler Building looking for the masquerade party where I was to get together with my old friend Elizabeth, who looks like a blond cheerleader from California. I had run into her accidentally one day last fall coming out of an Off-Track Betting Office. "It's just Fate," she said and hugged me lightly. Seeing her again after two years, I knew it was story time again and that I'd never get too close to her—this time she was hopelessly entangled with a compulsive gambler.

It was some kind of birthday party with a great big yellow sponge cake and an outrageous pink rose nestled on top. There was good old-time dancing music, too—not your modish punk rock or even Bob Marley and the Wailers, and I was dancing as close to Elizabeth as possible, long sliding dips and cosmic whirling. It was a great party, a real ball, and if I had stayed into it much longer she would have turned into the Waltz Queen herself, but Bliem came up and he was bored out of his mind and wanted to take a walk. He was looking for that basement again. We couldn't find it anywhere and sat down tired and sweaty on one of those rough old benches on a subway platform. When the droning work train came through, Bliem jumped aboard like a swashbuckling buccaneer. "O, Bliem," I cried, "why do you always want to do the same things?—you're forever looking for ratty old basements in the junkyard of modern therapy."

Just then I drifted off again (inside this dream) and had three very sexy dreams about being with Rhoda again. In one of them I look at her and want to hug her and I do. I do. And I look at her big inviting mouth and I want to get lost in it. She looks up at me with a mischievous smile, and she says, "Do you believe, Bill, do you really believe that you could do that without wanting the whole animal?"

In the second one, this poem buzzes itself into my head:

> that first birthday
> she wrapped herself up in a long dress
> and came over to his house.
> "here," she said, "open me.
> this is your present."

In the third and final dream, I was at the birthday party again, but Elizabeth had gone. I wandered everywhere looking for her and calling out her name and singing some of the Billie Holliday numbers she loves (like "The Lost Child" or "Smoke Gets in Your Eyes"), but I did not see a single familiar face, not even Bliem's. Finally a bitch lady came up to me with a superior and indulgent motherly air and said Elizabeth had called and left a message. "She was very nice," said the Dowager, "about your having left the party without her two years ago, but I got the distinct impression she did not want ever to see you again."

5. The Yellow Dusenberg

I saw Honey, my old actress friend, in a dream tonight, the same Honey who had rescued me once in a dark time with her amazing hands, and the same Honey I was supposed to visit the Sunday night I first met Rhoda in a Szechuan restaurant after her reading. We had all been sitting around eating exotic dishes that Mark, as usual, had ordered for everyone. He was, after all, the impresario of readings, the ring-giver as it were. His pairing of Rhoda with a droning rabbi-type poet was, in the light of what happened later, amusing—it worked too because that pompous seriousness set off Rhoda's delicious and eccentric sexuality. I knew only too well what Mark had in mind.

I got the jump on him (which surprised both of us)—I asked Rhoda if she wouldn't like to walk down by the River for awhile. We left then—Rhoda with her huge handbag containing all her manuscripts, a change of clothes, her toothbrush, and a bottle of Grand Marnier.

Along the way, I called up Honey to get out of that other arrangement. She hadn't really wanted to see me anyway, being nervous around my recent separation and being free herself (at least for a month or so) of my friend Jack who had gone to California. She really just wanted to talk on the phone. Except for this dream, which is beginning to unfold like an accordian, I haven't seen Honey in more than two years, but I see her clearly now in memory, a tall, full-bodied, dramatic woman with a face that could do or be anyone. (Jack once claimed he had recognized at least thirteen distinct persons in Honey, but Jack is therapy-saturated like many New Yorkers, neurotic, unsure of his own sexual identity, and prone to exaggeration.)

In this dream, Honey was reclining like a Fragonard nude on a huge frilly satin bed. She was wearing a fluffy white chemise and black underthings. The bed was on a raised dais and brightly floodlit. The walls around it were made of flimsy pasteboard with gaudily painted windows and other decorations sort of sketched in. Obviously, it was a stage set and Honey was some kind of actress! I didn't care—I was horny enough to fuck in a Jeep. I was starting to make love to her, fumbling around for her nipples and sucking at them. (They were very long, like small penises.) Suddenly, she leapt out of bed and started cavorting around the stage set, probably expecting me to pursue her, hotly. Instead, I saw that there were a lot of other people milling around in the loft-sized shadowy room where the bedroom set was located, among them Honey's children and my own, intent upon a TV screen.

A small wizened old man came running up to Honey and me and said that her husband was climbing up the fire escape and would be here in fewer than five minutes and that Professor Detective Alexander Snot, who had been pursuing me ever since I abandoned the Family Business and disappointed my father, was descending from the roof by means of a giant derrick . . .

❊ ❊ ❊

I am reclining upon a couch, my eyes intent on the TV screen. It is showing a movie I am also in, and I recognize a pan shot of one of the streets that Rhoda and I used many a-time for our Sunday getaways—like Todt Hill Road on Staten Island. I could see a long yellow convertible with Rhoda and me sitting up on the back flaunting the wind. We were smiling and waving like movie stars, like Gatsby and Daisy. And the wind sounds like applause in the trees . . .

❊ ❊ ❊

I was at the Print Center in Brooklyn watching them work a press that was scored like a jig-saw puzzle, the segments of which moved independently like each step of an escalator or a medieval torture machine. I identified myself to the printers as their President and Chairperson and asked them about how everything was going. Before they could respond—no doubt in disbelief and contempt—the huge double doors flew open and a masked musical procession filed in and began dancing around in their green harlequin outfits. They didn't say who they were but I knew they were all the crazy, wild, egotistical poets we had ever published

there. Among them was a plumpish girl I was attracted to. I
started bumping around with her and running my hands along
her body just below her balletic breasts. She used to be friends
with the Spice Lady, she said, and I thought she did look a little
familiar, under her bright yellow parrot mask. "My name's Kathleen," she said. "Well," I responded, "I'm sure I saw you at one of
her parties." And we just danced off then, gaily bumping one another like old buddies, towards the Fragonard set beside which
was parked a long bright yellow convertible, vintage 1922.

❊ ❊ ❊

I was jogging up a road near Rhoda's house on Ludwig Street
on the Island in my Indian moccasins and undershorts. A tour
bus rounded the corner by the drug store, because something Big
and Important was happening that day on the Island, maybe that
visit by Jackie Kennedy Onassis to Sailors' Snug Harbor. So there
I was just loping along when it suddenly dawned on me that it
wasn't exactly appropriate to be doing that out there in the middle
of a middle-class Italian neighborhood, almost stark naked. I was
awfully embarrassed and ran sheepishly back to find my clothes
which weren't where I'd left them, beside a bright yellow convertible, which the tour bus was just passing and in which some gorgeous plastic movie starlets were waving their hands and flaunting
their breasts.

6. Man-in-the-Moon Marigolds

In another dream, I saw Rhoda in a florid pantsuit, heavily
made-up, very attractive. She always looked best in gardens
(though she herself, a lousy gardener, is really a sort of animated
garden). We were going, late as usual, to a production of Paul
Zindel's *The Effect of Gamma Rays on Man-in-the-Moon Marigolds*. It was being done at a private school on Staten Island.

We could be seen walking along the outside gallery with white columns gleaming from the lights inside and the dreamy summer moonlight. The curtains were blowing in the breeze like the batik ones in the back window of my son's blue Datsun pickup, and people were leaning out through the curtains and shushing us, because Rhoda could never keep her mouth shut. She adored any kind of flute or recorder music, though she did not so much play as suck it up into herself. Technically speaking, she had a gifted mouth, with more feeling, for sure, than Ann Friday—that weird woman I slept with once who got all her stuff out of Burton's translations of Persian and Hindu erotica and was herself a somewhat frayed and much leafed through translation of a culture that was no more hers than mine.

Inside, groups of people were milling around the darkened auditorium and talking loudly, over the sound of Zindel's play— perhaps it dramatized just too closely a typical Staten Island household: failed, alcoholic parents and kids striving angrily and desperately towards a knowledge that was at once an escape and a judgment for them. To exist physically on one immediate level and be, simultaneously, an illustration (or translation) of a higher or at least a different reality. A bourgeois culture such as ours, and Staten Island, truly an island, set in the midst of one of the most sophisticated cities in the world, is just a parody of that—such a culture is bound to produce more than its share of strivers and especially dreamers, like the girl-child in Zindel's play whose gained knowledge and victory in the Science Fair was a real and fatal—if unconscious—indictment of her mother. The result is a garden alright, but an atomic one, full of grotesque mutations, anomalies, and emotions. Schizophrenia.

Inside, an usher came up and asked us was I fifty-five in which case my Lady could come in free.

"Not quite!" I laughed.

And she, Our Lady of the Rosebush, not so much laughed as exploded, and everything vanished. For a long time I could not get anything into focus, as though my eyes had been too close to a brilliant flashing light. I could see fragments of things, some real, some clearly fictive—the mossy woods up around Woodstock where we'd taken off all our clothes and wandered around like Adam and Eve and fucked again and again in broad daylight. And then two or three times on the upper deck of the Staten Island Ferry where she was shaking out old blues songs for silver in my Irish country hat. The graduation church where she'd stolen flowers right under the bishop's nose. The foldaway beds, the terrifying August storm over Long Beach Island. A coffee house she'd managed. A bus making all the hokey stops upstate. An airliner stretched out over Antarctica like an albatross.

It's all so difficult to hold on to anything so elusive, to keep things practically in focus . . .

As Bruno says, it's all just a dream, Bill, and she contained them all.

Just then I could see we were sitting at wide wooden tables, long enough for six to seven on a side. Was Bruno there? Staring at this garden she was? I asked her would she like to have played the Mother in *The Effect of Gamma Rays on Man-in-the-Moon Marigolds,* and she said, no. All that she had ever played was Thea Elvsted in *Hedda Gabler* and that must have been, I thought, like a nun coming out of a closet in a busty bikini, or Holly Woodlawn the transvestite playing Isabella in *Measure for Measure.*

At the next table over, a black-haired young man with black horn-rimmed glasses was sitting next to a lean and curly-headed young woman. Opposite them was a bald-headed old man with his back to us and a strange growth or wound near the top of his skull. The young man said, "He's dying, you know." (I wondered if he were syphillitic.)

At that very moment, the old man leaned his head way back and down, very loosely, into my lap (as though he owned it and it were the most natural thing in the world). His head was like a small medicine ball gleaming silver-gold in the light of that moving place. He looked just like an emaciated but grinning Ed Barry, who used to own the tavern down the street from me and Mr. Panzianni, the Flower-King, and now owns the Veterans Cab Company. He is an old sailing-man, I think—Coast Guard or Merchant Marine. Petulantly, I shoved his head up and away from me.

"You know, my dear," said the black-haired Young Man, "you *can* love three men at once you know—it *is,* well, not un*heard* of."

His lean, curly-headed young woman had vanished, and Rhoda was sitting next to him and talking intently with her hands about the Theatre and her glamorous aspirations. I told her fiercely to come back and sit down again where she belonged, by my side, but they all got up instead looking for bathrooms. Later I found her, defiantly, I thought, hugging and kissing that curvaceous simpering mortal in the foyer. It was like a movie.

7. Nirvana

I woke to a soft northern Minnesota rain and wondered aloud to Harry whether the lights we had seen in the north that night were gamma rays or just the auras of lush wildly flowering Lady Slippers, this wet summer.

"Just let go, Bill," he said.

Dear Harry, I thought, that's just like something you'd say. I went to you for the worst reasons. Being cured of anything like obsession—what you call "a dependency problem"—was the last thing on my mind. All I wanted was to get back what Rhoda and I had and I thought you could help. You said all the right things, Harry. You talked about addiction. About how much like my mother she was. How I had "to claim myself again, take control of my life." Vlado told me later I must have been a lousy patient because I wouldn't ever give you any of my dreams. And he was right too. I always nodded my head wisely but I could barely suppress the laughter and excitement in my heart and I went back to my own space next door and wrote poem after poem to her. I even showed some of them to you but you didn't have any imagination, Harry. God, Harry, she was the root, stalk, and flower of every fantasy I ever had, of every poem I ever wrote. I could go anywhere with her—to Hell, or Hades, or Nirvana or Paradise and back—or anywhere in my whole life. Child, father, mother, sister, brother. I could soar above her body (in which I was rooted) like a bird or a kite. She was my mother. I was her father. She would play with my Anger or Pain until we were both rolling in delight and laughter. If I were sick, she'd want to take that sickness into herself like a shaman. I never knew anyone so much in love with pleasure as she was.

8. Blitz and Bliss

There was a war going on and we could see flashes of light in the distance, as from bombs or lightning or some bi-centennial celebration on the Island. We were sitting around, a group of us, talking into the night (like Marlow and his friends reclining on the deck in the gathering gloom over the Thames in Conrad's *Heart of Darkness*).

But Harry, who seemed to be engaged in what was being said, turned suddenly and asked:

"Where are you really, Bill?"

"Harry, I'm over there in that other dream getting married."

And like a flash of lightning or one of those firebombs, I was in the light of that other dream unfolding like a procession: the Three Wise Men, the Magician, Rhoda, the poems I had been writing—all flared up briefly like a skyrocket, then vanished.

And Harry and I were sitting on the fire escape outside my window late spring 1940 watching storms come up over the trees and hearing Mother crying over the Blitz in London and wondering about Harrod's Department Store which used to ship her Ridgeway's Fine English Orange Pekoe Tea in beautiful tin boxes.

And Harry turned suddenly and asked: "Where are you really, Bill?"

And I was in my grandmother's garden, the trellis with the morning glories, the neat rows of zinnias and marigolds, and Rhoda in a long loose white dress and a huge floppy white straw summer hat. And my old family was there for the wedding and even my late mother, bless her soul. And they were standing around trying very hard to be sweetly polite to this fine, buxom lady. And she, Rhoda, was looking viciously voluptuous and she was yelling something out of one of my poems:

"I'm gonna take care of *me,* yeah, and you don't fit that sweet/ sour little picture, man, you just fuck off, yeah, and push some other sweet tart little ass around your ashram . . . "

And I was yelling back at her:

"Jesus fucking Christ, Rhoda, can't you shut up till it's over?"

And I was down on my knees then and grabbing her thighs and Harry was rolling over and laughing like jelly and my whole god-damned family blew away like a rocket and I didn't care anymore what my mouth was doing and Harry said it was just terrific I could look on the light side for a change.

9. Spear Flower Poem

Later that summer, we were just leaving somebody's country place—maybe it was Rosemary's place in Connecticut or Siv's. We were bound, I thought, for making one more try. There were lots and lots of other people there, storming about and laughing. And she had been laughing too, at me, about yet another breaking off of a branch already broken.

"This time," she said, "it's for your own good."

"Did you get my letter and the spear flower poem?"

"Yes," she said, "but I haven't read them yet—they came just before I left."

"When will you read them?"

"I don't think I will—I tore them all up in fact."

"I always make carbons," I said, laughing a little.

"Are you trying to blackmail me?"

"Of course not," I said. And I took out one of the pictures of her and her three kids I used to carry in my address book.

She said, "When did you grow that mustache? You look just like my ex-husband."

And there we were at her house (which he still owns) and I wouldn't leave and she could yell her head off and call the fucking police but I wouldn't leave and I wouldn't get out of that car or out of her house or out of her life. And she was petting my head a little, patronizingly. And she said:

"Nothing matters but Now. And Now's a sick little bull-calf with a black mustache and a chopped off tail. So get lost, little man."

So, helplessly, I look around at Anger now, sitting in the back-seat with Humiliation. He is red-faced and hairy. Now and then I see in that rippling face my own face, or my shrink Harry's, or my Dad's (the mornings he'd hit me with his razor strop). Anger is holding a little portable TV set in his lap which he lifts up to-wards my streaming eyes, and what I see there is this:

> She is wearing a red uniform
> that looks oddly like a general's.
> Her position is pregnable
> but messy—
> piles of old clothes, phonograph records, books,
> gifts, old manuscripts,
> and lovers who look like soldiers
> are lying around in her trenches
> playing with themselves.
> She seems to enjoy watching this.
>
> The sun drips in the sky
> like a tired and used up volcano.

I assault the summit
in my underpants,
my green shirt is a flag.

I have no weapon but this.

At first, the soldiers ignore me,
then universal laughter.
I rush at her like a bull
maddened by what I see.
She lies down immediately
and opens her legs.
Her cunt smiles up at me
like a peevish little girl.
I drive my weapon home
and feel just terrific,
like a child rapist.

When I wake in the morning,
the other inmates are hanging
all over my bed
and braying my poems at me,

like the Brementown Musicians.

10. Fire

I was moving again. Everything. An enormous, trucculent U-Haul van. Everything. Even the big wooden pelican we bought in Nasca, Peru. I waved goodbye to Bruno, knowing I would probably never see him again, and rolled on down Oxford Place toward the ferry terminal on Bay Street. Although I am in some respects strong as a stevedore, that truck was almost more than I could handle. It did not have power brakes, for one thing. It also had a governor that would not let me go more than 35 miles an hour, and it groaned up every little rise between New York and Minnesota as if it were an old fuddy-duddy and had a mind of—her—own. It was filled up to the brim with History and Romance, with good intentions and failed expectation, with Pride and Freedom and the

Open Road, with voices I had loved and hated, even the Farm I had abandoned years before—all neatly folded up and boxed and ready to spring into your eyes at the touch of this hand.

I've done it all before, many times—in fact, you could say I'm an old hand at new beginnings.

The place we had taken looked vaguely familiar, as though someone else had re-designed the house we had built near New Paltz. It was long and narrow, too long, in fact, to be really comfortable. The front part was two storeys high and rose all the way to a cathedral ceiling. The living quarters—our bed and other intimate furniture, the kitchen, the bathrooms—all of this was to the rear of the first floor. They were not damaged by the fire at all—in fact, we continued living there as though nothing had happened. Upstairs to the rear, I kept all my office gear—business records, files of correspondence, old journals, the books I had written or dreamed of writing.

When I was still very young, when my older brother fell down that cliff and nearly died, when my family used to go out from St. Louis on long wonderful picnics along the Merrimac River to, say, the old farm the Piatts had bought for weekends, I used always to take a complete kit with me—drawing paper, crayons, a notebook, pens and pencils, sharpeners, lengths of rope for climbing into trees or making rope ladders, and the books (like Will James' *Smoky* and the one about Neosha Bend, Missouri) I read over and over again—everything I needed to become the liberated Artist I always wanted to be, as soon as my Mom had taught me how to press wild flowers. I only dreamed then, and did nothing, my kit a future and a promise, or, as my Dad said, a goddamned nuisance.

I only dreamed then and did not know it, of some inchoate escape, a Tarzan swing full of krypton, and rescuing my Mother from her Fate or Virginia Magner from the Jaws of the death-dream I had so many nights, as later, perhaps, I was to swing through Rhoda's life and carry her, laughing, to the arced apex of

heights she only dreamed of, as now, though more and more
rarely I dream of her

> disrupting this page
> like an ambulance
> this false spring morning.
>
> Darling,
> if we go up in smoke tonight,
> the master of fires
> will be wearing an angry rubber coat,
> his boots will squeak like a farmer's
> across the porch of an old frame hotel
> where we are discovering
>
> the Spirit of Romance
> and the quicksilver slippery
> Ghost of Magic
> breaking into crocuses
> against the snowy sheets
>
> or fire

The fire was to the back or lee side of the house and confined to
my office area. For a long time I was afraid to go in because
Rhoda might be in there with my burned poems. Perhaps the fire
had not been as intense as I was pretty sure it was. Perhaps not
everything had been destroyed, only badly damaged and mostly
salvageable; perhaps everything I had built up and collected so
painstakingly over the years—these creatures that live only in my
fingers, in journal after journal, in that wonderful correspondence, in the not yet published or forgotten poems, in the Fiddle
Affair, in *Pope John's Motel*—perhaps all this was miraculously in-
tact and would not crumble away; perhaps only that dark wood
pelican we bought in Nazca had exploded and burned like an in-
cendiary bomb.

For days on end, I did nothing but brood in my journals—for
a thousand pages and more—and sleep and dream, lovely happy

dreams of human fellowship and reconciliation and Arabian marriages. Once I dreamed up some happy loose young lovers who had come to take care of us in their van, in our Golden Years.

Still I would not go into that burned-out area.

But one night I dreamed about a man who was struck by lightning.

He felt very small and distant, like a larva or chrysalis. He was very deep and small inside of himself, a pinprick of light, a sting of breath. He could not move his body—at least he did not think he could move and he did not want to move.

He could hear his children's voices faintly, like over water—"I . . . think . . . he's . . . don't . . . touch . . . him." He wanted to talk with them gently, in a fatherly way. "I . . . feel . . . alright . . . good . . . but . . . different." He wanted to talk with them, let his voice pass into the body of their ears, melodiously, like those two crows yesterday, answering one another over water.

In fact, he was moving now in a way he never had before. Her voice had split him easily like butter: "I wanted to kill you." He was swimming or flying, rising into the sputtering air or wind and something in him was splitting the whole dark world with a song answering a song, precisely, in the distance, maybe a thousand miles away over water and rising easily like a rush of wind in melodious trees. And he longed only a little for the body of his song, his habitation, and the dark where his mother had kept him until the sword of light split her and he was crying and it was beginning and it was raining again . . .

And what does it mean? That vast accumulation of papers and debris? The junk of a literary life? The dreams I had, like this one, recorded or invented, and now wasted, never to be recovered? And what does it mean? The photographs? The letters? My poems rejecting me?

("O Bill," she said once, "you're still sucking around in the past. All that matters is Now and the Flow and New Beginnings . . . ")

For a long time I mulled on that, an activity, mulling, which is exactly contrary to the philosophy embedded in what she said, an agreeable Philosophy, existential and modernist, consistent with all the best contemporary therapies, which is just great—until the pressure builds up, and you can't put your finger on what it is you have to know and it builds and it builds and you have to know, god, you have to know or you'll break into flames like that pelican and the past will spill out of your mouth like little blistering fish and she'd come in then like a malicious kid to watch the fire. Rhoda. Watching me watching Armand and his Pain.

11. Asking Directions

On the way to the church where I am to read poetry that night with Celestine, I encounter two policemen:

—Officers, do you know where St. Clements Church is?

—St. Clements? hm? hm? 40th and 9th, maybe? hm? Let me think. We would know the father there, wouldn't we?

—But it's not Catholic.

—O well, now, if it's not Catholic, we wouldn't know. Sorry, sir.

❋ ❋ ❋

If you want Tragedy, he thought, you go to Celestine. For Comedy perhaps Suzanne, who is screamingly funny about Men and Situations and who lives on Complication. For images, not Basil, though his faces haunt you like the ghost of Edvard Münch. For wisdom and serenity, only to yourself and what you could not have learned from your Mother (crisp as lettuce and rabbit-eared to your still childish hungers). For road maps and arterial systems, you go still to Harry in some abandoned church in a burnt-out part of the city.

❋ ❋ ❋

Talking with Celestine on the roof that night, the sky going dark, late summer, a sunset inferred behind that larger building capped off with water towers (like some small prairie market town, late thirties, driving home-free in a Ford V8 convertible, his suitcase crammed full with maps and directions to nowhere he would really know about until 40 years later), sitting on that roof with Celestine, she a dark swift snake coiling around his sinuous sentences, and they talking about and into his Passion and riding it through to the end when all would be lit up like some silly candle in a Church not of his choosing and abandoned, like that dark roof of all but him and Celestine.

There was an empty wheelchair at his poetry reading that night and it felt good to sit down in it and wheel it about like a real master because he felt crippled and was "recovering from heart failure." And the Idea of wheeling his poems and these dreams around and in and out of his audience was very comforting. And when he rose up out of it and it fell away collapsing like an exhausted and much-abused canvas director's chair, he felt as if he had been born again in some abandoned but once colorful church in a burnt-out part of the city and he no longer needed her or anyone else to push him around and control his direction. And he walked, O he strode clean free out of his sorrow into the light of his own laughter.

❄ ❄ ❄

Tonight I had a lovely dream and went on making it when I woke up. I was in the middle of a journey and the terrain was mountainous, as in that first dream long ago when he had been told that the end of the world was at hand. His world, anyway. Off to the north the new great glaciers were beginning to swell up and descend and would crack the earth and dry up the seas and there was a radiance to the south that glittered like the unearthly inside jewels that are like Rhoda's hard unmoving sweet eyes set in her Buddha face, that smile carved into softness out of the most perfect textured marble he could find. There was a radiance in the south as of sunlight in the dewy twilight of spring or cool warm early summer, as of clouds of incense rising from mown pastures, and the center of this radiance was a tall figure with a glittering jewel-like torch held pulsating aloft like the funny old Our Gray Lady of the Harbor beckoning not the lost and the forlorn, the hungry or the oppressed, but the living, the lighthearted . . .

And I found myself walking here in the streets of my City. And there was fear everywhere that the heavens were cracking and the sky was falling. And the mayor and his fat councilmen (like worried Cardinals) were eagerly and desperately passing resolutions as if tossing little pebbles into the great hungry mouth of a dragon or a volcano. The buildings, they said, were about to erupt and indeed there was a great trembling of buildings all around me. And I thought I could see at the very tip of an old yellow brick one the black edge of smoke and the glow of fire. And I looked and I looked and a smile broke through my fears and shone in that building. Before my very eyes it doubled itself like a huge penis, rose higher and higher, and the same thing was beginning to happen all around this place that was like a lovely old odd-angled square in this boisterous bustling city.

C. W. Truesdale. I have been greatly interested in dreaming and in its creative aspects for a very long time, and "Arabian Nights" was— and is—an attempt to see whether it was possible to incorporate a sequence of them that occurred in a period of a few weeks (for the most part) about 15 years ago. The story was originally composed within a year or two of the events which the dreams reflected and then set aside—simply because I had no confidence that the experiment worked at all.

Two or three years ago, I looked for a copy of the story because I knew it contained a dream record that I needed for some other (now forgotten) purpose. Out of some sort of vanity, I suppose, I reread the whole thing then and was intrigued by its possibilities, if still disturbed by some aspects of it. I reworked it extensively and then started showing it around to some of my good writing friends—Vivian Vie Balfour, Lisa Ruffolo, Pat Francisco, Celestine Frost, Roger Blakely, and Pat Barone among others—all of whom encouraged me to do something with it.

As it stands now, "Arabian Nights" is a story about the demise of a strong, intense relationship as it showed up in a number of strange and disconcerting dreams—something that often happens in traumatic situations of that sort. Real people, events, and places—like the old man Bruno, and the street where I lived at the time on Staten Island, Paul Zindel's play, The Effect of Gamma Rays on Man-in-the-Moon Marigolds—are freely intertwined with dream material as if the dreams themselves were real or real events had a dream-like effect on me.

Often what is strongest and most original in one's work is—simply for those reasons—the most disturbing. I think this was true in this case, but I leave it to the readers to make that judgment, one way or the other, for themselves.

MARCIA PECK

A Gingko in the Garden

F RANK THINKS I'M overprotective. I was cooking a bouill-
abaisse when he said to me, look, Daisy's got to start sometime.

But she's only in kindergarten, I objected, adding a teaspoon
of cayenne.

So if you're really so worried, then follow the bus to school.
Just the first day. If it'll make you feel better.

At dinner we explained it to Daisy. We would walk her to the
bus stop at the end of the driveway, then I would trail the bus to
school in the car. Do I *have* to take the bus? Daisy asked.

It'll be like field trips in nursery school, I told her. And you're
the last kid on the route. It will be a short ride. I'll be right behind
you the first day.

Could I just have plain mashed potatoes? Daisy asked, sneaking a forkful of cod to Ginger under the table.

❊ ❊ ❊

You know this is for you, Frank said later. It's not for Daisy;
it's for you. I suppose you'll be lurking around her junior prom.
You baby her. Ever since Colin, you baby her.

Give it a rest, Frank, I said. Since when can't a mother be concerned for the welfare of her child without somebody harping at her all the time. Besides, you're the one who fixed her tofu delight when she wouldn't eat my fish soup.

Frank said he didn't want to fight, he just wanted to watch the eleven o'clock news. So, making the final point, I sighed and went upstairs.

I smoothed the hair from Daisy's forehead, slipped one hand beneath the sheet to feel her heart pulsing like bubbles rising from a kettle of hot soup. Unfair, bringing Colin up. That was three years ago. The OB at Philadelphia General had asked if I wanted to hold him. I kissed his tiny swollen hands. Goodbye baby. Visit me in my dreams, I whispered to his silver eyelids. We had him cremated. Woodlawn Cemetery sent the ashes to us through the mail.

After a suitable time had passed, Frank raised the question of disposal of the ashes. We considered hiking up into the Wind River Mountains of Wyoming and sprinkling the ashes on the continent's triple divide. Rain would wash them into streams which flowed ultimately to the Missouri, Colorado, and Columbia Rivers. That seemed grand enough for Colin. But on further consideration, I said it smacked of mutilation, dividing him up like that. Anyway, Wyoming was so far from Philadelphia.

So I put off thinking about it. Now and then I would daydream about having a memorial service. But after a service wouldn't we be expected to scatter the ashes? Or bury them in the family plot at Woodlawn? Or something? I just couldn't come up with a good reason to move him from the bureau in the bedroom.

Two more years and he would have been starting kindergarten.

❊ ❊ ❊

Fall was in the air. Frank and I decided to plant a tree on Daisy's first day of school. Frank wanted a maple. I wanted something, oh, a little more special. One by one I dismissed the possibilities: a hackberry—too plain; an oak—but then there was oak wilt; a birch—we already had one; a mountain ash—maybe; a fernleaf buckthorn—Frank wasn't going to have any fancy dancy sickly buck whatever it was.

When I hit upon the gingko, I knew that was the tree it had to be. A what? said Frank.

It's one of the oldest trees on earth, I told him. It's genetically unique. And it has an edible nut that's been used for centuries.

Oh? a *gingko,* said Frank. You mean the one that *stinks.* That's what you want to plant?

Only the female stinks, you'll be smug to learn, I said. The male has no smell whatever. (I had researched this.) This tree is considered to be a living fossil, I said, resorting to the most irresistibly persuasive evidence in my possession.

Rosie, you're out of touch, said Frank, always the first to be judgmental.

❈ ❈ ❈

The day before school started I took Daisy to Wanamakers to shop for school clothes. I found a calico dress in fall colors with a smocked top, very like one Barbara Racioppi used to wear. Of all the girls in my kindergarten class at PS Number Three, Barbara Racioppi had the most cared for look about her. Daisy tried on a pink slip, trimmed in lace, with bands of satin and adjustable straps. Honey, I said, it's a size 8. It'll hang way down below your dress.

I'm not going to wear a dress. Just this.

Daisy, you can't wear a slip to school. The kids will . . .

Daisy was watching herself twirl from side to side. Smudges of face-paint from a recent birthday party decorated her cheeks. One pig tail sagged from its elastic band. Her fingertips held the slip delicately out to either side. In the mirror her face shone with pleasure, the face of a princess choosing her first ballgown.

Never mind. I'll pack a dress with your lunch in case you change your mind. I pictured her boarding the bus buttoned and zipped into the calico dress. She handed me the slip. I bought them both.

❊ ❊ ❊

But you should have seen her face, I said leafing through the September *Gourmet* that night in bed. You know, I've been thinking. Maybe we could just hang onto Colin's ashes until I die. You could mix his ashes up with mine and bury us together.

I don't think they do that.

Who?

You know. The crematoriums.

What have they got to say about it?

I don't know. Anyway, it sounds unsanitary.

That's ridiculous.

Well then, it sounds incestuous.

Frank, it's ashes! Ashes don't have sexual urges. This is ridiculous.

Don't use logic on me! Look, he's my son too. I've got something to say about this.

Well then let's all get mixed up together. An ashes milkshake. Or better yet, we can keep him in the spice cabinet. A dash here, a sprinkle there.

I mean it, Rose. This time you've gone too far.

Can we talk about this sometime?

Sometime, yes.

Now?

No. Frank snapped off the light.

We lay in the dark. A train passed in the distance. Daisy called for a glass of water.

What took you so long? Frank said when I got back into bed. What did you do, go out for *Perrier?*

I weighed the question and prudently glanced at Frank to judge whether he was as resentful as he sounded. He looked bemused. You know, I'm a good mother, I said. I take time in the dead of night to minister to my child. This is not something to tease a person about. I'm a person of character. It's all wasted on you.

Maybe, he said. He paused. But how about a quickie? he had the cockleshells to ask me. C'mon Rosie, he needled. You know you're a lifer.

That's how he thinks of marriage. Still, he has the sweetest breath of any man I've ever known. Sure, I said, just this once.

❊ ❊ ❊

Mama, said a small voice by my ear not long after sunrise.
Hi, Honey. All ready for your first day of school? I whispered.
Can I wear something of yours?
Like what, Honey?
Your banana necklace? Daisy searched my face. Please? I won't let any of the kids touch it.

The sun slanted across her hair. Frank stirred. Barbara Racioppi would never have worn her mother's banana necklace.
Please?
OK. Just this once. No precedents.

In the bathroom Daisy corrected me for brushing with the blue bedtime toothbrush instead of the morning yellow.

If you are half this observant, you are going to be a brilliant student, do you hear me? I said. Downstairs I wrapped a bagel with cream cheese in cellophane. Ginger licked the knife. I tucked a bag of dolphin fun fruits into the lunchbox. Two pencils and a fresh box of sixteen crayons. I peeked at Daisy in the family room talking to her dolls (now eat your spaghetti), absorbed, wearing the pink slip and a Barbie crown made of paper and glitter glue. When Frank wasn't around, I opened Daisy's backpack and slipped in the calico dress and a brand new imitation pink dia-mond ring.

You are spoiling her, he said from the kitchen door.

❋ ❋ ❋

We all walked out together. Daisy held Frank's hand. I juggled the lunchbox, her backpack, my car keys. When the bus came into view, I braced myself. Daisy would cry. She'd refuse to get on the bus. She would have to be coaxed. At the very least the step would be too high and she'd need a lift up. The bus groaned to a stop.

Where's the camera. We forgot the camera. Frank?

Rosie?

I'm such a dope. How could I forget the camera? Daisy?

Daisy was disappearing into the bus. The door closed.

Frank, she never even said good-bye. I stared after the bus. Did she get a seat? Frank, did you see if she got a seat? Shouldn't we have introduced her to the bus driver? Shouldn't we have found her a seat?

You'd better get going, he answered.

I plunged for the car. I lost sight of the bus at the light. In the schoolyard I glimpsed Daisy. She had memorized the route to her room on visiting day. Children poured into the school. I tried to catch her as she bore down on 1B like a spawning salmon, deaf to the ruckus around her.

You made it! I said, breathless, just outside the door to 1B. Daisy looked startled. How was the bus?

Not good. Daisy glanced around the hallway. Her chin trem-bled. She wiped her eyes with the hem of her slip.

What's wrong? Honey, what's wrong?

Mama . . . She reached for my hand.

I dropped to my knees. I drew her toward me, treasure of my life that no pain should touch. Her hair smelled of wildflowers on a damp day.

Mama . . .

What, little fish?

I'm the littlest kid. It's not like nursery school. The kids are all bigger than me. All the kids on the bus . . . Mom . . . they can *read,* she choked.

What do you mean? Were they mean to you?

Mama. Why can't I stay with you?

Her arms slid around my neck and her tears dropped to my shoulder like coins into a blind man's cup. If I cry, I thought, she'll never walk through that door.

But at that moment Mrs. Becker's blue pumps appeared on the linoleum next to Daisy. Hello Daisy, said her taffeta voice. Won't you come inside? I need someone to help me feed the guppies today.

And in the next moment she was gone. She looked back once, my Daisy did, but I was quick and I'm certain she saw only my sudden smile and the breezy wave of my hand. She turned to the guppies. Bye, Honey, I said after a while to the windowpane.

❀ ❀ ❀

Chunks of lamb sizzled on the stove. I shouldn't have gone. She had her strength until she saw me, I said, chopping onions.

She'll do fine. Come on. You want a cup of coffee? he asked, obviously intending to meander through his last day of vacation.

I know she'll do fine, I said, irritated. That's not the point. I slid the onions into the pot along with a liberal dash of brandy.

What's the point? Frank turned to face me.

I don't know, I faltered. She's all alone.

She's not alone. She's in capable hands. Frank stirred the stew. It's you who's alone. You don't want to let her go. He brought the spoon to his lips. Lemon, he stated. It needs lemon.

And who are you? Fucking Dr. Spock? I set the brandy bottle down hard.

No. I'm her father. I took the breathing classes. Remember me?

That's enough lemon, I said. I jabbed the stew with a spoon. I wasn't sure how high I was willing to escalate.

She's going to grow up, Rose. With us or without us she's going to grow up. Frank had an unnerving sanctimonious way about him in a fight.

Let Daisy grow up? I'm not letting Daisy grow up? My voice rose. You weren't there. She wasn't begging *you* to stay with her.

Damn it, Rosie. Frank wrung lemon into the pot.

Damn it, Frank! I smacked the spoon down on the counter. Sour cream splattered the floor. No, I'm not ready to let her go. I already let one of my children go.

Panic spurted across Frank's face. Don't, Rosie, he interrupted.

Well? I pushed. You never talk about him. He's dead, but he's still in this family.

Rosie! The word cracked across the room like lightning striking power lines.

Oh, make the stew yourself, I shouted. And I lifted the entire kettle of lamb stew from the burner and hurled it into the garbage.

The garbage tipped. The whole business hit the floor with the force of a grenade going off. Stew meat and coffee grounds skidded across the kitchen. A flurry of dust motes whirled in the light from the window. The sound of my voice hung in the air with the smell of garlic.

Frank was silent except that his breath came in huffs like little bursts from a bellows. We stood like that, in tableaux. Ginger nosed a piece of meat.

He was my son too, Frank said at last to a trickle of sauce near his shoe.

Why couldn't birthing babies be like planting a tree, I thought. If a tree withers, you plant another and another and another. But you can't do that when a baby dies. I had planned. I had watered. I had cherished. Where had I failed to tend my garden?

I took a step toward Frank, but he turned his shoulder to me. What did I do wrong? I said.

It wasn't your fault. It happened.

I wanted a garden. I got a desert.

How can you talk about a desert when there's . . .

Daisy? I know, I said, beaten. But Frank didn't know that sometimes my desert is so hot and dry and vast, I forget that I am shaded. I forget that the air is sweet with her fragrance. I forget she shields me from unbroken wilderness. I remember only that Colin is dead and I couldn't go there with him.

She sheltered me when I wanted to take care of him, I said. He shouldn't have had to make that journey alone. No child should have to make that journey alone. He was all alone.

Frank stared out the window, as though studying the last summer flowers. Finally he raised his hands and his head shook with a little shudder, making him appear leafless and unguarded. She shelters me too, he said. Then, still not looking at me he added, So do you, Rose.

That's all he said. I don't know if he said it to make me feel better or worse. Maybe he said it to make himself feel better. Who knows? But it did make me wish I'd said the same thing to him first. At any rate, he got a broom from the closet and began to sweep up the garbage. Ginger found the stew to his liking. Pretty soon I pulled out a mop. So the three of us swept and mopped and licked the place clean, and it felt good to do this small bit of housekeeping, to tidy up, side by side.

We went to House of India for lunch and ordered everything extra hot.

❊ ❊ ❊

The tree came at 2 o'clock. When the bus dropped Daisy at three o'clock, Frank was digging the hole. Well, how was it? I asked her.

Fine.

Do you like Mrs. Becker?

Yes. I like her hair. And her hand feels nice. Even though it's all wrinkled.

Daisy and I held the tree upright beside the hole.

You know, said Frank, when we plant the gingko tree, we could put Colin's ashes underneath. What do you say?

I looked away.

We could hold hands and sing a song, he said. What do *you* think, Daisy?

Daisy looked up at me. How about "Are You Sleeping Brother John?" We sang it in school today. I think that would be nice.

Frank folded his arm around my waist. What do you say?

I felt the bark under my hand, silver ridges, crusty, hard. All right, I sanctioned. Just this once.

Marcia Peck. *I grew up in New Jersey and on Cape Cod, went to school in Philadelphia and Duesseldorf, and came to the Twin Cities in 1971 to play with the Minnesota Orchestra. But it wasn't until the birth of my daughter here in 1982 that I felt grounded in Minnesota.*

I have come to believe that sticking with something—in my case the same job for twenty three years—gives us unique opportunities for transformation. Playing in an orchestra has taught me a lot about myself and about things larger than myself. After years of keeping a journal and trying to make a dent in the mushrooming stacks of books by my bed, I felt compelled to write about what moves me. I'm a Loft member and spend a week each year at the Iowa Summer Writing Festival. The discipline of music helps me with writing. I'm grateful to spend every day in contact with the Masters through their music. It is a humbling experience. And expanding.

My loves: husband, horn player Dave Kamminga, and daughter

Hadley; my women's group of ten years; music; anything well-written; mycology; rocks; backpacking; life.

"Abe" won the Castalia Bookmakers' 1989 Fiction Award and I received Honorable Mention in the 1993 Tamarack Awards for "An Unexpected Cadence."

Marcia Peck

PAUL MICHEL BAEPLER

Travel

A LONG PLASTIC JUMBO jet floats at the end of three almost invisible threads in one of the large gallery windows
at the Travel Bureau where I work. People rarely notice
the glassine threads. They see the white jet soaring in the sky,
wings tilted gracefully, landing gear in mid-retraction. Little boys
walking along Michigan Avenue stop to watch the landing bea-
cons blink on and off and to leave their oily finger, palm and nose
prints on the glass. I love that model. Sometimes, when I have
nothing to do at night, I stay late at the office and look more
closely at the jumbo jet. I peer in the cabin windows and search
for the tiny stewardess as she bumps the tiny cocktail cart down
the aisle with her hip. I see her calming smile as she passes out
stethoscopic earphones, half-pillows and small shiny packages of
almonds. Sometimes I can even see the ultra-tiny subliminal
women in the iced-drink advertisements on the back of the magazines my beautiful stewardess hands to me.

My lover is a stewardess for Pan Am. She flies in jumbo jets
and brings me miniature bottles of Tanqueray Gin. She brings me
cellophaned croissant sandwiches for my lunch and leaves packets
of scented towelettes in my car. She's always trying to please me.

After long flights, I massage her cramped feet and the tiny

face muscles which ache from being expressive and sincere all day. I feed her a dinner of heavily garlicked spaghetti and cheap beer which she devours lustfully. In the evenings, I slip Bob Marley into the tape deck and we limbo and lose ourselves.

When we are together, the time flies. And when we're apart, we're never really apart. Our love is perfect.

❊ ❊ ❊

For as long as I've worked at the Travel Bureau, which is nearly three years now, that magnificent airliner has flown in the window. I never tire of watching her figure gleam. I work alone in Promotions and she inspires me.

When I was commissioned to design the new corporate logo, I knew exactly where to turn. I drew a stylized jet in blue with a long jet stream rule for flare and "Travel Bureau" lettered in twelve point Gothic. Now it's on every piece of letterhead, every envelope and everything official that leaves this office. Sometimes I look at the Pan Am routing map with all the red arcs leaping from the point marked Chicago to places like Paris and Jakharta, and I think of all my little airplanes, sealed in airplane envelopes and air-mailed all over the world.

My lover envies me; she thinks my work is very important. Without Promotions, she says, people might never leave their homes and that would be tragic. She says travel brings the world closer, and she calls me a peace-worker and a man of vision. I can only smile at her adoringly because these are her convictions and they come to her naturally.

My lover is a fantastic stewardess. She finished first in flight training. She is always well groomed and poised, her drink orders are never misguided, and she's saved the lives of two passengers with the Heimlich maneuver. Even the pilots tell me her sense of humor is a relief to the flight crew. When she was named hostess of the month, the in-flight magazine called her a highly trained professional and "everything a stewardess ought to be." She loves her job and recognizes just how rare that is. Unlike so many people, she's always known what she wanted to be. She laughs when she says it, but she's serious; she was *born* to be a stewardess.

❀ ❀ ❀

Sometimes when I'm staring at my CRT, the red button on my phone flashes and I know it's my stewardess. She calls me from the credit card phone aboard the jet just to say she's thinking about me. She's at 40,000, no turbulence, and the sky is always an unbelievable azure.

We read each other's minds like that—almost telepathically, so I know how lonely she can be. She's always leaving me, but from her view, she says, I'm always travelling away from her, and I admit she is at least half right. We dream of a place together, but I tell her it will always be a dream, somewhere in mid-air. I call her my aero-mermaid because she must always return to the sky. This is unsettling to her because she knows it's true. She's terrified that she doesn't have a life, but like many women her age, she refuses to forfeit her career only to be earth-bound. My stewardess wants it all.

❀ ❀ ❀

Often when I return to my desk after lunch I find powder blue note squares adhering to my CRT. Usually the Art Director has called with the silvers for a brochure I'm designing, or Audiovisual needs script copy for a promotional campaign. I never expect to find personal notes.

My lover was going to have a baby but she didn't. The note said she had seen the doctor and it was all over. This was the first news I had of any baby.

Before I saw her again, I met up with my lover's brother who is a Hydraulic Systems Engineer and also works for Pan-Am. He said everyone thought she was going to have a baby. She had told her mother and sister and father and Jill, the stewardess she overnights with in London. It troubles me that I didn't sense what was going on. I should have been the first to know. She had even told her boss and her boss grounded her until after the baby was due.

But the baby never came. The doctor said she had never been pregnant. My lover cried because she believed she had been. The baby had slipped away in the night, she said, like a lost thought.

I held her tightly in my arms, tightly to let her know I was with her.

Now my lover wants me to make a new baby with her.

❊ ❊ ❊

I love being a stewardess, but recently I've begun to wonder. I've begun to think about life. Since the miscarriage I've questioned everything. But my friend Jill says it's more than just the baby. Jill's been so good to me. Sometimes I think she knows me better than I know myself. My lover knows me, but in a different way than Jill. Jill says she's seen other girls go through changes like this. It always starts with a lie, she says, some warp in the mirror —you don't see yourself in the same way. I could tell she was a little scared to tell me this. Maybe a little envious too. She made it sound so revolutionary and frightening—I think maybe it's what she secretly wants for herself. But I honestly think it's the baby that upsets me.

Who really knows what they're getting into when they decide to create a baby? Everything happened so quickly, I don't think my lover ever believed it was possible. You should have seen his face when I tried to tell him. For an instant he was shocked. And almost as quickly I could tell he didn't believe me, like it was only a wish that had gone out of control—a rogue desire. But I would never lie to him, at least I haven't so far, and I don't understand why he reacted this way. It's all so confusing. I feel anxious all the time and uncertain of everything. At least when I'm flying, I have a lot of time to think about these questions.

I think babies are called into this world almost as an act of imagination. I mean we never actually see the sperm invading the individual egg. We rely on scientists to tell us how procreation works. And we believe them because they make logical sense, because logic has a value, drives business, fills planes with thousands and thousands of business people who fly to places like Bangkok and Jakharta. So many of these people fly weekly, even daily, and their ride is like logical sex. But for children flight is still a mystery and you can see it in their faces pressed so hard against the tiny oval windows, leaving their individual finger, palm and nose prints.

It's difficult for me to be like those children when I fly. I fly every day, and even though it's still miraculous, there's nothing like the first time. But it's not routine, like it is for so many. I see some who don't lift their eyes from the reports they're reading during takeoff, others who only pause momentarily from their dictation to endure the momentary annoyance of turbulence. Their confidence is an unshakeable form of arrogance, their belief in air tables, crash statistics, the FAA, the strength of Boeing stock, the fluctuating price of OPEC air fuel, the reliability of Air Force flight training, and the great myth that man has tamed nature. But to me, flight is still a miracle, and one trip is *not* like the other. Flight is a form, like drama—the rise, the spectacle, and the fall—and each flight has its own life with innumerable variations.

My lover works for the Travel Bureau and he only begins to understand the importance of flight in my life. In many ways, I think I am his creation. I am the inheritor of his vision, just as he is created by others and by forces he has yet to recognize. I see this, and yet I don't feel superior. I don't have the power to escape the gravity of generations.

❊ ❊ ❊

My stewardess pays an exorbitant rent to live in a high-rise, she says, for the view. Often when she's home she'll climb the stairs to the roof to visit the peregrine falcons that the Department of Natural Resources is trying to reintroduce into the wild. She loves the thought of rare birds in a nesting box on top of her building. If they're successful, the newly hatched chicks will fly off and return to the high-rise next year to lay their new eggs. She likes to think that one day the entire roof top will be feathered with young falcons. She sees them riding invisible air currents all over the world, wheeling and swooping, flaunting their freedom until the nesting instinct radios them back to the high-rise and they lock in a return flight pattern for home.

My lover doesn't keep pets because she's seldom at home, but her overnight bag has a leash and it follows her obediently on hidden wheels that squeak. The high-rise doesn't allow animals, and besides, her apartment is very small. But my stewardess is a model of efficiency and used to tight quarters. Her kitchen is packed with time and space savers, and she's the first to admit that she's overly reliant on Lean Cuisine to keep her weight at the optimum level set by the airline. Except for a Chagal print of a free-floating man, her living room walls are bare (she likes the dimensionless feel of the color white). When we sleep at her apartment I slide open the door to her closet and find her blue uniforms. She keeps six, all clean and pressed and hanging next to each other like in a dispenser. On her dresser, in the jewel box she picked up from the duty free shop at the Hong Kong airport, she keeps three pairs of little pin-on golden wings and her enamel name tags. And suspended in her window is a scaled down model of the Concorde which is her dream machine.

Blue and red airplanes soar and dive on my lover's see-through shower curtain. When we let the bathroom fog up with steam, the planes are lost in a cloud bank. In the morning, without our contacts, my lover and I can barely see in the shower. With the dwarfed soap bars she takes from the jumbo jets, we feel for each other and soap each other's backs. The small soaps nest perfectly in my palm, slowly dissolving against my lover's skin until they disappear in the water and gray steam like lost babies.

On special evenings, nights when she has been delayed in Singapore, I meet my lover at the airport and we have drinks at the Seven Continents Lounge on the Blue Concourse. The cocktail waitress serves our Manhattans with plastic airplane swizzle sticks speared through our cherries. And we watch the taxiway as jumbo jets slowly nose past each other like steel geese.

On these nights, I drive my lover to her apartment and lead her to the bedroom. Her blue uniform falls freely to her waist. Since she has had no time to change, she is still wearing her flight underwear. Quarter-sized black dots are painted on the tips of each white bra cup like the nose cones of twin Boeings. She steps closer and the blue uniform lands gently on the ground. My stewardess wears V-cut panties that are shaped like the wings of a Jumbo Jet. We embrace and we fly.

Later, when all is still, we float on her water bed and listen for the falcons above. Glow from the moon slowly uncovers us and the muted sounds of night pass through the glass window. I don't have to see tears to know my lover is crying.

She can never have a baby with me. I think she knows this, but she doesn't know why. Always she looks at me to find the answer but never asks. There's nothing I could tell her, and instead our bodies meet and the waves beneath us roll.

❀ ❀ ❀

He is silent, my lover, and he believes his silence conveys meaning. I respect silence too, but not as an explanation.

All day I am silent at my job. It's part of being an Air Hostess. When a well-meaning passenger asks me how I am, I can't confide to her. I can't say how much I crave a child by my darling lover; a child both perfect and flawed in spectacular ways, whom I will teach and by whom I will be taught the meaning of love and creation. No. I am a model of professionalism and I maintain a certain artificial distance at all times. I provide hospitality, the illusion that I am happy to please everyone, that I will bestow miniature tokens of my affection—Tanqueray Gin, almonds, half-pillows—selflessly. Of course, I am not happy, but like a convincing actress, I have learned to lie to myself. And only when the truth is flung at me in a loud rubbery screech at the end of the day am I filled with diving despair.

But I love my sweet travel man. I love his red tie with the small jet clip, his suit, his fanciful nature, his tiny insecurities, even that misextension of his love which believes he has some power over what he has created. I love his physical being, how he fills his suit, the press of his warm body, the pulse of blood that traffics through his neck. I love that his beard grows even when we sleep, that wrinkles slowly erode his face, even that he will eventually die. And yet, at times, he seems imaginary. His world, his expectations, his endearing fetishes are unreal to me. Perhaps, now that I think about it, it's this foreign quality which attracts me.

And I hesitate to mention this, but there are times when he *is* purely imaginary. When we make love, well, when I make love . . . I mean it helps that he looks a little like Patrick Swayze. And then it just goes on from there. He reads as featureless movie star or construction worker or Cameron, the gay steward I work with. Sometimes he's even a woman. It's limitless, really, and I don't mean that to be crass. I love him, and I don't want anyone else, but sometimes I like to indulge. I know I'd be terrified if I woke up with Patrick Swayze or an astronaut or some crazy exotic someone, so I transform my travel man. It's odd to think he must do the same with me.

Sometimes I wonder how my first class passengers see me.

Their world seems far more unreal than my dear travel man's. I watch as they sip champagne while steerage passengers cattle by. I suppose it's their deluxe illusion, what they call success. And although it's my job to cater to their fantasies, and I have done this seemingly all my life, I still don't understand the supreme orgiastic pleasure of endless indulgence. It's a little like using oral sex as birth control, wonderfully satisfying to a point, but what does it have to do with the real business of life? What does it have to do with making babies?

❁ ❁ ❁

My lover is always the last off every plane. She tells the other flight attendants to leave while she stays to straighten up the galley or tally up the cash receipts from the mini-bar. Everyone realizes how much she loves travelling—the anticipation, the speed, the excitement—and they give her these few moments to be all alone in the jumbo jet. Though they work with her every day, nobody suspects my lover's terror each time the plane descends, terminating her flight. My lover's joy is the buoyancy of flight. For her, the darkest moment of each trip is that sinking feeling when the wheels touch down. The screech of rubber against the runway is a cry of pain. She lives with it each day, and at night the cry of a dying child invades her dreams.

❁ ❁ ❁

There are moments as I'm flying when I'm overcome with sadness. We fly in machines, great mechanical tubes, and it only reminds me that I can't escape the ground, that I'm fooling myself as much as I'm fooling gravity. And it makes me wonder about my desire to have a child. Is it only some blood drive to push beyond myself, to escape mortality? There must be something more.

I like to think the illusions and the stories we tell ourselves are more important than we admit. I believe in the designed beauty of the airplane—the balance of aerodynamics and aeroaesthetics is the delight which comprises life. Have you noticed how the wing of an aircraft curves just slightly, causing a discrepancy in airspeed between the underside and top? This unevenness creates tension. Love between two people, I think, is like this. One moves and acts and feels with a different intensity than the other. The result is lift, the experience of flight.

❀ ❀ ❀

On her layover days, my lover likes to picnic in the park. We unfurl the tightly wrapped Pan Am blankets and patch them together on the grass. Sometimes when it's overcast we lie on our backs and lose our thoughts in the clouds. On brilliant days, when the sky is clear and jet streams cross-hatch the sky, my lover tries to read the vapor trails like the Head, Heart and Life lines on my palm. She says no two patterns are alike and they mean something to her that I'll never understand. There is mystery and also great trust between us.

Outside in the clean air, everyone imaginable pushes babies. On our blankets in the middle of the park, we watch as parents fill their babies' lungs with fresh oxygen. Dr. Spock suggests wheeling newborns for three hours daily and the older, plumper ones for an additional hour. I like the eight-wheel, all-terrain moon buggies, but my lover prefers the collapsible umbrella-handle type because they travel easily, even on an airplane. These movable babies go everywhere; they criss-cross the nation. And there are more babies and more buggies waiting to fill the streets. I tell my stewardess I love her and she knows this. I lie and tell her she will have my baby. She smiles peacefully, unsurprised. We sip from the same half liter of complimentary Chablis and watch the baby traffic.

Every six seconds another baby is born and my stewardess waits calmly for her late arrival.

❅ ❅ ❅

I love my Travel Man, but I'm capable of so much more than he imagines. I am pregnant.

I haven't told him yet. I haven't thought he was ready for it. But maybe that's a lie. We tell each other lies out of kindness. We think the truth has the power to crush and I suppose we see each other's weakness as a form of adoration. But how did we make each other so dependent? Isn't that the real lie? I know he'll love the baby. Tom's such a tender man. Once he recognizes how things are he'll adjust. He'll be the model father of a model baby girl.

Tom will want to call her Ariel or Angelica, an airy name, but I won't have it. She'll be Ruth or Lucy or Sara, and she'll play in the dirt and swim at the ocean. She'll want a toy six-shooter for Christmas and nothing else, or an old iron typewriter to take apart with a screwdriver and pliers. She'll fall out of trees and fight with the boys; I'll yell at her to come down off the roof, and she'll listen to the same Edith Piaf song over and again until it becomes a Zen-like child's anthem. She'll forget where she buried things in the yard, and my gold pin-on wings will go missing, as will the gerbil when she sets him free. There will be knee scrapes and stitches and small uncontained fires in the woods. And until she's five, she'll point to every plane in the sky and say, "Mama, Mama."

And Tom will love her dearly, all his preconceived ideas of her rushed away in her cyclonic activity and perpetual shifts and changes. How we'll both try to capture her over and again as she eludes our grasping attempts. And, without knowing it, some day Tom and I will blunder into each other, tripping over our own astonishment for little Ruthy, and realize suddenly, oh quite by accident, where we have been and just how far we have travelled.

Paul Michel Baepler. *In Chaos Theory, people talk about something called the Butterfly Effect. It's the notion that the innocent flutter of a butterfly's wing today in Hong Kong can transform storm fronts next month in Maine. I like the "Butterfly Effect" as a metaphor for writing. I know that when I write I start with something small—an image or a smell or a chance encounter—and over time my imagination whips it up in ways I couldn't have predicted. Something chaotic happens. Or in the language of my story "Travel," flight occurs. I don't mean to sound mystical by any means, but I think there's a tendency to overestimate the crafting of a story . . . and for a good reason: we can learn control. Chaos is a different matter. It's always new.*

My work has appeared in several journals, most recently in Negative Capability *and* Exquisite Corpse.

JOHN TOREN

Mountain Upside Down

I F YOU'VE SEEN THE "David Letterman Show" even once, you won't have any difficulty envisioning the evening he telephoned a woman operating a concession at the Grand Canyon, and asked her to describe the view. He was hoping, as he told the audience, to get her to say "breathtaking," and he was more than a little incensed when she failed to provide him with the expected cliché. We can safely conclude on the basis of this episode, I think, that David Letterman has never seen the Grand Canyon. He may have been there, but he's never really *seen* it. Why? Because whatever else it may be, the Grand Canyon actually is breathtaking.

After a long day at the office, or the challenge of getting the kids fed and to bed, the stuff and nonsense of late-night T.V. can be invigorating and relaxing. I don't find baiting people by phone amusing, however lighthearted it may be, though many viewers no doubt do. What troubles me is the evident glee with which the studio (and presumably the home) audience enters into this kind of project, oblivious to the fact that the joke is actually on them. Letterman's banter and hijinks may be entertaining, but they're often depreciative. The Grand Canyon, on the other hand, has no entertainment value whatsoever, yet the mere sight of it can be ennobling. If the remarks we make about this august hole in the ground are cliché-ridden and flat, it isn't because the Canyon itself has become a cliché but because it stands, even in this age of instantaneous electronic communication, beyond reckoning or description. When our late-night comic turns his (and our) attention in that direction, we run the risk of enjoying a cheap laugh, while subtly defiling a great natural wonder, and also ourselves, in the process.

❊ ❊ ❊

"Noble deeds are possible only in periods when self-irony is not yet rife," the French essayist E.M. Cioran remarks. Noble sights as well?

❊ ❊ ❊

Yes, I visited the Grand Canyon not long ago. I'd seen the pictures, had vicariously ridden the whitewater in rafting sequences of "National Geographic" and "Nature" specials and accompanied mule trains as they plodded along on dusty trails with a thousand feet of empty air dropping away below them. Yet the first time that desert wonder actually came into view through the trees at Mather Point, I realized that I'd never seen the Grand Canyon. At that moment it became clear instantly why, to those who haven't seen it, the Grand Canyon can hardly be more than a cliché. Everyone knows that it's big and colorful, that there isn't anything else in the world remotely like it. What you cannot know, until you look down into it, is what it's really like.

❊ ❊ ❊

In one of his letters Flaubert identifies *Hamlet, Don Giovanni,* and the sea as three incontestably sublime things. He hadn't seen the Grand Canyon.

❋ ❋ ❋

Many visitors to the Grand Canyon tarry only briefly before continuing on to Monument Valley, the Petrified Forest, Las Vegas, Disneyland, or Mesa Verde. The world's biggest hole in the ground. Yes, but what, precisely, are you supposed to *do* there?

Mary McCarty once remarked with respect to Venice that everything that can be said about it already has been said . . . including the quip that everything that can be said about it already has been said. It seems to me that nothing of real substance or relevance has yet been said about the Grand Canyon, and nothing ever will be . . . including the remark that nothing of real substance or relevance. . . . Its vastness, its intricacy, its beauty, its mercuriality, its threatening presence, are not the stuff of language. All the talk about geology, about eons of uplift and erosion, the various named and unnamed strata; about Colonel Powell, the one-armed officer who first navigated the depths of the Canyon in a wooden boat; about the peculiar breed of squirrels that have evolved on either side of the crevise; all of this information, which the museums and park rangers dispense on a daily basis throughout the year, may be interesting, but with respect to the colossal presence and impact of the canyon itself, it's merely a distraction. The canyon is there, it confronts you, imperturbable and unique.

The bigness of the Grand Canyon is unlike any other bigness. Mountains are big, it's true, but to see their bigness, you have to remove yourself from them, at which point they become remote. The ocean is big, but it's a flat receding bigness: You're always struggling to see what's "out there." The bigness of the Grand Canyon, on the other hand, is yawning right in front of you. Vast though it is, you see it in what seems to be perfect detail. The light at a hot dry 7000 feet above sea-level is bright and clear. The fact that the inner gorge is of darker rock and largely hidden from view gives it added mystery. Oriental names have been given to many of the buttes and spires—Shiva Temple, Zoroaster Temple, Cheops

Pyramid, Rama Shrine—which is unfortunate in some ways, I think; the names seem contrived and unimaginative. On the other hand, these promontories largely lack human associations, because few humans have ever visited them. Meanwhile, the fact that there is no readily identifiable point of reference within the canyon gives its contours a bewildering otherworldliness.

The Grand Canyon may be the ultimate mandala.

❀ ❀ ❀

It's been a recurrent theme in European philosophy since the time of Emmanual Kant that space and time don't really exist. No, these qualities are the creation of the human mind, which makes use of them to bring order to experience. On the face of it this theory is simply ridiculous. Why build an addition to your house, after all, if the extra space you need is already present inside your head!

Kant would probably find this common-sense view of things risable, yet consider his own argument: "Space is not a discursive or, as we say, general concept of relations of things in general, but a pure intuition. For, in the first place, we can represent to ourselves only one space; and if we speak of diverse spaces, we mean thereby only parts of one and the same unique space."

We ought to give Kant credit for taking an argument to extremes, but in fact what Kant describes is the reverse of what we actually experience. We'd be closer to the truth if we accepted the opposite proposition: We can represent to ourselves only particular spaces; and if we speak of space in general, we mean thereby only a collection of discrete and familiar spaces. Space makes itself felt *between* things. From that concrete experience of what artists call "negative space" we generalize an abstract and infinite "positive space" stretching out in all directions like a vast empty sea.

Though he loved to read travel books, Kant never actually saw the Grand Canyon. If he had, it might have occurred to him that he was in the presence of a space such as he could never have conceived intuitively if he hadn't actually seen it.

Claude Monet never saw the Grand Canyon either. Maybe it's just as well. He might have been unhinged by the experience. Yet as you watch the light change on the face of the innumerable crevises, gullies, outcrops, and buttes that make up the canyon walls, you can't help but think of Monet's famous renderings of the façade of Rouen Cathedral. The same subtlety, the same luminescence. You might, perhaps, have expected that the paintings he executed in the Cevennes, or on Belle Isle, being more "geological," would make a more fitting comparison. Yet the Grand Canyon is not primarily geological in appearance. This is perhaps the strangest thing about it. It speaks to us on a personal level; it arouses admiration and respect. Reverence. Whereas Monet's Cathedral façades offer us a heightened and energized vision of an architectural pile that may or may not be quite so vibrant in and of itself, the Grand Canyon offers us an array of shifting shadows and colors well beyond our ability to adequately absorb. I might even argue, against all commonly accepted notions of space, time, and art, that the Grand Canyon is Claude Monet's greatest achievement, or at least, that only he could really have "seen" it fully.

Taking nonsense one step further, let me suggest that we consider the Grand Canyon as a cunning collaboration between Monet, the master of evanescent nuances of shifting light, and Marcel Duchamp, who, by exhibiting a porcelain urinal as a work of art, taught us to look at things twice.

It took a million years to make the Grand Canyon, so we're told. Well, it took the history of our universe—ten billion years, that is—to make the glass of cheap Spanish wine that sits on my desk as I write. So what? It's diurnal time, not geological time, that's really interesting. Predawn light. The sunrise. The creeping greens and reds of mid-morning brilliance. The fiery glare of midday. The shifting shadows of the afternoon's progress, and the poetry of the sun's descent. A series that lacks unit structures. Things haven't changed, but now they have. One stares out across the ridges and buttes and spires and valleys as the clouds pass and the shadows shift.

A hodgepodge of buildings sits on the south rim of the canyon. Hotels, restaurants, mule pens, gift shops. I bought a deck of Grand Canyon playing cards, after considering but rejecting the Grand Canyon shot glass. I saw a number of people buying or wearing "I Hiked the Canyon" sweatshirts, some of whom I felt the urge to confront: "Did you *really* hike the canyon?" A flagstone patio stretches for several hundred yards in the narrow space between the buildings—all of which are rustic in one way or another—and the edge of the canyon. A low rock wall prevents tourists from tumbling into it. Crows sit in the branches of the trees that rise up from the escarpment below the terrace, scrutinizing passing humans at eye level before lifting off and out and down into the yawning abyss. A footpath leads from the end of the terrace out along the canyon rim. Before long a second path breaks off to the right, dropping immediately and precipitously as it enters the canyon itself. This is the famous Bright Angel Trail, the most popular avenue of access to the Tonto plateau and ultimately to the river itself. (There is no sign identifying it, though you can't wander far down that decline without beginning to wonder precisely where you're on your way to.) The main path ascends slightly as it follows the rim, leading out to the west past a series of promontories, spaced at roughly a half-mile from one another, which provide the breathtaking views we so often see reproduced in travel and nature magazines. These promontories can also be reached by car, and they usually are, I think, judging from the fact that we met almost no one on our walk from point to point. As evening descends on the Canyon, tourists, many of them speaking German or French, gather at these overlooks, which bear names like Hopi Point and Maricopa Point. Conversation is muted and intermittent, in part because so many people are taking pictures, in part because the intensifying beauty of the vistas drives onlookers into a state of stupified awe. In fact, the word "tourist" doesn't adequately convey the spirit of those individuals and families who have travelled great distances and arranged for accomodations, simply to see this tranformation of the canyon into night.

The sinister aspect of the Canyon emerges at the moment it occurs to you that wherever your eye takes you across the seemingly endless miles of ridges and buttes and ravines, you will, in all likelihood, be looking at a place where no one has ever been, and no one will ever be. This combination of brash visibility and utter inaccessibility is both tantilizing and unnerving. You find yourself reflecting, "If I were right *there*, I would be dead before long. If I fell in over there, there is no way I could get out, even if I survived the fall." This continual emotional vacillation between, on the one hand, expansive beauty and peace, and on the other, imminent injury and death, brings to the Grand Canyon an element which the German Romantics would have referred to as sublime.

All the same, I doubt whether anyone could look for long into the Grand Canyon from any angle without forming a childish desire to go down into it. Nor is such a desire difficult to fulfill. Although the Canyon is 227 miles long, there are hardly more than a dozen well-known trails leading in, and only three are actually maintained by the Park Service. Well, how many do you need? From the south rim, for the beginner, either the Bright Angel or the South Kaibab will do nicely. My wife Hilary and I had considered attempting the precipitous Grandview trail, as a means of avoiding the crowds, but our enthusiasm for this slightly less well-travelled, and considerably less well-maintained, avenue of descent cooled when we learned that a hiker, stepping back to frame a photograph, had fallen to his death there three days earlier.

We arrived at the South Kaibab trailhead at 8:30 in the morning. The parking lot was full. Many of the cars belonged to men and women who were camping down in the canyon, but as we negotiated the sharp switchbacks that bring one from the rim down the sheer face of the upper canyon wall we passed a number of hikers who were returning to the top, having gone down in the dark to view or photograph the sunrise. It was cold in the shadow of the canyon wall. The fine dust on the heavily travelled path was red, then yellow, then white, as we moved slowly down through the layers of ancient sediment. The path itself had been pounded to a smooth and beautiful trough. Turkey vultures soared in the sun above the pines of a side canyon hundreds of feet below us. Signs posted at several places early in the descent warned of dehydration and death, and cautioned hikers to carry at least a gallon of water per person per day. We had dutifully brought two gallons of water in a day pack, though it became clear in retrospect that these warnings were directed at midsummer hikers: At the end of the day, we had a gallon and a half left.

I was surprised at how lightly dressed many of the hikers were. Thirty minutes later we came out of the shadows into the blazing Arizona sun once and for all, and I immediately cursed myself for having worn the sweatshirt that would be wrapped awkwardly around my waist for the next five hours.

Walking into the Grand Canyon is like walking down a long steep hill. People with baby strollers go down into it. Youths jog down to the river and back. One spindly and apparently disoriented individual we passed was dressed entirely in black; he shuffled and stumbled and rested frequently on rocks and sloping walls with one arm outstretched for support, looking more like someone returning out after a long hot hike than someone going down in. He was swinging a large black boom-box at arm's length, which he used to record his impressions on tape with a little microphone. Two men, evidently oblivious to the majesty of the country they were passing through, avidly discussed the recent firing of a major league baseball manager as they loped along. One woman's knees began to shake uncontrollably as we approached the first major rest area. "My knees are shaking," she yelped, half-laughing, half-crying. "Get a grip on yourself," her husband shot back. "We've been on more strenuous hikes than this back in Seattle."

But the delight you feel at entering into the Grand Canyon, and of seeing close-up what you had previously seen only at a distance, and of feeling the walls of the Canyon rise behind you as you descend, so that you find yourself at last approaching the bottom of an immense and gorgeous domain—this delight never frees itself entirely from the accompanying thought that before long you're going to have to retrace your steps, climb up and out of that gaping and infernal hole. The desire is ever to go further down; the calculation is, "If we drop to the next level, will what we see justify the added agony of coming out?" Behind that question lies another one that beginners like ourselves can't help asking ourselves: "If we drop to the next level, will we *be able* to get back out?"

Hilary and I chose to stop our descent at the end of the long and relatively flat ridge that extends out from O'Brian Butte, three and a half miles along the Kaibab Trail, a third of the way down to the river. At this point, called "Skeleton Ridge" on the maps, the trail cuts sharply downward and to the east. Climbing over a small ridge off the trail to the west, we sat dangling our legs over the edge of the canyon wall, out of sight and of hearing of the hikers that were passing at intervals on their way both into and out of the lower canyon. The Tonto Plateau spread itself a thousand feet below us, its green sward now recognizable as a stubble of naturally-spaced stunted bushes, and in the distance we could see the Bright Angel Trail, draped like a piece of thin white thread down the south wall of the Canyon twelve miles away. Far below us to the north a switch-back of the Kaibab Trail reappeared—perhaps an hour of hiking away—from which point, we guessed, it would be possible to view the inner gorge. Looking back at where we'd come from, it seemed we'd hardly begun to enter the canyon! But from this vantage point we could, for the

first time, see a thin ribbon of brown water—the river itself!—
through a break in the ridges and waves of rock. We sat, and
gazed, and sat some more in the brilliant sunlight, surrounded by
energy and color and light and space, staring off and down at
places we wanted to get to, but would not. Not this time, anyway.
Three rubber rafts the size of grains of rice came into view in the
silence below us, drifting slowly down the river, and then vanished into the rocks again.

❊ ❊ ❊

I dreamed I was on the David Letterman show. It went something like this:

LETTERMAN: So, John, I hear you've been to the Grand Canyon. What was it like?

ME: I tell you Dave, it was simply breathtaking.

LETTERMAN: You mean the canyon actually took your breath
away. How do you explain it?

ME: I don't know what it is, exactly, this immensity, and
beauty, something indescribably big and powerful and . . .

LETTERMAN: But is this merely a physiological response? Can't
breathe, wind knocked out of you, that kind of thing?

ME: I don't think so. And besides, when you use the word
"merely" you seem to be implying that there's some other
kind of response that would be more meaningful. What
that might be I don't know. Maybe we should call it a
cerebro-sensual response.

LETTERMAN: (rubbing his chin thoughtfully): There's a passage in Spinoza's *Ethics* that may be to the point here. I'm
thinking of his definition of the emotions in Part Three,
where he remarks, simply enough, that pleasure is the result of a transition from a lesser to a greater perfection.

ME: You may be on to something there, Dave. The idea of coming into a greater and fuller realm of experience, something expansive and agreeable but not quite manageable. I'm not sure the reference to perfection is appropriate, though. A remark Max Scheler made may be even more germane. Something like this: 'There is a "hearkening" to what a feeling of the beauty of a landscape, of a work of art, says to us, or to what is conveyed by our response to a person standing in front of us. There is a heedful "going-along-with" this feeling and a serene acceptance of what stands at the point where it ends. We can have a good ear for what stands before us and a sharp testing of whether what we experience in this way is clear, unambiguous, determinate. We can cultivate a critical sense of what is "genuine" and "not genuine" here, or what lies in the line of *pure feeling* and what is only a subjective wish. All of this has been lost in the constitution of modern man. He has no trust in, no seriousness for, his own latent affection for particular things.'

LETTERMAN: I like that last part, John, which reminds me of the observation E. M. Cioran made. A funny guy, do you know his work? He said, "Noble deeds are possible only in periods when self-irony is not yet rife." (Sigh and impish smile). But tell me, did Max Scheler really say all that? You mean Max Scheler the little guy who runs the bagel shop on 42nd street? Well, I'll be . . . Hey! We're going to break for a commercial and when we come back Pavarotti, Roman Polanski, and Terri Garr will be joining us . . .

❋ ❋ ❋

The novelist Julian Green, who lived for many years in Paris, once remarked: "During the long war years, when I was living far

from Paris, I often used to wonder how so large a city found room
inside a tiny compartment of the human brain."

❊ ❊ ❊

Not that the Grand Canyon actually *means* anything. There is
no message there, no sign from above. It's a freak of nature, pure
and simple. Then again, everything that exists—you, me, Radio
City Music Hall, the snow on Mt. Kilimanjaro—is a freak of nature. As the Japanese philosopher Kitaro Nishida wrote, "A truly
pure experience has no meaning whatsoever; it is simply a present
consciousness of facts just as they are."

The Grand Canyon reminds us of how engaging, bewildering, threatening, and generally uplifting "facts just as they are"
can be.

John Toren. *Born in Minneapolis, I spent my formative years amid
the crabgrass, chiggers, and horny toads of Bartlesville, Oklahoma.
My family returned north when I was seven to the village of Mah-
tomedi, which some scholars believe was the model for the community
Dylan Thomas describes in "Under Milkwood." I became a Star
Scout, and I also played my best poker there.*

*I entered the University of Minnesota with an interest in math
and Spinoza, and left with degrees in European History and Anthro-
pology. Following a lengthy and intellectually feverish stint in Graduate School, my wife Hilary and I packed our furniture into my parents' garage and spent several months travelling in France—a
pleasure we've returned to repeatedly in subsequent years. Since that
time I've worked on the receiving dock of a local book distributor. The
air is brisk, interactions with my colleagues are seldom other than engaging, and, if the truth be known, moving boxes from point A to
point B offers satisfactions that the act of writing A, crossing it out,
and then writing B, sometimes does not.*

Still, writing is important to me. Fiction is out of the question—I have no imagination—and friends tell me my poetry is pretty bad; but several of my personal essays—on subjects ranging from croquet to alternative agriculture to modern dance—have made their way into the pages of Minnesota Monthly, Twin Cities Magazine, *and other regional publications. Since 1989 I've been responsible for the text of a quarterly pamphlet called* MACARONI *(available at select bookstores everywhere), in the pages of which I explore aspects of history, opera, birdwatching, religion, travel, cooking, film, literature, sports . . . sometimes all at the same time. I've long had it in mind to write a brief, scintillating, and erudite history of the glory years of modern European art and thought—in the American afterglow of which we've been groping now for half a century—but somehow, I haven't been able to get a weekend free.*

To me, writing is the same thing as talking. Of course, nearly everyone over the age of three knows how to talk. To the writer is given the opportunity to move, change, expand and alter his or her utterances, the theory being that, as a result of this privilege, the talking may occasionally rise to the level of singing.

MARIANNE LUBAN

Romance Language

WHEN MY BOOK, *The Samaritan Treasure*, first came out, people, especially the elderly, would stop me at the Jewish Community Center where I was often to be found. Some congratulated me on getting published, others expressed amazement at the fact of my having become an author, nothing about me having given any indication, in their opinion, that I might be up to anything of that sort.

"I wish I could write," some of them added. "The stories I've got in my head!"

Most were content to let those stories stay up there, it seemed, but a few participated in a creative writing workshop for seniors at the center, out of which came some marvelous things.

I, myself, took courses in Yiddish from time to time. While I'm fairly fluent in this language, I like to be around people who study it for fun. It brings back memories for many of them and they laugh at their own tripping tongues. I've noticed that Yiddish brings with it its own good time. Yiddish classes and groups have, these days, become a sort of indoor sport.

One day an elderly lady came up to me after class and said, "You're the youngest one here. Why old timers like myself want to talk Yiddish now is a mystery and an irony because, when I was

young, you couldn't give Yiddish away. The reason was everybody's parents spoke it and whatever your parents did was, naturally, just plain gauche."

"Some things never change," I said.

I offered the woman a ride home, which she accepted gladly.
She introduced herself as Fanny. When we arrived at her apartment building, she said, "If you're interested, I could tell you a
story that has to do with Yiddish. Since you're a writer, maybe
you'll put me in a book."

Fanny's apartment was orderly and imaginatively furnished.
Out of the ordinary, really. While most older Jewish women have
an abundant exhibit of photographs of children and grandchildren, Fanny's pictures were of a different kind. On her living
room walls I was surprised to see 8 x 10 glossies and film posters.
Rudolph Valentino as the Sheik was there as was a pert Clara Bow
with cupid's bow lips and spidery lashes. Jean Harlow and Lana
Turner glowed as though lit from within, and Clark Gable dis-
played dimples to die for. There were even a few Jewish stars,
Fanny told me as she pointed out Tony Curtis, Joan Blondell and
Leo Genn, whom Fanny pronounced the handsomest Jew ever on
the silver screen. Genn's huge, dark eyes stared at us from his picture with a mournful expression like that of a wounded stag.

I sat down, impressed but speechless. Fanny took a seat beside me.

"Some of these people were works of art," she remarked. "A
lot better than a Picasso, in my opinion, or even the Mona Lisa. A
beautiful face is God's masterpiece, I like to believe."

"Faces can fool you," I couldn't help commenting.

Fanny surprised me by agreeing with me. "You'd better believe
it! That's what I wanted to tell you about in the first place. This
story takes place in the old days, in the Twenties. It has to do with
Yiddish, too."

"I notice you speak it pretty well," I told her.

"Yeah, yeah," said Fanny with a dismissive gesture. "Too bad I
couldn't have been bothered to learn it better while my grand-

mother was alive so she and I could have gotten to know one another. My *bobbe* died when I was eleven and she didn't know English. Whenever I tried to talk to her in Yiddish, the result was somewhat like that explorer, Dr. Livingstone, trying out his Swahili on the natives for the first time. Come to think of it, no African ever looked with more suspicion on a strange white man than my grandmother looked on me. While I was too young at that time to be considered a real Jazz Baby, I was, to my family, a casualty of pagan times. The word 'neurosis' wasn't bantered about during the Twenties like it is today. *Meshuggeh* took its place very adequately, however. Even Freud, I'll bet, used the term from time to time.

"I kept mainly to myself at home, which wasn't difficult considering I was an only child. Harboring guilt feelings over not supplying me with brothers and sisters, my parents gave me a dime a week, which easily enabled me to support my habit.

"I was a movie maniac. My mind was not only one-track, it was sound-track, very convenient in that Silent Era. I lived in the real world only in a grudging way. Alone in my photo-papered room, I created sequels to the film I had seen the Saturday before. Once, my mother took me to see a doctor about my reclusive tendency. Probably due to my discomfort at being so closely examined by a stranger, the doctor pronounced me a nervous child. This gave no satisfaction whatsoever to my Russian-born, pogrom-veteran mother. To her, high-strung nerves were a Jewish condition, almost a monopoly, like a knack for playing the violin. On the other hand, there were types like my father's Aunt Rokhel, an eccentric of legendary stature. Whenever I caught my mother studying my face, I knew she was searching for the stamp of Aunt Rokhel in my features.

"However, this is not really my story. I was just there as a sort of curious bystander. There was an incident in our home when I was about fourteen that I have never forgotten. It had to do with boarders.

"Anyone who knows what a nickelodeon was, who recalls the

effects of Pluto Water and remembers silk stockings held up by blood-stopping garters, probably knew a boarder or two. When I was growing up, our family circle would have seemed incomplete without the various gentlemen who stayed with us. Ours was an undistinguished two-story house on the old West Side of St. Paul. Generally, our boarders were not quite greenhorns. Most of them had made a beginning out East and, oppressed by the pace and sheer numbers, had moved farther west where they had been told life was more like back home in the *shtetls* of Eastern Europe. I don't know if St. Paul in those days resembled a European hamlet, but, for four months out of the year, things were certainly nice and green and beautiful. During the winter, people soon grasped the fact that they had come to another Siberia.

"The turnover was constant. The men brought over their families or got married. Sometimes they left to go even farther west. One boarder, a cutter from Warsaw, moved to California and, like so many others from the garment industry, somehow became involved in motion pictures. I was thrilled, naturally, but my father found it inconceivable that a man could swerve so radically from the respectable trade he had followed since his youth. 'Wild horses couldn't drag me,' was his usual dismissal of the movies. I, myself, could barely envision our former boarder, neither sheik nor cowboy, in so romantic a business, but it occurred to me much later that, to a cutter of cloth, snipping film must have seemed rather an enticing challenge.

"What am I going on about? This story isn't about anybody from Warsaw. It really concerns an American woman who came to our door one day while I was upstairs practicing how to smoke an unlit cigarette (stolen from my father) in the most provocative way possible. My mother was in the cellar 'cleaning from the spiders', as she would put it.

"The young lady, apparently in her twenties and very conservatively dressed, was accompanied by two suitcases. She had come about our sign, which meant she intended to be our new boarder.

I should have explained to her immediately that my mother never took in ladies, but, to be honest, something about her intimidated me. Sitting in our parlor, she proceeded to interrogate me. What was our family name?

"'Nudel,' I told her. 'Ain't it awful? The kids at school razz me constantly. It gives me *weltschmerz* in the you-know-what.'

"'Build your character so as to rise above such nonsense,' the young woman advised. 'And don't say ain't. Do you think you might try to find your mother for me?'

"I yelled down the cellar. 'Ma, for pity's sake! There's a lady here with her luggage, Ma! . . . That'll make her shake a leg,' I assured our visitor.

"'Two seconds!' was the reply from down below.

"The young woman folded her gloved hands in her lap and gazed at me in that cool, unblinking way that has always made me say and do crazy things.

"'What's in the suitcases? Your lingerie, I suppose. Have you read *Stella Dallas?*'

"She replied quietly, 'Yes, I have.'

"'Risky, isn't it?' I submitted.

"'*Risqué,* you mean. Not very. Are you reading it?'

"'Just for the vicarious experience. Do you think vicarious experiences are best—or the real thing? You know, for emotional growth and all.'

"I never did receive an answer, for at that moment my mother came into the room and I was edged into the background as usual.

"As my mother often later explained, the house was empty and the young woman presented herself as very serious and spoke in a refined way. Plus, she was all alone in the world. To my mother, having no relatives was the worst misfortune that could befall a single girl—almost. But best of all, as I overheard my mother tell our neighbor, Mrs. Farber, the woman was a schoolteacher who might be available to help me with my homework!

"Mrs. Farber was eventually to form her own opinion of the female boarder:

"'Skinny and stuck up. A Mrs. Vanderbilt without the money and without the bilt.'

"As it turned out, the schoolteacher scarcely took any notice of me, much less offered to help me with my studies. And she wasn't exactly a blessing to my social life, either. Her presence in our home made me the object of even more teasing at my school where, the Fates would have it, she taught.

"Our boarder proved to be an unpopular teacher from the start. She was unsmiling, unbending and, of course, unattractive. Some spiteful students started the rumor that she wore a wig. Others said they had heard that one of her legs was a wooden one. I, being in a position to know that it was all nonsense, found myself having to take her part. Teacher's Pet became the least of the names I was called, although I was not even in her class. The two of us were barely on speaking terms, at home or at school. I had the feeling that she was even an anti-Semite until my mother told me with a laugh that the teacher was as Jewish as gefilte fish. Cold fish was more like it, I thought, wondering what could have happened to a Jewish girl to make her as stiff and unspontaneous as a DAR matron.

"But this she and I had in common—unfortunate names. Our boarder was called Sarah Bernath and some of her pupils, in order to entertain their classmates, would deliberately confuse her with the great French tragedienne, Sarah Bernhardt, who had died in 1923. It became not extraordinary to hear Miss Bernath (as portrayed by a seventh-grade girl) declaiming, 'Oh, Antoine, don't leave me!' or what fell on my unacculturated ears as 'My cherry' to an imaginary lover in the schoolyard.

"In reality, the Miss Bernath who lived with us never had gentleman callers and no more resembled a French actress than did my father, an Orthodox Jew who wore a skullcap and put on phylacteries every morning. However, when I got up the nerve to ask her about the 'cherry' business, she did explain and said the word *'cheri'* in such a way that I began to wonder if there wasn't more to Sarah Bernath than met the eye.

"Several months after Miss Bernath came to us, my father received a letter from Bucharest in Roumania, the place where he was born. He read it to my mother after supper, whereas I learned that Leon Hirsch would soon be arriving in St. Paul. This was hardly the first I had heard of the famous Leon, who, as a boy, had been a brilliant scholar. The family in Bucharest had thought Leon would become a doctor or a professor or something difficult, but he became an art dealer instead. In the end it hardly mattered what he did for a living as he had married a girl from a very wealthy family. Since my father had always thought of Leon as flourishing, he couldn't figure out why he wanted to leave Roumania. Leon's letters had offered no clues, but my father felt obligated to become his sponsor.

"Miss Bernath being absent, my parents began to argue the advisability of a young single woman and an unattached man living under one roof—ours. In the end, my mother had to admit that Miss Bernath's charms were none too apparent and my father took the position that Leon Hirsch was, after all, a married man and, like all the members of his family, a pious Jew.

"'A man with his wife in another country is still unattached,' maintained my mother, and before my father could say another word she fell to lamenting Miss Bernath's own unmarried state and the fact that the latter was looking increasingly gaunt and unwell.

"'She makes a mouth like my Aunt Rokhel in Roumania,' observed my father. 'That one was an old maid, too, and as lean as leather. A man could have shaved himself on her hipbone.'

"My mother gave vent to her worst fear.

"'Maybe she's got consumption—not that she doesn't eat well by us.'

"'Have you ever heard her cough?' asked my father.

"'No, but she's so yellow in the face.'

"'So tonight you'll ask her if she has consumption and she'll give you one of her looks and *you'll* drop dead!'

"'She never laughs,' persisted my mother.

"'What's an orphan got to laugh?' said my father, to whom life was simple.

"The next day my mother remarked to Mrs. Farber that Miss Bernath needed a husband to put roses in her cheeks, whereas Mrs. Farber cynically stated that men were best suited to blowing up bellies, not putting roses. It seemed to me that Mrs. Farber, a childless widow, had little to complain of on that score.

"Leon Hirsch arrived one afternoon just in time for dinner. Although dressed like a European merchant in a black suit and Homburg hat, he came up our walk rather like Lancelot crossing the drawbridge to Camelot. He moved slowly, taking in his first close-up view of an American neighborhood. When he caught sight of me staring at him from an upstairs window, he smiled, and I believe that, even as a grown woman, I have never been so affected by a man's appearance.

"If this Roumanian cousin was an observant Jew or any sort of Jew at all, he gave no outward sign of it. He was two heads taller than my father, beardless, slender, and his collar fit him. While his eyes were dark, he had hair of an ash-blonde shade that Miss Vilma Banky or Miss Mae Murrays themselves, might have envied.

"It was apparent that my father, also, was somewhat unsettled by the splendor of this *landsman* he had not seen for so many years. When my father left Roumania, his young cousin had been a *yeshiva* prodigy in a baggy black coat wearing dangling earlocks. At that point Leon Hirsch had been scheduled to become a rabbi, but he gave it up to study at a secular university. When this cosmopolitan gentleman greeted my mother and me, it seemed startling to hear familiar Yiddish come out of his mouth.

"Somewhat later in the kitchen, my mother handed me a dish

to bring to the table, whispering, 'A prince we've got now! A regular count!' and then for some reason added, *'Oy vey iz mir!'*

"The only one who seemed unimpressed by Cousin Leon was Miss Bernath. She was introduced, replied politely, and began eating her dinner in silence. Not so indifferent was Cousin Leon. He addressed Miss Bernath but was coolly informed by her that she did not speak or understand Yiddish.

"'My English is not so good,' Leon admitted.

"'Miss Bernath knows French!' I couldn't resist putting in.

"My mother made shushing sounds at me and Miss Bernath even blushed a little, I thought. Cousin Leon said something to the lady boarder in what I'm sure was excellent French. She replied and they had a brief conversation that might have been very ordinary but that sounded wonderful. My father seemed greatly pleased at this demonstration of the erudition of his family, something of which he had often tried, but in his opinion, failed, to convince Miss Bernath.

"After that, the dinner conversation consisted of father and Cousin Leon discussing, in Yiddish, relations in Roumania and Leon's plans in America. It had been decided long before that Leon would board with us until he had found employment and was ready to bring his wife and son over from the Old Country.

"Looking at him more closely, I decided that Leon Hirsch was far from being a young man. He had quite a few white hairs mixed in with the blonde ones and there were tired lines around his mouth. His hands, so unlike my father's in their pale slimness, trembled from time to time, betraying the strain of his journey. Somehow, I found myself wishing that Miss Bernath did not wear her hair brushed back so tightly from the part in the middle and that she would raise her eyes, which were blue and not unattractive. I wished, against logic, that she would break out with some line of witticism or flirtation even that would put another smile on the face of this greenhorn who had made so dashing a start in the New Land. But Miss Bernath was quiet and ate diligently.

"Cousin Leon made no further effort to engage her in conversation, that is, until after dinner when she excused herself to correct papers. He looked up then and said in Yiddish, 'How very strange that a Jewish daughter does not know the language of her people,' to which she answered, *'Bon soir. Monsieur.'* At that Cousin Leon laughed in a manner I was certain no woman except Miss Bernath could have resisted.

"Cousin Leon or 'Uncle', as I was told to call him, did not open an art gallery nor owned so much as a picture postcard. He found a job in, of all places, a cigar factory. I couldn't picture him happy in such work, but I never heard him complain. He also seemed content to stay at home and spend the evenings with my parents. During their long discussions, I noticed that it was my father who gesticulated and changed his tone for emphasis while Uncle never seemed to have any strong opinions but simply sat and listened, his tobacco-stained fingers forming a placid tent. Occasionally Uncle went for long walks, returning with books in French from the library or just some new words for his English vocabulary that he had picked up. One time, after my mother had rebuked me for behaving like a 'wild beast', as she put it, Uncle Leon put his arm around me and declared that I was just 'a young flepper'. Greenhorn or no, it was Uncle Leon who turned out to be the one who helped me with my homework.

"Except with my English papers. Since all those with whom he worked spoke Yiddish, there seemed no pressing need for Uncle to learn English. But one night as Miss Bernath returned from one of her 'concerts', I saw him say something to her in reply to which she nodded gravely. After that, each evening Miss Bernath gave Uncle Leon an hour's lesson in English. I, too, was forced to attend by my mother with the idea that I might learn to speak a more dignified English myself. During those lessons Uncle Leon made the teacher laugh quite often, although she did her noblest not to.

"In spite of the tutoring and preparation for her daily classes, Miss Bernath still managed to go out several nights a week. None of us had any real idea where she went, although my father always asked the same question the following morning in a tone that struck me as all too nonchalant.

"'How was the concert?'

"'Very moving, thank you,' Miss Bernath would say crisply, and, without further comment, gave all her attention to her breakfast.

"One evening, in the middle of a lesson, Uncle Leon suddenly asked, 'What do they play at these concerts? I would like to hear Tchaikovsky again.'

"Miss Bernath stared at him for a moment.

"'Is your outlook really so consistently frivolous?' she asked and even made Uncle look up the word 'frivolous' in the dictionary. The next night, however, they were both gone.

"Something began to worry my mother. I heard her remark to my father that she never saw Uncle Leon write any letters to Roumania.

"'Give him time,' my father told her. 'He's not used to rolling cigars. Besides, maybe his wife can't read.'

"That seemed to satisfy my mother, who also had difficulty signing her own name.

"As he grew more Americanized, Uncle Leon, with much encouragement from me, acquired an enthusiasm for the movies. He went with me every Saturday, which I knew distressed my father. But I think my father finally decided that attending the pictures was not work and therefore did not desecrate the Sabbath. Father had never protested my going. He was far too kind a man to watch a child sit at home restricted and restless.

"Because of my handsome escort, I became the envy of all the girls in the neighborhood, not to mention a good many older women. We were walking home from a Theda Bara film and I casually asked Uncle if he thought Miss Bara pretty. I, personally, found the vamp with her black eye-shadow a bit on the sinister side.

"He answered, 'Very. She reminds me of Miss Bernath with her dark and mysterious glances.'

"'But Miss Bernath is homely!' I burst out.

"'Nu,' chuckled my uncle, 'do you think everyone can be a milk and roses beauty like you?'

"Receiving such a compliment from my uncle did not lessen the shock of his comment about Miss Bernath, for I now realized he was in love with her. Aloof, astringent, plain Miss Bernath, what was there about her that could possibly attract a man? After that I spent much time speculating about what she would think if she knew. That led to thoughts of what my parents would say if *they* knew, and so I hoped my uncle would get over his infatuation very quickly. Besides, I loved him far too much myself.

"Yet my chief concern was for Miss Bernath. Somehow I sensed she would be made to suffer. She was altogether too ordinary. In the pictures, the very good-looking people, like Uncle Leon, never seemed to be the losers. They always went on, seldom more than momentarily crestfallen, armed with their beauty. One felt it would never fail them.

"Other irregular things began to happen. Mrs. Farber, the 'nextdoorike,' took to acting very peculiar. She stopped in twice as much as before, carrying bakery, which she always 'hoped Mr. Hirsch would enjoy.' She ignored my mother's hints that Mr. Hirsch had a family in Bucharest, as though suspecting my mother of denying her her chances in favor of a match that my mother wanted to engineer.

"One Sunday afternoon Uncle transfixed Mrs. Farber with his natural gift for conversation while my father sat by, glowering. He had never liked Mrs. Farber much, and I never knew what prevented him from strangling her now that she was behaving so annoyingly. I will never forget the expression on Uncle Leon's face when Miss Bernath walked out onto the porch where they were sitting, nodded at them and sailed off. I hoped it was obvious only to me that Uncle longed to spring up and run after her, if only to escape Mrs. Farber. The neighbor was whispering of how she could have sworn that yesterday she had seen Miss Bernath lighting up a cigarette behind the shed in our backyard. My father, dependably tolerant of the habits of others, merely raised an eyebrow and shrugged. Uncle Leon took a sip of his tea. 'Even the coldest flint can make a spark,' was his odd comment.

"Miss Bernath did not return that entire day. As I passed her room on the way to my own, I noticed one of her suitcases standing near her bed. All right, the door was open a crack, so I pushed it open a little more. Was the teacher thinking of leaving us?

"Then I did something I had never done before. I went into Miss Bernath's private domain. Not only that, I also opened the suitcase, which was not locked as the device was broken.

"At first I was disappointed; it contained only books. But, on closer inspection, I saw that the books were not those ordinarily used by teachers of the seventh grade. It occurred to me that *Class Struggles in France* had nothing to do with rebellious schoolchildren and that the *Code de la Nature* was not a science textbook. There were pamphlets that spoke of capitalism and the *bourgeoisie*. One bore the legend: 'From each according to his capacity, to each according to his needs.'

"Other books, far more interesting to me, were novels of the dimestore variety whose covers hinted of sizzling romance. The last thing I looked at in the suitcase was a dance card with a silk tassle, devoid of names, but with the word 'beasts' scrawled across it in a bold hand. I was relentless that day. In Miss Bernath's wastebasket I found a crumpled note that cautioned 'Burn everything. Hard times are near.' Perhaps Mrs. Farber had witnessed the teacher striking up a match, after all, but for a different purpose than smoking. Somehow I became convinced that Miss Bernath would not be stopping with us much longer, but I said nothing to my mother. I had little warmth toward the hard-faced spinster, yet I knew for certain that, had she discovered something about me that I wished to hide, my secret would have been safe with her.

"Two days later the mailman brought Uncle a letter from

Roumania. Having read it, he went to the window and stared outside for awhile, tapping himself absently on the brow with the rolled-up paper. Later, he told my father that his wife had written him that he need no longer concern himself about the funds for her passage to America. Her father had relented, had given her the money, and she and their son planned to come as soon as possible. When my father offered his congratulations, Uncle Leon merely said, 'Yes, her father is a rich man and I am a poor one.'

"It was then that my father and I realized that Uncle Leon had either cut himself off from the fortune of his wife's family or been disenfranchised for some reason.

"At that same time Uncle developed a cough he claimed was due to the particles of tobacco that floated around the shop where he worked. He declined to attend a wedding with my parents that Sunday, saying that he did not feel well. As usual, when my parents wanted to go out, I begged them to let me go to the movies instead of tagging along. Uncle Leon didn't want to go with me either. To my mind, he looked more worried than ill.

"Arriving at the movie house, I discovered the film was one I had already seen and hadn't cared too much for the first time. Having spent my money on ice cream, instead, I went back home. The scene I found there was a frightening one.

"Knees shaking, I stood in the hallway, unnoticed by Uncle and Miss Bernath who were having a terrific argument. That is, Miss Bernath was shouting at Uncle. Her usually-neat black hair hung in strands over her face and she kept pushing at it. Her cheeks were red as though she'd been slapped and her eyes were as I'd never seen them. The pitch of her voice was high and savage. It was not a Miss Bernath I knew. In fact, it came to me that Miss Bernath had not been herself for quite some time. Hadn't my mother said just the day before that while Uncle seemed poorly, Miss Bernath was flourishing at last?

"'Perhaps she has stolen a bit of his beauty away,' she had remarked with a sigh.

"But even my mother would not have believed me had I described our lady boarder as I saw her that day. For a moment I thought perhaps Uncle Leon had assaulted her in some way, but knowing him, it seemed hardly possible.

"'You are a spineless worm!' she screamed at him. 'All you need to do is write one letter, yet you haven't that much backbone. You told me you loved me and not her. Her father will take care of her. She isn't even in sympathy with the cause. Tell her to stay where she belongs!'

"Uncle told her that she was too young to fully understand such matters. The thing she wanted him to do was not honorable. Besides that, Miss Bernath had her whole life ahead of her and was too educated to saddle herself with a failure who might never be able to make a decent living in America. As for the cause, Uncle wanted to hear no more about it. He no longer cared about the communist ideology. Too many causes had forced him to a strange land where his tongue was clumsy and his lungs were filled with filth in a stinking cigar factory. In spite of that, Uncle told Miss Bernath he liked America and that he felt communism had no place here. It was like putting a bandage where there was no wound, he said.

"'I love you,' he finally declared. 'You mustn't doubt that I admire you enormously. But I have nothing else to give.'

"Miss Bernath's fury seemed to mount with every word Uncle spoke.

"'You are not honorable,' she shouted. 'You are a coward! A coward and a fool like all the rest!' Then she ran upstairs and I heard the door to her room slam.

"Uncle Leon wiped his face with his handkerchief. After a moment, he started up the stairs, but changed his mind and went into the kitchen instead. Apparently Uncle had gone to get a drink of water because a glass smashed on the kitchen floor.

"I know; I swept up the shards myself. I had to go into that kitchen, you see. I was afraid that Uncle Leon would cut his beautiful hands even though a part of me was angry at him, at how miserably he had failed Miss Bernath. That is how I first came to realize how devastating certain men could be.

"Yet Miss Bernath, I thought, had been too greedy. Maybe if she, like myself, had gone to the movies, she would have known that women who looked like she did simply never aspired to men like Leon Hirsch. Beauty deserved beauty; that was the rule. At fourteen I was positive that was how nature had intended it to be."

❊ ❊ ❊

Fanny removed her eye-glasses and wiped them with a tissue concealed in her sleeve.

"You're the only person I've ever told this story to," she said. "I certainly never told my parents. I never liked Sarah Bernath much, but I thought of her several times over the years when I became better acquainted with her pain."

My eyes were drawn back to those photographs. How few of these glamorous individuals were actually still living. I recalled having read in the paper or in some magazine recently where someone had said they had seen that greatest of beauties, Hedy Lamarr, in her apartment building and had actually been startled at how grotesque she appeared.

"Do you still believe that," I had to know, "about beauty deserving beauty? Is that what you think really makes men and women fall in love with one another?"

Fanny gave a little laugh. "Are you kidding? Could I be this old and still believe such nonsense? I don't care what he told her—Uncle Leon never loved Miss Bernath. Men never love the women they admire. They only love women who are somehow, in some basic way, worse than themselves. The strong fall in love with the weak and the weak devour them. Love is not such a pretty thing when you put it under a microscope and the beauty of the people involved only adds to the confusion."

I thanked Fanny for her story and told her I would be in touch. I had the idea this woman had more stories than just one.

As I rose to leave, Fanny took hold of my arm.

"What's the matter with me? I forgot to tell you something about that quarrel. This occurred to me only many years afterward, but I'm sure I heard right. The entire argument between the teacher and my uncle had taken place not in French, not in English, but in everyday, homey Yiddish."

Marianne Luban. My family and I were immigrants shortly after the Second World War. I recall, as a little girl of six, going to school without a word of English. Six years later I had developed a love for language and was writing all the time. I had a rinky-dink typewriter, parts of which were held together with rubber bands. Since those days it has become clear to me why I write. I agree with William Faulkner when he said that writers are people who don't want to pass through the wall without leaving a mark on it.

My "mark" is to be found in my short fiction collection, The Samaritan Treasure *(Coffee House Press). This book is described in the forthcoming 500* Great Books By Women *(Viking Penguin), which makes me feel rather vindicated for the years of patient perseverance against the odds. I have learned that perseverance is the key word in the writing game, something I am trying to remember as I try to find a publisher for my new collection,* Death-Defying Thoughts.

Most of my stories are on Jewish themes. The well-known Jewish writers are nearly all men. Why this is I'm not sure, but it looks like just another set of odds to me. My dream is to nudge these great men over just far enough so that I can squeeze myself into the portrait.

Marianne Luban

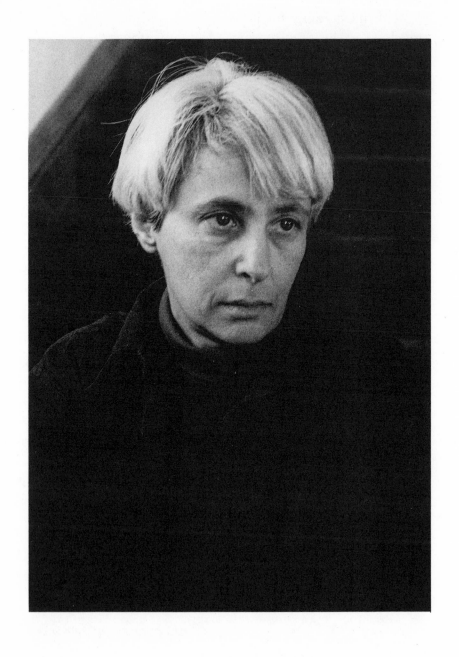

ELLEN HAWLEY

Remembering Anna

My father's sister was a psychoanalyst—a Freudian, a recorder of early trauma. She saw patients in her apartment and they waited for her in the living room, sitting where we sat when we visited. From the couch they looked at the oddly flattened picture of a walled city and from the chairs backed stiffly against the opposite wall they saw the portrait of Anna as a young woman.

Then Anna herself would appear, short and bargelike in the doorway, and they'd follow her into the next room, which held the couch, her chair, and a desk. At the end of their time they left the inner room through a converted closet which led directly out to the hall, a dozen paces from where they'd come in.

As a child I knew this, that Anna hid her patients from one another. So I knew that what she did was shameful.

When I was supposed to go out with Anna, I lost things. My shoes and barettes disappeared. I cried because I had to wear a dress, or because the snarls pulled when my mother brushed my hair.

Anna took me to museums or to the zoo, and I became aware, in her presence, of my behavior—not of whether it was good or bad, but of what it might signal. I became aware of interpretation. I felt her there, watching me.

In return I watched back. I was her only niece and I knew she favored my cousins, Danny and Jay. I also knew I was expected to like her. She told me she enjoyed having a girl to buy presents for. She bought me a rag doll I could strap on my feet and dance with; she bought me an embroidered Mexican blouse. She pinched my cheeks and asked, "How's my ootsa pootsa pootsa?" and she encased me in the smell of powder and perfume. I rubbed at my cheeks to remove her touch and when that didn't work I splashed them with water.

We struck a balance, Anna and I. She wanted and I withheld. She wanted to be a second mother; she wanted to understand me. She talked to me in that voice adults save for children, and I answered her in sentence fragments. I wasn't sure I wanted anyone to understand me, but especially not her.

In case anything happened to my parents, she was to be my guardian.

"In case anything had happened to us" was the phrase my mother used, years later when she told me about the arrangement. I was sixteen and we were sitting at the supper table over a final cup of coffee, which I was just learning to drink. I'd added sugar and cream that night, and the sugar outlined the bitterness until I swallowed it like aspirin. My parents drank theirs black throughout the meal, and this presented itself to me as a virtue.

Why had they chosen Anna? Expertise. What else was there? I drank my coffee, which I held in my mouth for a minute before I could get my throat to accept it. I looked at the table and felt my lips pushing out into a pout.

"The fifties were a terrifying period," my mother said, answering the question that must have been on her mind. "Especially after the Rosenbergs were arrested. If it happened to them it could have happened to anybody. Any left-winger. It could as easily have been us. People were losing their jobs; people were turning their backs on everything they believed in."

"Paulie, you can't explain the fifties if you just breeze by the Rosenbergs like that," my father said.

"I already know about the fifties," I said.

"When the Rosenbergs were first arrested," he said, "their boys were shipped from one relative to another, and then for a while they were in a children's home. One never has the advantage of foresight and there was no way to tell what was going to happen, but in case the worst should have come to the worst, we wanted to work out something more stable for you."

"How come you didn't tell me?"

"It was a terrifying period," my mother said again. "We tried not to let it affect you."

"We wanted to find a middle ground," my father said, "between your need for security and the sense that we had to teach you some kind of caution."

Caution. The susceptibility of children to trauma was as accepted in our household as their susceptibility to chicken pox, so my sense of security took precedence. I had no idea that throughout the fifties my parents half-expected a visit from the F.B.I., although if I had known I doubt I would have understood the threat that implied. It would have been exciting; in fact, it would have been an honor.

As it happened, the F.B.I. didn't visit my parents. They went instead to my mother's mother, a gentle, late-Victorian lady. They asked about my parents. Did she know they susbscribed to *The Worker*? Did she know what meetings they attended? Did she know their friends? She'd been coached not to talk to them. My parents had told her, as they told me later, that there was nothing illegal or unpatriotic about that.

My grandmother told the agents they should be ashamed of themselves, worrying innocent people while gangsters walked around shooting each other. They were very polite, she said. Well dressed young men. Well spoken. And couldn't my parents—*I know you haven't done anything wrong but there's the child to con-sider*—couldn't my parents be more careful?

This too I learned later.

At the time, what I received were hazy warnings: don't talk to strangers; don't accept candy; don't get into cars and don't answer questions. I wondered if these were rules for all children or only for me. They made no sense to me but I don't remember being frightened.

My memory of the fifties is spotty though. My father was broad-shouldered in his suit, slender without it. When my mother dressed up she carried white cotton gloves, which I never saw her wear. She collected money for the Rosenberg defense fund and she stored it in a milk bottle in the linen closet. On the day the Rosenbergs were executed, I added three pennies. I remember it clearly. My parents had gone to the vigil in Union Square and the woman who stayed with me kept the radio on. When the news came that they were dead, I asked her to bring the bottle down and I dropped the pennies in one by one. She replaced the bottle between two stacks of blue towels and for the rest of the evening I smelled copper on my hands.

It was during the fifties that my mother ran for City Council on the American Labor Party ticket. This meant nothing to me except that I got to stand in a crowd and watch her speak from a sound truck. God, she was beautiful. She narrowed her eyes like a sailor keeping watch in a storm and her voice came to me doubled, first her natural voice, pitched to carry past the crowd and into the bricks of the wall behind us, then metallic words, pounding through the loudspeakers. I rode first on one voice and then on the other, then tried to decipher both at once. The wind drove her hair back. She leaned into the microphone and the men and women around me tipped their heads to watch her as if they were pulled. When she climbed down the ladder, I wrapped myself around her.

I wanted to be like her.

This was a part of my life I couldn't talk about at school. Or to Anna. As she asked about my life, it sounded pointless and average. She asked about my girlfriends, as she called them, or my boyfriends; as though the word friends wasn't good enough, they had to be sorted and tagged by sex.

"What kinds of games do you play with your girlfriends?" she asked.

"I dunno. Just games."

"Do you play counting games?"

I shrugged. "I s'pose. That's what kids do, isn't it?"

My rudeness went unacknowledged and I confused it with freedom. Anna became more distant, which we never mentioned. I was asked to go places with her less often. I saw her when she visited my parents or when we visited her, although it seems to me the visits became less frequent. Mostly I saw her at family parties, where we were buffered.

Family parties were ritualized events, permanently scheduled and impossible to miss. Thanksgiving was at Nora's; Christmas was at our house. We celebrated Christmas. My father's parents had been militant atheists and their children abandoned the Jewish holidays for Christmas, which, I think, struck them as less religious. It was a national holiday, my father said. Like Thanksgiving.

Anna's parties alone bore no relation to the calendar. She invited us when it suited her. The adults pulled chairs out to complete a circle at the coffee table. They drank Dry Sack, or Cherry Kijafa, or Kahlua, names I remember because with each new arrival Anna pushed the conversation back to whatever it was they were drinking. Around those embedded sounds I formed my picture of sophistication.

I drifted back and forth between the adults and my cousins, who played games which excluded me in the inner room, and on my way between the two rooms I stopped at the dresser that faced the front door and I eased the lid off the squat blue jar that always sat there, being careful not to let it clink.

This was where Anna kept candy—raspberry-shaped drops with a liquid center; flat candies with a colored flower that ran all the way through. Sometimes I eased the lid back on and took nothing. More often I reached in with two fingers and lifted one out by the twisted end of the wrapper, being careful so the cellophane wouldn't crackle.

I hadn't been forbidden to take the candy, but I couldn't remember having been told it was there. So to ask permission would have meant I'd been snooping.

My cousins clanked the lid. They reached their hands in to dig for the piece they wanted. No one objected, and it had absolutely no bearing on my approach.

It was at one of those parties that Anna told a story she'd heard: A woman in a mink coat walked into a delicatessen on the Lower East Side and pushed in front of several customers. She waved her hand at the man behind the counter and said, "Listen, I won't take a minute. All I want is a herring. No, you better make that two herring. And will you hurry? My chauffeur's double-parked outside."

The man behind the counter didn't move.

"Listen," she said, "I came all the way down here for a herring. The least you can do it sell me one. What's the matter? You don't want to do business? Will you listen a minute? Do you hear that? That's cars. Outside. They're honking. My chauffeur's blocking traffic."

So the man behind the counter lifted a herring out of the barrel and he held it out on a level with his face. He looked at the fish, and he looked at the woman. And he looked at the fish again and he looked at her again. And he shook his head and he said, "Lady. It doesn't want to go with you."

The story stayed with me. That anyone in my family would

be Jewish enough to tell it surprised me. So I remember the adults eating fish at those parties: pickled herring dripping its juice as they lifted it onto crackers; bright pink lox that left the smell of low tide on my fingers. And I think of Anna, almost square in her fur coat and fur hat, which is the way I remember her from the time when she still took me out afternoons, although I must have gone out with her in the summer too when she wouldn't have worn a coat. We walked down 75th Street to Second Avenue, past the kids I played with, and the fur coat marked us, at least in my mind, even more than the fact that I lived in the only elevator building on a block of five-storey walk-ups.

Neither the coat nor anything else embarrassed Anna. In front of the kids on the block; in front of the black woman who cleaned her apartment, whom, as my mother commented, she called Alice and who called her Miss Siegel; in front of the waitresses in the restaurants she took me to and the elevator man in her building, she was at ease. Commanding. Like gravity itself. In tow beside her, I felt glaringly white and more than ever like one of New York's middle-class brats.

Not that I didn't feel that way without Anna. I heard the kids on the block say things like "borrow me the ball" and knew I was supposed to say "lend me." To keep from setting myself too far apart, I said "loan me." But I was usually the one doing the lending. I owned a carriage I could push my dolls in. I owned books. When the ice cream truck stopped on our street and I shouted up from the sidewalk, I could count on my mother dropping coins down, folded in a piece of white paper.

The other kids from my building didn't play on the street. I remember the first time a girl named Sharon came upstairs to play with me. She wanted to ride the elevator so I pushed the button for the second floor. Then we hung out the window in my room and she called down to the kids on the street, "Hey! Look where I am."

I knew exactly what my role was.

The stories my mother relayed to me about my father's childhood, and therefore also, of course, about Anna's, stood in contrast to all this. I knew they'd grown up in a cold-water walk-up with the toilet in the hall—five kids and two adults in three rooms. I knew that my grandfather had taught Hebrew in the Old Country and that he was an educated man. I knew that in this country he lost job after job, and I knew that once a week my grandmother had boiled the wash on the stove and that the steam had packed the rooms until it squeezed out the air.

I went over and over these fragments. They formed a picture, but it wasn't one I could put my relatives into. Not the real people—not Anna, not my father. I accepted the stories, but I accepted them as mythology. The world before I was born was hazy to me and nothing I could do would make it solidify. As far back as I could trace the people I knew, they never matched up with the people my mother said they'd once been.

I was in my twenties and Anna was well into her seventies before it occurred to me to ask her about herself. What I was groping for, I think, was the person underneath the aunt—someone I could afford to like. We were sharing the piano bench at a party at my parents' house when I asked about her original interest in psychoanalysis. She answered me briefly and dismissed the question.

Then, a few days after the party, she asked me to have lunch with her at Schrafft's. We hadn't been alone together since I was a child, and I watched, fascinated, as she settled her fur coat and hat into a mound on the chair between us. The waitress came and went. I drank my beer with real concentration and resisted the urge to pet her hat. We talked awkwardly—about food, about wine, about beer.

"You asked me the other day why I entered analysis," she said finally, "and I didn't answer you adequately."

I couldn't remember having asked her anything that intimate.

"I had ended a love relationship," she said, "and I hadn't been able to come out of it properly. So I began seeing an analyst."

I held my fingertip flat on my beer mug, the moisture gathering around it. As far as I could remember our conversation, what I'd asked her was nothing more than how she decided to become an analyst, although in the language of the time I may have said, literally, "How'd you get *into* analysis?" So I asked again what I'd meant to ask, and she said analysis was new at the time. It was in the air everywhere. It was tremendously exciting. She talked about the fascination of studying the human psyche in its endless complexity, and we were on safe ground again. I settled into a half-trance and listened while she spoke in generalities. Already I regretted the conversation we hadn't had.

The next time I saw Anna, we were no closer for having talked. She was concerned that the woman who cleaned for her was stealing tablecloths, and I had fallen in love, first with a woman named Lucy and then, to make up for lost time, with women in general.

When about a year later Denise and I moved in together, I introduced her into the family. She took a liking to Anna and at parties she asked about the evolution of psychoanalysis and about Vienna in the twenties. She didn't mention the vaginal orgasm or Freud's famous faux pas, *What do women want,* and I'd mellowed enough to be grateful.

I was thirty-five when Anna died. My parents called with the news and when I put down the phone, to my own surprise, I cried. There followed several weeks of slow, continuous eating, which I recognized about halfway through as a form of mourning.

My aunts Sylvie and Nora took the job of sifting Anna's apartment and they asked me to choose something to remember her by. We walked a path through the boxes into which her dressers and closets had been emptied. Her portrait still hung in the living room—round-faced, serious, sterner than I'd known her but also less overwhelming. On the floor below it the picture of the walled city stood on its end. I chose the blue jar Anna had kept candy in.

Then we sat in the dismantled living room and I asked about the affair Anna hadn't come out of properly.

"There was no one man that I know of," Sylvie said.

Sylvie is the eldest now, with Anna gone. She was very much the Bohemian in her day and even now wears long scarves around her throat. She's a thin-boned woman and, like Anna, she never married.

"What about that one," Nora said. "With the hair." She ran a hand from her hairline down over her forehead to indicate the way his hair fell.

"Red hair? Thin little eyebrows?"

"No, no. Dark hair. Black hair. Fell forward like a bush."

Sylvie shook her head. "I don't remember that there was anyone in particular. Anna always had someone."

"Ach," Nora said. "You never paid attention."

Nora is the only one of my father's sisters to have had children. She is heavy, but not the way Anna was heavy. She carries it softly.

"Who was he?" I asked. "When was this?"

"She used to bring him home on weekends, for dinner. He gave me chocolates wrapped in foil. If I was eight or ten, Anna would have been—what? Twenty-three? Twenty-five? He had a beautiful laugh. I remember that. And he and Father could go on at each other for hours."

"What did they talk about?"

"At that age who listened. Sylvie, what did they talk about?"

"How would I know? I don't remember him. Religion maybe. Palestine. Socialism. What Father always came around to."

"I don't remember that he ever cared for the theater."

"The theater," Nora said. "Father loved the Yiddish theater."

"And you don't remember the one with the hair? Such beautiful hair. God, I was half in love with him myself."

"You see?" Sylvie turned to me. "It's not Anna's affair we're talking about here, it's Nora's."

"What ever happened to him?"

"He stopped coming with her."

"She never said why?"

Nora shook her head and I shrugged. Of course Anna never said why. If there had been anything to say. Maybe it was someone else—the man with the red hair, or someone none of them had met. Some married man with three kids and a balding skull. A Hassid. A stockbroker. It was all beyond imagination. I couldn't picture Anna in love. Nora yes; even Sylvie. But not Anna.

❊ ❊ ❊

So this is what I know of Anna. Or this is what I don't know of Anna. I'm not sure which tells me more.

I know that Anna went to Vienna to study psychoanalysis. How she financed the trip I don't know. I know that before she went there was a love relationship which she failed to come out of properly; and I know I never asked what that meant.

As I get older, I think more about the lives my father's family lived before I was born, the lives they live apart from me. They say very little about themselves and it works at me like a hunger.

The apartment where Denise and I live is laid out like the one in which they grew up—a railroad flat with the bathtub in the kitchen. We have six people fewer and much of the time we have hot water, but even so it's small and awkward, with grates on the windows and roaches in the kitchen. Both of us work and we talk sometimes about moving. I'm not sure whether it's to deny the family that fought its way out of an apartment like this or to keep faith with them, but I'm reluctant to leave.

Denise tells me I should buy a tape recorder and interview the family. She reminds me that they're aging, that what Anna might have said is already lost. I tell her that she's right and I do nothing. I'm a respecter of silence, I've come to realize, collecting what stories are given, marking the gaps, assembling and reassembling them as if they would make a whole.

And so I own a blue jar in which I keep nothing—because candy makes my teeth ache; because nothing I can think of lives up to my idea of what it should contain; and because the candy I used to pick out of that jar never tasted as good in my mouth as it did while I was lifting the lid off, keeping it centered so it wouldn't clink.

Ellen Hawley. *"Remembering Anna" is part of a series of short stories and fragments about a group of people that in many ways resembles my father's family and in many ways does not—as the family will be quick to tell you. I decided to write the stories as fiction rather than nonfiction because I needed the narrator to be someone who was not exactly me. That decision carried some negatives, the most important of which is that I gave up the authority that flows from telling the truth as nearly as I know it. Writing, at least in my experience, is full of the uncontrollable, the inexplicable. At our best, or our luckiest, we're calling up elements of ourselves that we don't fully control, or fully know.*

So, what facts can you trust to be true? I moved from New York to Minnesota in 1966. I edit A View from the Loft, *a monthly writers' magazine published by the Loft. My work has been published by* The Threepenny Review, The Quarterly, *The PEN Syndication Project and a variety of small—but, ah, discerning—magazines.*

Photo by Kathy Corey

CHET COREY

Stash

THE BOY LEANED against the garage, tapping his shirt pocket with his fingers as though he were distractedly saying the Pledge of Allegiance, something he wouldn't need to do in junior high that fall. He could feel each of the cigarettes as he rolled them back and forth against his chest with his fingertips where he definitely knew he was gaining muscle from doing a summer of lawns.

Luckies, this time. The last time, he couldn't remember. Maybe Pall Malls. He hadn't liked them much and was glad the guy hadn't stayed with his mother more than the weekend. His first two fingers worked beneath the flap of the pocket so that he didn't have to unsnap the mother-of-pearl button to fish out the first cigarette. The shirt was his favorite, even if the trucker who had left it behind one morning wasn't.

To get one cigarette from his mother's pack, whether it was on her dresser or in her purse, was nothing. Two were easy enough, as long as it was a new pack and late at night or early in the morning. But three were out of the question unless she'd been out drinking and had brought someone home. And then, if he could, he would always try for a brand other than what his mother smoked. The guy would usually forget his pack on an end table in the living room, and the boy could easily come out of his bedroom unnoticed after his mother had closed the door to hers. By the time he'd smoked all three, the noises they would make would have stopped and he could sneak back into the house and get some sleep.

He fished into his jeans pocket with his other hand for the lighter. Because it had an insignia on it, he was sure the guy who had left it behind missed it. He bet the guy had even carried it through Vietnam. Even in the shadow beneath the overhang, the metal was smooth and shiny as he rubbed his thumb across it before he flicked back the top with a snap of his wrist and spun the wheel against the flint. When he first found it, he had worn the end of his thumb sore making it light over and over. Since he had replaced the flint and filled it with fluid, it always lit on the first try. Zippo!

His mother did not say anything the first time he wore the shirt with the white ribbing and mother-of-pearl buttons. If she noticed it was big for him in the shoulders, she didn't say. But once after she had done the laundry, he noticed that she had taken in the seams and made it fit more the way a cowboy shirt should. After that he washed it out by hand himself and let it hang dry in his room. He planned to grow into it. He only wore it nights when she would go out drinking and he knew she would bring someone home.

As he slipped the lighter back into his jeans pocket, he wondered if someday the guy might come back for it. Or maybe one day he would be in a bar and offer a light to an old guy and it would turn out to be that guy. But by then he could say something, like he got it from his uncle or a pawn shop or won it in a poker game or he'd been in the 101st Airborne too.

He had mastered smoke rings. He formed his mouth in a perfect O and with a glottal chugging sent a series of o o o's up into a spider's web. As they entered the web and broke apart, they were like the wisps of clouds beneath the moon. Then he tried larger rings that encircled even the moon.

Because they lived close to the end of town, the night was quiet. And he had two choices. He could walk out toward the fields and along a gravel road or down the alleyways and further into town. He always avoided streets and sidewalks. He'd discovered that he could tell more about people from walking the alleys—especially rich people—than he ever could from their front sidewalks. You could tell more about rich people at night, too, especially because rich people always left more lights on. He figured that was where someone got the expression "Money to burn," though they didn't pay any more for lawnwork than the old ladies in his neighborhood. They just had more yard.

He chose the alleyways. The moon was too full for the fields, and they looked so lonely laid out as they were. He could even see the creek highlighted by moonlight, like a chrome bumper or the barrel of a nickel-plated revolver.

Within minutes he was behind the girl's house. Since he had been coming to that spot, he had learned a lot about her. For one thing, she was Catholic. That was easy. She had to be. She didn't attend his school. But he was sure he would meet her that fall in junior high and he knew that he would ask her to the first dance and that she would accept and agree to meet him at the gym, even walk her home. There wasn't a Catholic high school in town anymore. She didn't have a choice. He didn't know much about Catholics, but he knew she was one and that made her all the more mysterious.

He straddled the big oak that had almost hit her father's garage when it came down in the first summer's storm. It hadn't been sawed up yet for fireplace wood. They had one, he knew that. He'd smelled the wood burning one night that last winter when he'd stood in the tire tracks, careful not to leave his footprints in the deep snow. They were celebrating something, maybe even her birthday.

The talk of the town after the storm was about all the virgin timber that had come down. All he cared about was his favorite tree. It was so easy to climb you could almost walk up it. And the bark was so deeply rutted it provided perfect hand-holds. He could get up to a second storey limb and have a cigarette. And he could see into her bedroom, but never much because her mother drew the curtains. His house only had shades, and they were always down, except in his own room at night when he would go to bed and let the shade snap up so that whatever light the night held would fall into his dark room. The light off the snow when it was a clear night was the best for sleeping because it looked so cold outside but felt so warm beneath the blankets. Tonight he would have to settle for straddling the tree trunk, broader than any horse's back, instead of the comfortable limb.

Again he fished into his shirt pocket and tweezered out the second of the cigarettes between his fingertips. He snapped the cover of the lighter back and guarded the flame from detection within his cupped hands. As quickly as it was lit, a snap of the cover snuffed the flame out. As he smoked, he stared at her dark house. They were gone for the second week. Perhaps they had a cabin or had gone out west to a dude ranch to ride horses through the draws and hollows he'd read about in *Boy's Life* at the library. For a moment he panicked. Perhaps they had moved. He took such a deep drag that he choked; quickly he ducked behind the broken oak, his nostrils puffing smoke and his eyes watering. He wiped his eyes with his sleeve, then cupped the cigarette within his other hand until he was sure no one had heard him. But he was alone in the night.

He stood up and flicked the unfinished cigarette deep into the tree roots that had been torn from earth. Then he unzipped and pissed the last of its fire out. He was getting a lot bigger and had grown more hair all right. Maybe he wouldn't have to worry about showering after gym, as he heard they had to in junior high. He'd just watch the other boys to see how they turned the shower on. Or maybe the teachers would do it, like the Gestapo gassed all those Jews in the history book with its picture of a pile of white bodies that looked almost like the twisted roots of the dead oak or more like the pile of buffalo bones in that same book. He smelled his warm urine as a wind came up, and for a moment he felt afraid. He finished zipping up as he walked back down her alley toward his.

He carried the lighter clenched in his fist and looked over his shoulder twice before he had finished crossing the first street. In one of the houses a dog barked, and that started another dog barking in another house. He hurried. He hadn't been afraid since the night a man his mother had brought home started shoving her around. Somehow—he didn't know how—she got him to stop. He stayed in his room that night with three knives from the silverware drawer stuck into the woodwork to keep the door locked the way she had taught him. Later that week he saw the bruises on her arms when they were turning from black to brown. She'd said it was nothing. If he were older and knew how, he'd have killed the son-of-a-bitch. He didn't keep anything the guy left behind—and went without smoking for a week.

As he got to their garage, the bathroom light shut off. He knew that she had gone back to her bedroom. He let himself slide down beside the side door to the garage where he could rest against its framework. He felt older looking at the rusted clothes-line poles with only two of their six lines strung. He had thought once of spending his lawn money for paint and painting them just to surprise her, but he found that they were so rusted away he could push a ten penny nail through parts of them, so he bought her a clothespin bag at the hardware. It hung on one of the lines all through that next winter and summer; then it just fell apart.

The garage itself was empty. If it had a big door, they could've rented it out in the winter. Some of the neighbors didn't have garages. He didn't know how he'd ever learn to drive a car, but he knew that when he could earn enough money to get one he would. Sometimes when the men his mother brought home left their cars or rigs unlocked out front, he would sit in them. Once he had even sat high up in a semi that had chrome stacks and air horns. And there had been an opened pack of Camels behind the visor. So he took two. But he'd rather have set all the dogs in the neighborhood barking with a blast on the airhorns.

They were stronger than the Lucky Strike he sat smoking down to almost where it burnt his fingers. One of the men had his first two fingers yellowed from smoking them down too short. One of his fingers was missing too.

The boy walked over to the clothesline pole and stuck the cigarette through a hole the size of his little finger. It was where he always got rid of his last butt. Better than any ashtray, and he never had to empty it.

In summer the boy could go out and come in through his bedroom window. But with the house so quiet and dark, he went in through the front door. And anyway, he was feeling older. If she heard him and came out, what would she say? No more than she had when he'd thrown out all of the things the men had left behind, except the footlocker. Some of the stuff was good, too, but he didn't want any of it. He only kept the footlocker because it had compartments for the stuff he'd kept from the others. The guy had stayed the longest, but so what? Maybe she was glad he'd kept it because she'd really liked him. Maybe she thought he'd kept it because the guy had taken him bowling for the first time ever and had talked about going fishing. What did she know anyway? Summer came and he was gone.

She didn't know half the stuff he had—and half the stuff he could've had. And he'd bought the lock and she'd never know. Not a combination lock either, but a padlock that looked right and made it *really* look like a seaman's chest, which he didn't believe for a minute it was. The bullshitter, the loser. Never said anything he meant anyway.

In the half-light coming in through the windows, the boy crossed the room and took one more cigarette from the package

on the end table. The guy would never miss it, probably never remember how he got where he was if he was like all the rest. Maybe
he'd just get up in the night and be gone. That'd be good. She'd
sleep late and he'd mow Mrs. Williams' lawn for the third time
that summer. And if she offered him a glass of milk and some
cookies or cake or whatever, he'd say sure.

Quietly he opened his bedroom door and closed it behind
him. He was glad he'd taken a leak back at the girl's house. But he
wondered if her father'd see the cigarette butt he'd pissed out. Instead of switching on the ceiling light, the boy used the flashlight
he kept on his dresser. He set it lens-down on top of the footlocker so that the only light was the glow from its lens cap. First
he unsnapped the mother-of-pearl buttons from the cuffs and
then down the front. Standing at the foot of the bed in the red
glow, his upper body and face looked deformed to him and much
older in the dresser mirror. He laid the flashlight on the bed so
that its light bathed the bedsheet and pillow, creating a rounded
headboard against the wall.

He knelt down beside the footlocker and, without removing
the string with its key from around his neck, unlocked the padlock. The inside drawer with its partitions had been painted white
and the sides of the footlocker had wallpaper-like designs of island people. He fished into his jeans pocket for the lighter and set
it in its compartment. Then he sat on the bed and, using the toe
of one foot and then the other, worked off his tennis shoes without untying them. He pulled off his jeans and socks. Where they
were was where he would find them in the morning. He stood in
his underwear for a moment before the mirror. He looked like the
islanders rowing out to the masted ships or climbing up the ropes
to come on board to trade their goods. He picked up the shirt
from the bed and carefully folded it before setting it down again.
Then he lifted the drawer out of the footlocker and set it on the
bed. Finally he reached down into the bottom of the footlocker,

lifted the cover of the Dutch Masters cigar box and removed the nickel-plated revolver. He wasn't sure how to fire it or that it would if he pulled the trigger, but he was sure it was loaded.

The revolver was one of the things that hadn't been left behind. He'd discovered it underneath the seat of that semi with the chrome stacks. He'd taken it because he knew he might need it. He had the old silverware knives, but what did his mother have? The trucker would be weeks on the road before his hand would feel for it and find it gone.

The boy set the revolver back within the cigar box and took one of the magazines from the small stack beside it. He remembered what each of the men were like who had left them behind and where he had found them. One in the bathroom wastebasket; another beside his mother's bed while she'd slept the night off long after that man had left. And the first one—the one that a salesman had shown him in his bedroom after his mother had fallen asleep. But he didn't want to think about that. He didn't feel right when he thought about it. He was tired. He didn't want to get hard. He dropped the magazine on top of the others, picked up his shirt and laid it across his knees. Slowly he snapped the second and third mother-of-pearl buttons. Then he placed the shirt on top of the cigar box and magazines. He straightened its collar. Then he replaced the drawer, the insignia on the lighter glinting in the glow from the flashlight. Finally he closed the lid and snapped the padlock to the seamen's chest.

He went over to the door and wedged the knives into the woodwork above and below the handle. He crossed to the window, raised its shade and stood for a moment looking out at the shadow of the clothesline pole falling across the yard. Finally he sat down on the bed, pushed the flashlight beneath the pillow and pulled the sheet up to where it covered all but his ears and eyes.

The night sky clouded over and the room darkened while the boy dreamt of riding with the girl on the limbs of trees through draws and hollows.

Chet Corey. *I was born and raised in Minneapolis in a neighborhood with defined borders, a few streets on either side, and rigid divisions by age, boys my brother's age or older. I was either a tag-along or alone. I spent hours playing my parents' thick twelve-inch records; I would buy* Hit Parade, *which only printed lyrics, and memorize its songs. Figures cut from comic books and kept in a shoebox gave me my earliest experiences creating stories. My neighborhood of hills, alleys, and vacant lots gave me a sense of place, a healthy feel for loneliness, and images—cars with running boards, men pitching horseshoes in backyards, leaves burning in piles along curbs. I had to walk past a public grade school four times a day to attend Catholic grade school. The liturgy of the Mass increased my love of words; I remember waiting each Christmas Eve for* O Holy Night. *But I was a poor student and lasted only one year at De La Salle, failing Algebra, Spanish and English. And I remember reading only two books,* Swamp Fox *and* Lord Grizzly, *before I entered the army and began to read—Hemingway, Kerouac, O'Hara, Steinbeck. At Mankato State I took Robert Wright's course in writing fiction and wrote my first story, which* The Laurel Review *published. As a writer, I see myself as a man in a rowboat who is keeping his eyes on where he has been to get to where he is going in spite of the chop.*

Photo by Peterson Portraits

VICKY LETTMANN

The Sheep, the Cow, the Rooster

MY MOM IS RUNNING her fingers through my hair. I can feel the way she lets my hair lift and fall, like feathers, back on my head. I close my eyes and wonder how long she will stay.

She says, "Robert, when are we going to give up our rituals?" She means the soft things that put me to sleep every night. I remember when she would only blow me a kiss at the door. The next night she rubbed my back and blew me a kiss at the door. A few weeks would go by and I would ask for a new thing: Rub my back, massage my neck, kiss, plain hug, run your fingers through my hair, and finally blow me a kiss from the door.

It's like the story we read about the boy who lost his hat. First he passes the sheep and asks the sheep where he can find his hat. The sheep doesn't know but says, "Come. We will ask the cow." The sheep and the boy go to the cow. The cow doesn't know and says, "Come. We will ask the rooster." The boy, the sheep, and the cow go to the rooster. And so it continues until there is this big crowd looking for the hat.

Sometimes we talk about the day, my mom and I. Sometimes we say nothing. As she sits on the side of my bed tonight, I have almost forgotten about what had happened at Jens' house. Tonight she says, "Do you want to talk about the fire?" I want to say, "Fire? What fire?"

I say, "No."

I push my head deeper into my pillow. I can see Mickey Mouse on my sheets, close next to my eye. He looks huge and black.

❋ ❋ ❋

It wasn't so bad. I remember Jens saying, "Hey, Robert. Let's make a little fire under the tree."

Sometimes we would take out our big magnifying glass. Usually in the summer when it's hot and the sun is bright. We would sit in the driveway and focus the sun into a bright spot right on the center of a leaf. The leaf begins to smoke in that one spot, then it turns brown, then red and a little flame poofs out of the center. It all happens without a match.

Jens and I had just finished watching that movie on the VCR. His sister's boyfriend, who is sixteen and drives, rented it from Buster's Video. When he left, he said, "You two are too young to watch this movie. It's not for eight-year-olds."

Faces of Death. We were just going to see what it was about. Just watch a little bit. Blood was everywhere in it. First it's just a regular movie with people going to work. Then a pit bull attacks a man getting out of a big truck. The dog charges and charges at the man—darting at him and away. The dog's teeth bare, snarling and growling. He is all teeth. The man screams and holds out his hands but the dog is low and charges at him again and again. The man tries to run and falls. The dog keeps biting and biting him. Until his leg is off.

That wasn't all. But I can't talk about it.

I thought the fire would be okay. Like the hot spot on the center of the leaf. It would be the porch light shining in the night, lighting up the dark green trees whose branches stretch black arms against a dark sky. Magic. It would take my mind off the blood.

Jens said, "We can even smoke some." He pulled his Cardinal's baseball hat down on his head, backwards so that the brim made a dark shadow on the back of his neck and the big red Cardinal was in back like a red flag. "I know how to make cigarettes out of pine needles," he said.

He took me to this big tree by the house. We crawled under the branches. No one could see us under there, Jens told me.

"See here's where we can build it," he said. The ground under the tree was packed dirt, dry and dusty. It smelled like the inside of a tent—musty, like old canvas and dried pine needles.

❅ ❅ ❅

Aunt Sally smokes. She sits on the stool by her vanity in her slip and pulls on the cigarette as if it were happiness to her and she couldn't get it into her fast enough. She has a big jewelry box full of earrings and necklaces. She lifts out a long strand of purple cut glass beads and dangles it in front of her. "Should I wear this one, Robert?"

I nod my head and watch her squint at the beads and then at me through the ring of smoke around her dresser.

I stay with her after school some days, the days when my mother has to work at night. "Robert," Aunt Sally calls. "Robert, bring me a drink." I bring it to her even though I don't want to because I know she will sit and call and call until I do. She looks at me, takes a lungful of cigarette smoke and holds it there, then smiles at me so that I forget about the television show I was watching and sit down on her chenille bedspread to talk to her. "Robert, you are the best," she says.

Aunt Sally is always sitting at her dresser deciding on what shade of eyeshadow or which piece of jewelry to wear. She doesn't go anywhere to work. She just seems to float through her apartment in a thin blue housecoat and slippers with chiffon flowers on the toes. When I ask my mother what Aunt Sally does, she just looks away. Sometimes she tells me about when she and Sally were children and how in the summer they went to stay on their uncle's farm. That was in North Carolina where my mother grew up. We live in Minnesota now, but my mother keeps talking about North Carolina, even though she has lived here for many years. We were all born here. My sister and brother. Aunt Sally moved up here too.

I've been to the farm a few times and don't see what was so great about it. A swing still hangs in the big pecan tree by the side of the house, but the only animals are cats that seem to live everywhere. My favorite thing when I go there is to take the cats bowls of warm milk from the kitchen and watch them come from all over and stick their pink tongues in the saucer making bubbles in the milk and a soft slurping sound until the milk is all gone and they lick the bowl dry.

While I sit on the bed talking to Sally, I seem almost to understand things that I believe will be clearer someday.

"Robert," she says. "For a boy your age you are wise, so I'm going to give you a problem to figure out for me." Aunt Sally likes to read puzzle books and so she'll flip open a wrinkled paperback on her dresser and read a puzzle to me. Sometimes they have to do with deciding who the right person is if two people are fishing on the river and one is related to the other, but the other is not the father. I usually want to know more about the people and somehow I know that a big part has been left out.

Something horrible happened on that afternoon when Jens and I lit a few leaves under the tree. I didn't know it at the time. I was just like one of those people in Aunt Sally's puzzle, but you can't be in the puzzle and figure it out at the same time. Jens and I had both felt a little weak from watching *Faces of Death*. We went to the kitchen and made ourselves some grape Kool-aid and slabbed a thick pad of peanut butter on two pieces of bread. Some of the Kool-aid spilled on the counter and left a deep purple stain when we tried to wipe it up. Some dripped on the floor and our feet stuck in it as we walked around the kitchen.

Jens' mother was shopping or playing golf. We weren't exactly sure, and his older sister was sleeping in the basement. She was always sleeping in the basement, even though it was well past noon when we decided to take the matches underneath the tree next to the house.

You could tell that other kids had played under this tree before. The ground was swept clean and the sand packed solid under the branches that hung down all around. It was a giant pine tree, like a big Christmas tree, and the pine needles were pushed against the trunk.

Jens leaned against the trunk of the tree and let the pine needles run through his fingers. "I can make a cigarette out of these," he said.

"With what?" I asked him. "You can't make a cigarette without cigarette paper." I was thinking of the thin paper—like I had seen on Sally's dresser, the kind she used to make her funny smelling cigarettes.

"That's right. I forgot the paper. I'll be right back."

I sat under the tree waiting for Jens to come back and watched the way the July sun came through the pine needles and made patterns on the smooth dirt. The summer was getting long and I was wishing every day that my dad was home again. I never said anything to Mom or Aunt Sally but deep down I was sad all the time about it. I had tried different tricks to bring him back, like one day I swam twenty laps of the pool remembering how proud of me he was when he came to my swimming lessons that one time and how he said, "Now you swim a few laps like that every day and soon you'll be another Mark Spitz." I didn't know who Mark Spitz was, but after I swam twenty laps I kept hoping I would look up at the end of the pool and see my dad standing there and hear him saying, "Just like a regular Mark Spitz."

When I finally stopped there were the same moms sunbathing and yakking in their chairs, not even looking at their kids in the pool.

"Ow." Jens was back and he scratched his cheek on the low branch as he squeezed in under the tree. He was holding some notebook paper in one hand and held a pair of scissors in his mouth while he pushed aside the branch. "Here hold these," he said, pushing the scissors into my hand. "We'll have to cut the paper first."

I took the lined paper from him and began to cut out a rectangle through several sheets. The paper reminded me of desks and blackboards, but today all I could hear was the recycling truck moving down the street in the block behind us. Glass cracked and broke and the tires of the truck roared as it moved from house to house. I cut carefully, imagining in my mind the length of Aunt Sally's cigarettes. Jens was gathering little piles of pine needles. "We'll make a whole pack," he said.

I handed him my stack of papers and he took one and carefully placed a line of pine needles down the center. Then he tried to roll the paper around the needles, but the paper was much too thick and the needles kept falling out.

"Here, let me try," I said. I took the paper and folded it over in a crease on the edges and then rolled it so that the needles stayed in. Then I bent the ends together.

"Great," said Jens. "That's just the way I was thinking of doing it. It's hot under here," he said. "Let's take our clothes off."

Jens was a scrawny kid with thin hair that fanned out from under his baseball cap. He ate strange things, like dog biscuits and goldfish food. I had never actually seen him eating those things, but my friend Eric had and when I told my mom about it one night, she said he was possibly missing something in his diet. Nothing seemed to surprise Mom. "Maybe he should take some vitamins," she said.

I wasn't too shocked when he began taking off his shirt. His ribs stuck out and I could see that his collarbones made a kind of shelf for his head.

"I think I'll keep my shirt on," I said.

"Men take their shirts off when they smoke," he said. He tore a match out of the book and bent the cover back. "Can you light a match like this?" he said. He held the matchbook in one hand and pulled the end of the match between the cover and the brown sandpaper on the back. Nothing happened.

He tried again, and finally the match burst into flames, scaring us both. He dropped the match quickly into one of the small mounds of pine needles. We watched it burn down and blew on it to keep the needles around it glowing for a few minutes. There was a nice smell to the air after that—warm and like marshmallows.

"Your turn," he said handing me the matches. "But you have to take your shirt off." I slipped my T-shirt over my head and reached for the matches. It felt cool under the tree and I didn't like the way my stomach stuck out and my chest went in.

It took me a lot of tries before I was able to light the matches by pulling them between the covers, but when I finally was able to it was like when I learned to snap my fingers. I couldn't stop. Even Jens liked the way I was able to light them so fast until all the matches were gone. We had forgotten about the cigarettes and were busy trying to see how long we could keep a small pile of needles going before it smoldered and went out. Jens kept going back into the house to get more matches from the jar his mother kept in the dining room. It was a big brandy snifter of matches that she and her ex had collected all over the world. "We have enough to last forever," said Jens. By now he was down to his underwear, a pair of Jockey briefs that kind of hung around his thin white legs.

I was beginning to wonder how long we had been under the tree and remembered how my mother said, "Never play with matches." But we loved the way the matches burst into flames and burned down. The smell after each lighting was so delicious and I liked the way the matches curled into circles as they burned on top of the pine needles. Jens showed me a trick where he pulled the paper matches apart to make arms and legs and then twisted two matches together and lit them so they looked like a couple screwing as they burned down. The legs and arms moved together and around each other. Jens laughed his Beavis and Butthead laugh as we watched the matches burn like two people. "Heh, heh. Look at that. They're screwing," he said. "They should have had that in the movie. Be good, huh?" He turned to me and stuck a match between his teeth.

"Did you like the movie?" he asked. He decided to try one of his cigarettes and took the match from between his teeth to light the end of the pinched notebook paper.

"It was kind of gross," I said. I didn't really want to talk about the movie.

"Maybe we could light a bug or something," said Jens. "We could take a picture of it with our VCR."

❀ ❀ ❀

In the movie were jerky scenes filmed by someone with a home video camera. One showed a cow being chopped apart. The eyes bulged out and the intestines were everywhere. I suppose that was where Jens got the idea of the video camera. We had done that before, making up little skits and funny fight scenes and recording them. My mom laughed when she saw them, said we should become actors.

We went back into the house and searched in the dark basement for the video camera. Jens' sister was sleeping in the corner on a big double bed. She was just a bump under the comforter with her foot hanging over the side. Jens tiptoed over to her and made out like he was going to pull her foot. We looked right at her face, but she didn't even move.

We finally found the camera and took pictures of each other

shooting baskets and then lifting some old weights we found in the basement. We kind of forgot about our cigarettes under the tree. Jens was running around the house in his underwear pretending to be a famous film director. He was still wearing his red baseball cap, and he looked funny with bare chest and skinny white legs. We took some shots of his sister sleeping and then dressed the dog up in my shirt and tried to get him to do tricks while we filmed him.

After about an hour we went back out under the tree where I tried a pine needle cigarette and we burned a few ants. Jens had the power pack in the video camera so we were able to get a few close-up shots of the ants turning into tiny flakes of cinders. I didn't mind the ants burning, but the grasshopper jumped around and tried to get away. That was like in the video when the chicken had its head pulled off. Then we stomped on the fire and put it out.

Later that afternoon the wind picked up and the temperature fell. Jens and I messed around for a while down by the creek and then went back to my house around supper time. Mother was home from work and Aunt Sally had stopped over. She leaned down and gave me a hug and I could smell her perfume, sweet and strong, mixed in with cigarette smoke. "Hi, Robert," she said in her deep voice. "How's my favorite boy?"

Her new perfume was called "Obsession," she said. I thought it sounded like "Of sex on." "No, Obsession," she laughed. "Do you like it?"

She looked at me with such heavy dark eyes. I could tell she was crazy about me. Jens always got a little jealous of her, I think. His mom was rich, since her daddy had been a big shot at Cargill, and even though Jens didn't have a dad either, like me, his mom didn't have to work like mine. Still—she was never home, always shopping or playing golf or tennis at the country club. She was beautiful with a real tiny waist and long black hair that she always held back with a headband.

"We're going up to Perkins for some dinner," my mom was

saying. "And no, you can't invite Jens." She laughed because she knew that was the question ready to come out of my mouth.

When we came back from the restaurant and Mom turned down Jens' street, we saw the sky brighten and then the fire trucks lined up on the street.

The night was cool and the wind was blowing hard so the smell of burning things was strong. Lots of people were standing around on the sidewalk in clumps. I could see women fanning their faces with their hands.

"Oh my God," Mother was saying. "It's Jens' house."

At first I didn't think what I was seeing had anything to do with me. We parked the car. For a moment the wind seemed to die down and the night felt warm and sticky, much like the afternoon.

I stood between my mother and Aunt Sally and felt happy in-side. It was something about the fire engines, the flashing lights, the people—all with a bright look on their faces. It reminded me of those cool fall nights when we circled around the fire in the family room—before my dad left us. He always made the fire—arranging the kindling in careful rows around the wads of paper, then putting the soft birch next, and above that the solid oak logs. He would crack the window just a bit to allow a draft for good ventilation. Sometimes he let me throw a match in, and we all watched the sudden blaze as the paper and the little pieces of kin-dling began to burn.

Then I saw as clear as could be that the place under the tree where we had been smoking and making cigarettes that morning was where the fire started. Suddenly I felt very cold and wanted to go home.

I suppose I could tell more about the rest of the night, how Jens' sister had discovered that the fire had blown under the back wood steps, how she had seen smoke creeping in around the win-dows of her basement room, how the fire somehow leaped over to a roll of old carpeting in the basement and began to smolder more and more—how she felt her way out and called 911.

Then Jens and I were taken to the police station and questioned and the house was full of smoke and totally damaged because of it. We both had to go see a psychologist where I drew pictures about the fire.

❀ ❀ ❀

"You can talk about it when you want to." The words of my mother move smoothly into my sleep. I can still feel the warmth of her hand by my neck. She is a shadow moving out my door now. My room is much darker.

To start the story again: I was a little boy whose mother loved him—and who had a father who took him on fishing trips. I heard stories, easy ones like the cow, the sheep, the rooster that became bloody and violent in the movie I watched one day with a friend. I went looking for something every day and carried with me all those people who had been with me from the day I was born. We were not like the sheep, the cow, and the rooster looking for a hat, but we were looking for someone. I really liked having Aunt Sally with me because she was a mystery—a story like mine without a clear beginning or ending but full of love, as were her eyes when she looked at me, and her words that told me that I was smart.

Now I hear my mother say as she moves toward the black rectangle of the doorway, "Goodnight, Robert. I love you." She blows me a kiss from the door. It's like glitter in the dark. Like sparks.

Vicky Lettmann. *All through my twenties and thirties, writing was a "maybe someday" for me: maybe someday when I have more time, maybe someday when the children are older, maybe someday when I'm not teaching. True, I wrote, but only in jerks—journal entries, a poem or two, the beginning of a short story. I took workshops and* classes, became inspired, wrote during the class and for a short time thereafter, and then I'd slip back into the busy-ness of my life.

In 1985, I took a workshop at the Split Rock Summer Arts Institute with Natalie Goldberg whose book Writing Down the Bones was in galleys. Her advice, "Shut up and write," forced me to stop talking about writing and do it. It was also during that workshop that I met two writing friends. We started meeting in restaurants and cafes, huddled over a table covered with left-over sandwiches and cold cups of coffee, and wrote. Then we would read to each other, not worried if other diners craned their necks to hear what we were saying. Those other diners were our first audiences. And slowly I began to see myself as a writer.

In 1987, I won a Loft-McKnight Award and received an extra boost of encouragement. Since then I have completed an M. F. A. in Writing at Warren Wilson College and am now on a leave from teaching writing and literature at North Hennepin Community College (where I have taught since 1968). I see that "maybe someday" is here.

I'm completing a collection of short stories, The Polly Stories, about life as a displaced Southerner, change, disappointment, family, money, time, and memory. "The Sheep, the Cow, the Rooster" is from that collection and is told from the point of view of Polly's eight-year-old son, Robert.

Vicky Lettmann

Photo by Pete Crouser

JON HASSLER

Peggy

THE MYSTERIOUS AND handsome new music teacher
came to Peggy's high school the year she was a sophomore,
and under his direction, the music program, never strong,
took a turn for the worse. Membership in his choir soon dropped
from thirty-two students to nineteen, and about half of them had
no talent. His band, at their spring concert, got lost in the middle
of "The Skater's Waltz" and had to leave it unfinished and go on to
something harder, an arrangement for brass of a Rossini overture.
This they stumbled through to the end, but shouldn't have, because the disharmony was so hard on the ears that a committee of
parents was formed to seek the director's dismissal.

The principal, sent by the committee to confront the music
teacher, advised him to resign his position, effective in June.

He said, after a long, thoughtful pause, "I have no intention
of resigning."

"Resign this year," countered the principal, "or I'll fire you
next year."

"I'll not resign," he said.

His name was Tillemans. He was a heavy-shouldered, dark-
haired man who lived alone in a small apartment and seemed to
have no friends. Students called him Tillie the Turtle, a reference

to his deliberate movements and manner of speaking. Ask him a question or say good morning, and he needed time to formulate a reply. Climbing the school stairways or moving along the narrow passageway leading to the music room, he caused traffic jams. He was about thirty-five years old, not as old as he acted, and the tip of his right forefinger was missing—shot off, it was said, in Korea. While most of his students paid him very little respect, Peggy thought him a genius.

Peggy loved music. Beginning in the seventh grade, she'd sung in the choir, played the saxophone in the band, and now, as a sophomore, she went to Mr. Tillemans for piano lessons. It was clear to Peggy that his shortcomings as a teacher lay in the area of classroom management and had nothing to do with his musical talent. One on one, she found him patient and wise.

She also witnessed, in November and December, the wonders he could work with older, more serious musicians. Having put out a call for adult voices and instrumentalists, with a view to performing Handel's *Messiah* at Christmas, he was gratified by the great number of singers who turned out, along with a few string players and a trumpeter. Peggy's brother and sister, Kenny and Connie, were among them. Both Kenny and Connie had moved away from home, Connie to take a job in the city, and Kenny to attend law school. Peggy missed them acutely, and it was in order to be near them that she first went to watch them rehearse. Loving the music and intrigued by Mr. Tillemans' methods of putting the choir together, she went back to all the subsequent rehearsals and attended the single public performance, which she thought exquisite beyond any concert she'd ever heard.

She was particularly impressed by three of the soloists: a baritone with a beard who'd come to rehearsals straight from his job as a meatcutter in a packing plant, a radiologist who despite missing three of the six rehearsals sang tenor like James Melton, and a soprano named Diane Kunkel who moved Peggy practically to tears every time she opened her mouth. When Diane Kunkel sang

"I know that my redeemer liveth," Peggy was overtaken by the closest thing she'd ever had to a religious impulse, a feeling that her soul was leaving her body and floating to heights of pure satisfaction. That's when Peggy knew what she must do with her life. She must sing.

The following year, Mr. Tillemans did it again, rose above the discouraging chaos of his high school classes and put together a choir and orchestra of even greater beauty than last time. This year it was Haydn's *Creation*. Again Diane Kunkel was the star, but she didn't monopolize Peggy's admiration quite so much as before, because Peggy herself was now in the choir, the only high school student who tried out, and she was enchanted by the graceful way Mr. Tillemans drew melodies in the air with his baton. Her own voice in particular he seemed able to pull effortlessly and magically out of her chest. That's when she made up her mind to do more with her life than simply sing. She must direct other singers.

It was about this time that Peggy began to sense Mr. Tillemans' fondness for her. He liked to talk with her in the privacy of the practice room during her piano lessons. He told her she was destined for a musical career, perhaps not in piano, for her keyboard accomplishments were quite ordinary, but most certainly in voice because of her timbre and perfect pitch and enunciation and sense of pacing.

"How about band?" she asked breezily, half expecting him to say something scornful about her saxophone playing, which she'd never taken very seriously.

"Yes, band, too," he said, "because band is enjoyable for you, more enjoyable than piano, but your voice is your treasure, Peggy." Here he pulled his chair up close to the piano bench and studied her face very intently in an odd way he had, as though her expression were telling him more than she meant it to. She was made uncomfortable by the silence that ensued. Coming back to himself finally, he sat back in his chair, drew in a deep breath and spoke very ponderously, like someone drugged or brain damaged. "It will be a very great tragedy . . . if you don't become a professional singer or teacher of singing." Then he sat forward again, and laid his hand on her arm, brushing his fingertips lightly across her breast as he did so. "Peggy, you owe the world . . . the gift of your voice."

She laughed self-consciously, while resolving to become worthy of his praise.

When in the spring his teaching contract wasn't renewed, Peggy was both sad and relieved. She still felt privileged to be taking lessons from a genius, but less and less of her lesson was devoted to her playing and more and more of it to conversations which, given his long pauses and penetrating gaze, she found hard to sustain. Filling one such pause one day, she asked, "What have you composed lately, Mr. Tillemans?" During rehearsal for *Creation*, he'd asked the choir to run through a brief hymn of his own, something about the Christ Child, which everyone had thought very beautiful. They suggested it be sung in performance, as a lead-in to the oratorio, but he scoffed at the idea, claiming that not only was it unfinished, it would be presumptious to ally himself with anyone so gifted as the incomparable Haydn.

"Oh, I have not composed for three or four years," he told Peggy.

"What about that little hymn at Christmas?"

"Oh, that old thing . . . very old . . . no, nothing new for three or four years."

"Why?"

"Because when I try to work on something, all I do is doodle."

"Doodling's a start," she told him.

Two lessons later, he placed on the piano a sheet of music with the notation done in his own hand, in pencil, with many erasures. It was called "Bagatelle Number Six."

"Something new?" she asked.

"I wrote it because of what you said."

"What did I say?"

"Doodling was a start, you said."

"Oh." She'd forgotten. "Well, I'm glad I said it then."

"It isn't finished, but I would like to play it for you."

She started to rise from the bench, but he insisted she remain there, and he sat down beside her. He hunched over the keys for a time, as though he were praying or working up courage, and then he began playing very deliberately, holding the chords much longer than Peggy would have, playing it so slowly, in fact, that it wasn't until the second time through that the melody came clear to her. It sounded like a lullaby, slow and then slower and all of it quite beautiful—though it was hard for her to concentrate on the music rather than the movements of his mutilated finger. The piece ended in midphrase, and he held the last chord until long after its sound had died away. Then he lifted his hands and looked at her.

"Beautiful," she said. "Just beautiful."

"I know it," he said. "I can't believe I wrote it." He said the conclusion had been coming together in his head, and he asked if she would make the notations while he worked it out on the keyboard.

"Oh, yes," she said, eager to be his accessory.

"It saves time if I don't have to interrupt myself to write." He went to his desk and found new sheets of staff paper and returned to sit beside her, on her left so her right arm would be free for writing.

It was slow work. When the half hour drew to a close, they had covered only four measures. She thought it sounded odd, mostly music for the left hand, and therefore darker and more disturbing than what had gone before. At one point he dropped his idle right hand, not onto his own lap, but onto her left forearm, and this aroused her to feelings far greater than admiration. It set off the alarms of love. She kept glancing at him, unsure if he realized where his hand was. He seemed too engrossed in composing to notice. At the bell, she hurried off to her English class, feeling feverish.

The next week, they went at it again. This time, late in the session, she was startled to feel his hand on her shoulder.

"I'm afraid this is turning very somber," he said. "What do you think?"

She thought of pointing out that perhaps the piece needed more of his right hand, but she was breathless and didn't trust her voice. Nor was she sure what she ought to be feeling. His hand was very warm and comforting, but when he moved it slightly toward her neck, she flinched. Again the bell rang, as though his advances were carefully timed to be interrupted. For the rest of that week she thought of little else but her body and how its various parts would feel if touched by the hand of the composer.

At the next session, her last before summer vacation, Mr. Tillemans' hand was very low on her back when the bell rang. She didn't get up to go. She'd confided in her best friend about the composer's wandering hand and this friend, a boy-crazy girl named Anita, had shrieked excitedly and said kissing was next. Peggy sincerely hoped so. She wasn't yet permitted to date boys, not till next year, and had never kissed one. She was certain that no boy her age could ever measure up to this sensitive man home from the war with a shortened finger and mysterious, penetrating eyes. She lost sleep yearning for the kiss of this genius and imagining intimacies beyond that.

But there was no kiss, only the hand on her lower spine. "I guess this is as far as we can go," said Mr. Tillemans, his eyes on the unfinished score. Withdrawing his hand, he rose from the bench. She rose too, and studied his face for a sign of longing or love, but she saw nothing of the sort. When he offered to shake her hand, she ran from the room and wept in the lavatory.

The rest of the week she skipped choir and band, and avoided running into him in the hallways. When she got her report card and found her grade lowered from A to B for these absences, she felt no resentment or anger. What she felt was sad for a while, then wistful, and finally privileged to have known Mr. Tillemans and to have been some small help to him as a composer, and to have learned so much by his example as a director, and perhaps—who knows?—to have been a bit of a comfort to him as a lonely, friendless man. She would go looking elsewhere for the kiss of a genius.

Jon Hassler. Writing is what I was born to do, though it took me an awfully long time to get around to it. I have the novelist's temperament. I can work happily and solitarily away at a project for two or three years with little or no feedback. It's only when I finish a novel, as I did very recently, that I grow anxious and aimless and begin rather desperately searching my journals and memory and imagination for a new plot and cast of characters.

In the mid-1970's, I spent five years writing a children's book (Four Miles to Pinecone) *and five months writing* Staggerford, *which were published simultaneously in the spring of 1977. The book I've just written the last word of—"music"—is novel number ten. It's called* Rookery Blues, *and concerns the faculty of Rookery State, a remote northern Minnesota campus where the college motto is "Paul Bunyan's Alma Mater." Readers will insist it's really Bemidji State, where I once taught, and they'll be correct, but only in so far as the physical setting is concerned. The plot never happened in Bemidji; the characters never lived there. "Peggy" is one of its many wholly imagined chapters.*

Photo by Pam Leschak

PETER M. LESCHAK

The Viridian Gate

WHEN I GOT to the shore of the lake I saw the island was back. It was nestled against our dock, pinned by a gentle southeasterly breeze. I hadn't seen it for a month.

The island is roughly seven feet on a side, and about two-and-a-half feet thick. It's a durable mat of muskeg, supporting a lush verdure of Labrador tea, leatherleaf, pitcher plants, cranberry vines, and sphagnum moss. It roams Secret Lake with the wind, occasionally passing a day or two bumping the poles of our tiny pier—like a moored boat. It's a little world on waves, independent of its bog mother; a chunk of shoreline that somehow broke free several years ago. My theory is this: a large bull moose ambled too near the edge of the floating muskeg and ripped through. As he lunged and thrashed, finally kicking into open water and swimming away, the island was torn loose. It continues to thrive, a mobile ecosystem that goes with the flow.

I've portaged a lawn chair down to the dock this evening, and as I unfold it the dog leans out to sniff at the island. He's half lab, and it's been a bad day for a black dog—sunny and in the high eighties. The Reverend spent the afternoon panting under the back porch. He likes the lake, but doesn't come down alone. He used to enjoy the water more before his accident. One day he was hanging far over the edge of the dock, peering at something in the water, when his paws let go and he plunged nose-first. He sank like a waterlogged beaver cutting, vanishing completely; a gulp of bubbles broke the surface. After a long moment he burst out of the depths, snorting and wild-eyed, paddling in panic for shore. Dogs are good swimmers but only inadvertant divers. He shook and coughed and wouldn't set foot on the dock again that day. Now it must be scorching hot before he'll go in.

After a cautious olfactory sweep, The Reverend hops onto the island and starts shoving his snout into the moss. Something's caught his attention, and he's unfazed by the quaking of the mat. I consider giving the island a push and sending The Rev for a ride, but it's been a long day and I ease into the lawn chair. I'll settle for more subtle entertainment than a surprised, betrayed dog.

It's a few minutes past nine, and the solstice sun has just set. We'll have a luxurious hour of June twilight, and if the mosquitoes don't drive me off, I'll watch some lingering cumulous clouds stained into rainbows—one color at a time, until the stars take over. I'm anxious to see the most enlightening shade, the delicate blend of yellowish blue-green that tints the western horizon at deep dusk. Vega and Altair will already be winking in the east, and this resonant hue will only endure a few minutes. A good thing, for it's much too beautiful. It's the color of God's eyes, a reflection of eternity. If I could leave this planet at will, rising up in a quantum leap, that narrow band of viridian would serve as the gate to another universe.

In the meantime we've got action. A solitary loon offers a tremolo to the air, and it strums my spine. She's just twenty yards from the dock. She? Only an expert could determine loon gender at that distance, but the call struck me as feminine siren-like, yet soft and virginal. She breaks into a long performance of rapturous yodels, and in the enhanced silence that follows I'm startled by a whoosh directly overhead. Another loon is banking over the dock

—wings spread wide, feathers splayed—"flaps down" as it were. The sound is identical to that of a landing aircraft in the moment when the Doppler effect has sent the engine noise the other way, and you can clearly hear the sigh of wings. With my eyes closed there'd be little difference between Cessna and loon. It's amusing how technology imitates biology, but what could be more natural?

The loon curves into the breeze and drops at a steep angle, canting almost perpendicular to the water before its tail hits, gracefully ruddering its torso into an extended splashdown as wings are folded into the amphibious mode. The transition from flying to swimming is as smooth as synchro-mesh, and is greeted with a single high note (appreciative?) from the female. The loons immediately begin preening and fishing, and it occurs to me that the island would provide an excellent nesting site for them—if it wasn't so vagrant. Most creatures get tense when their eggs go roaming.

Above, I notice the bright contrail of an airliner, a 727 I suppose, still lit by the sun I can no longer see. The vapor is dyed orange—a cloud created by jet engines, and for a moment I'm on the verge of another biology/technology analogy. But a beaver slaps its tail not ten yards away, and I almost spill my beer. The Rev leaps back onto the dock, ears perked, tail rigid. Old Castor has snuck up on us again.

The beavers moved in three years ago, raising a lodge on the northern shore. It's true, they stay busy. Three or four have virtually clearcut five acres of aspen and birch—pretty amazing when you're using your teeth and you waddle on land. (And only work the night shift and take winters off.) Last autumn I planned to drop a log across the stream that flows out of Secret Lake. I enjoy walking that way, and it would serve as a crude, low-impact bridge. No need. When I hiked over I discovered the stream no longer existed. The compulsive beavers had replaced it with a hundred-foot long dam. So, that's why the lake level rose all last summer.

What intrigues me (and The Rev) about the beavers is that they always approach the dock. One or two will swim over when we arrive and cruise back and forth in front—sometimes a mere ten feet away. I can see their pupils and hear them breathe. Periodically they slap and dive, but nobody seems terribly excited. I assume this promenade is a defensive measure, perhaps a warning; sure enough, The Rev and I never assault beavers nor pilfer aspen cuttings.

However, I have toyed with the idea of climbing aboard the island and paddling it to the vicinity of the beaver lodge during the day. I'd half burrow into the moss, then cover myself with fresh aspen limbs. When the beavers emerged at dusk, I'd try to pat one on the head when it came over to check out the aspen. It would be "counting coup"—gentle revenge for all the times I've been startled by tail slaps.

There's only one beaver this evening and The Reverend quickly loses interest. The first time he saw one near the dock he jumped in. But the beaver vanished, and I yelled, and that was the end of it. He's still fascinated, but only for one minute at a time.

A pair of mallards zip by at spruce-top level—quacking—and Rev looks up, but he's ready to return to the house. He's truly a domestic animal. On the other hand, his nose has probably told him all he needs to know about the lake this evening, and it's likely he's gleaned more information than I have. But he won't leave alone.

I'm hoping we'll hear The Screamer; that would keep the dog interested. For the past twelve years we've regularly heard an awful squawking/keening at night—more often than not from the direction of the lake. It drives The Reverend crazy. He growls and barks and charges off into the woods with hackles high. Our previous dog reacted the same. In fact, other than trespassing ATVs, it was the only thing that ever upset him. I assume The Screamer is a bird, since it seems to travel so fast. (Unless we're surrounded by Screamers.) Is it an owl? I imagine I could find out with a little research, but it's more fun to leave it enigmatic. Still, I'd be thrilled to actually see a creature generate that hair-raising cry. Maybe if I spent a night on the dock, or better yet, on the island.

Hearing The Screamer would be appropriate this evening, because one reason I've come down to the lake is that I'm disturbed. I need the therapy of water and twilight. It was nothing specific at first, but now I keep focusing on a news item I heard on the radio. There's been a major earthquake in Iran, and it's reported that over 30,000 people have died—many of them horribly, no doubt. But of course for the dead it's over, the pain is done. Many thousands more are still alive—bereaved, homeless, utterly shocked. Some have probably gone insane, their world literally shattered. It's the island that keeps me thinking of them.

Rather, I saw the mat of muskeg and the word "island" came to mind. That led me to recall the once-profundity/now-cliché of the preacher John Donne: "No man is an island . . . " And I was forcefully struck by the apparent. Those humans in Iran news items—really exist. If I headed for that band of blue-green sky (a mere 727 would do), I could be with them in a few hours. It's not another universe; they're just around the curve of the globe, and we share the same atmosphere. We're linked, and their suffering disturbs me. " . . . any man's death diminishes me . . . " wrote Donne.

And yet it's astonishing that I can sit in my lawn chair, relaxing with loons and beavers, scratching the ears of a beloved dog, and being mesmerized by a kaleidoscopic sunset. How can I be so blessed, the Iranians so cursed? At the same time on the same planet? Is simple distance that potent? Apparently. For I also recall a saying from The Talmud: "Every man has the right to believe that just for him was the world created." I'm privileged; this light and these animals are mine. Death belongs to the faraway, unfortunate Iranians.

And here is the paradox: we are not islands; we are indeed islands. Both. I'm the only human on the lake, but the sunset glows for millions. I'm a wandering island—touching here, bumping there. The big question, of course, is where did I come from? I trust I was not set afloat by a careless bull moose. Nor by any other accident. I like to fancy there's salvation beyond that viridian gate. Perhaps we'll make the quantum leap someday. Perhaps 30,000 Iranians have just done it. Meanwhile, a donation to the Red Cross for earthquake relief is as good as anything.

Before I leave the dock, I give the island a shove. It's time to touch somewhere else. The Reverend sprints for the house. It's been a bad day for a black dog.

Peter Leschak. *Last night I returned from three weeks of duty on the firelines of central Washington. The Tyee Creek fire was at 1000 acres when we arrived, and totaled 122,000 acres when we left. The hours were good. It's supposed to be contained next week, but everyone knows that only rain (or snow) will actually put it out. Neither is in the forecast, and my colleagues will be busy there for a long time. Some are happy about that, others unhappy; some don't care much either way. It's a job.*

Despite the beguiling TV images and the body of romantic lore surrounding firefighters, the job is chiefly drudgery, encompassing precious little glamour. It's dangerous, but in a mostly banal way: sprained ankles, saw cuts, carbon monoxide overdose, infected blisters, poison oak, bee stings. Only rarely is anyone seriously burned. When the fire itself is in the mood to kill, we just stay the hell out of the way. The bees are harder to avoid. Above all else the job is dirty. My fingernails and my snot are pitch black. So why do it? 1. for the money (which many Americans would rate from poor to fair), 2. for the occasional excitement, 3. for the status—deserved or not, 4. for the fellowship of colleagues, 5. for the drudgery—which brings its own rewards of potent brain chemicals and the wondrous relief of being done with it, 6. to contribute, in some small way, to the community, 7. for the risk, the energizing realization that one day this job might kill me.

These are also the reasons I write.

Peter M. Leschak

Photo by Juanita Garciagodoy

GEORGE RABASA

Jimmy Pearl's Blue Oyster

O N NICE DAYS I enjoy sitting in the parlor. At my age all days are nice days if you happen to be up and about, with good digestion. The days are especially fine if the joints are flexible and the pain that occasionally starts in the middle of my right buttock and runs down the leg like a red-hot wire to the back of my knee is somewhat subdued and buried deep in the muscle tissue rather than snaking its way through the flesh until it strikes raw bone and gristle. I don't complain; it gets me a government check once a month.

A particularly good day in the parlor of the Grand Hotel Winfield, which is no longer a real hotel but close enough if you don't insist on a reception desk or room service or bellmen, would be a warm spring afternoon with the sun smack against the windows as it courses above the alley that runs between the Tuck-A-Way self-storage and the Labor Exchange across the street. The dust that hangs in the air, swirls and glows in the light makes a man feel downright peaceful.

Most of the other residents are too dimwitted or crisped out to care whether the sun shines or not, and, since the TV died two years ago, not likely to get the oomph to hike up their sweat pants or tie their ratty bathrobes around their clacking bones and jiggling adipose and amble down to the parlor. Moira and Jimmy Pearl and I have the room to ourselves.

We call the others the Living Dead after the famous movie because you can see them coming into the cafeteria at meal times, their slippered-sneakered-duckshoed feet shuffling in unison like they were some kind of dance group. Not kicking like the Rockettes, though.

After dinner, they scurry right back into their rooms, afraid to be left out in the dark. I'll ask Jimmy what time it is, and he'll say "Oh, about quarter till the night of the living dead." That means it's ten PM, because in about fifteen minutes management starts turning off the lights. The three of us will chuckle as we huddle together around our special table in the cafeteria. As many times as we've gone through the Living Dead routine, it still cracks us up. We just can't get our minds away from all that grumbling and moaning as deep and mournful as the hooting of a distant wind.

Talk about the consequences of living a hard, fast life. Just the thought of Mildred Higging and Casey Stanfeld and Sollie Rosen tripping back in the sixties is enough to give you a side-stitch. The long faces and the disheveled hair and the blank eyeballs tell the tale. I mean, did they really think that becoming one with the trees and the moon and the tiny little blades of grass wasn't going to cost them, somehow?

"I don't know what's keeping him," Moira grumbles from the other end of the parlor.

Startled, I drop last week's copy of the *Wall Street Journal* onto my lap. "Jesus, Moira, I didn't know you were here."

"Who did you think I was anyway, the wicked witch?"

"No, Moira. I knew it was you. That raspy cigarette wheeze of yours is fucking unmistakable."

"Are you through abusing me?"

"I was concentrating on something."

"On last week's stock prices?"

"I'm after perspective, not immediacy. I can spot the trends,

see the flow and ebb of the market's tides better when there's a little time between my attention and the events themselves. It's
called perspective."

"You said that already."

"I know I said 'perspective' twice. For your benefit."

"You read the old *Journals* because it's Jimmy's subscription,
and he's been a week behind in his reading since the fourth
grade."

Once again our conversation comes around to Jimmy Pearl.
Of the three of us, he is by far the most worldly. And the best
looking. And at seventysomething, old enough to be our father.
So when the three of us are together, we let Jimmy do the talking.
Even when he's not around, sooner or later Moira and I will end
up talking about him, or about something he said, or about what
he does when he's not here.

"Where is he anyway?" Moira asks, rhetorically I'm sure, since
I don't keep track of Jimmy as closely as she does, mainly because
she is in love with him. I personally love the man too, in a broth-
erly way. I just don't get so wrapped up in his comings and goings.

It's bad enough that Jimmy's bladder and mine are in sync.
Have been for about ten years. Even on days when we don't see
each other, I can always count on running into him in the men's
room when we both wake up at all hours of the night damn near
the bursting point, and we wander into the stalls to let out a few
measly droplets, because our bladders have all the elasticity of
shoe leather and our prostates are as big as persimmons. I mean
we would like to piss out real gushers, but we end up simply
marking our territory like dogs encountering hydrants on a walk.

When I first moved to the Winfield Hotel and noticed this little guy who always, winter or summer, wore a double breasted
white suit, I knew we were going to be friends. We got acquainted
while leaning into the urinal waiting for the flow, and then shaking our wrinkled little puds for a long time knowing there would
always be one last dribble after we'd tucked them back in.

"You're too young for this kind of routine," he said sympathetically. "How many times do you do it?"

"During the night? Or in a twenty-four hour period?"

"Don't get technical on me," he said.

"Five, six times."

"Eight to ten for me." He nodded thoughtfully. "It's a pisser, isn't it?" He laughed uproariously. "It's unnatural. The night was made for sleeping and boffing."

"I haven't done much of either in years."

He squeezed his eyes shut and gritted his teeth and parted his lips in a grimace. "This place doesn't really lend itself to sex. The only good-looking woman around here is Moira Jones. Great personality too. Find me in the cafeteria one of these days. I'll introduce you."

That's how I met Moira, although in all these years I've never harbored romantic hopes about her. She's a fine looking woman too; she just thinks she's smarter than the rest of us. Falling in love requires a measure of stupidity, and women like Moira never let their mental guards down enough to get involved. That's what I told her when she was complaining about not having married. I said to her that she was just too damn smart for her own good. She said she didn't think she was a genius or anything, but certainly a lot brighter than any man she'd ever met. Except for Jimmy Pearl.

I think she would've fallen for him years ago, but he was just not interested in catching her. Why would a man who has topless dancers on his payroll waste his time on some crank?

"I don't think I've seen him since supper last night," she says.

"He must've taken one of his trips to Jersey," I venture, remembering that I haven't seen him in the men's room.

"He just came back from Jersey."

"Owning a topless bar is complicated. Butko the Bouncer was threatening to quit. He probably had to rush back and hire another big guy."

"It wasn't Butko that was leaving. It was that other guy, the bar tender."

"Jimmy calls him Lloyd the Slice, on account that he puts a slice of lime on every drink he mixes whether it calls for it or not."

"I know as much about The Blue Oyster as you do," Moira snaps impatiently.

"I was just making conversation. I know you knew about Lloyd's nickname."

"You were patronizing me."

"I like it when you sulk. It makes you look sultry and animal-like. Why don't you come over and sit a little closer?" I slide to the side of the sagging brown couch.

"Thank you, no."

"You're a treacherous tease, Moira."

All the repartée in the world was not going to make us forget that Jimmy Pearl was not around. He had gone off before, for days at a time. But he'd say his good-byes before he left.

When he returned he'd be full of stories about his little bar in Newark, The Blue Oyster. That was why he wore a white linen suit, because the owner of a club had to project class. That was also the reason he talked on the phone so much, settling arguments among the three topless dancers who were forever breaking the rules—pay for drinks or get some schmo to pay for them, don't date customers, don't dope on the premises, don't fight, and share your tips with Butko because he is your protector, and nobody ever, ever tips the bouncer. The Blue Oyster was a big headache but he stayed with it because, he said, it was a little gold mine.

When I asked him if he had so much money why did he live in the Hotel Winfield, Jimmy just said he liked the people, that it was people that made a place home. He was talking about Moira and me. I know.

"You should go to his room and see if he's all right," Moira suggests after a while. I thought she had fallen asleep; her head had toppled forward, and her chin was grazing the top of her blue dress with the big paisley print. Under the bright sunlight her red hair gave off tiny reflections that looked like sparks.

"You go see. I think he's fine."

"I bet he's not," she insists. "Besides, I've never been to his room."

"That's not what I've heard," I sing softly.

"Jimmy tell you something?"

"Right from the horse's mouth."

"Well, that proves you're lying. Even if it were true, which it is not, Jimmy is too much of a gentleman to blab."

"You think so? All guys blab. Blabbing is the best thing about having sex. Blabbing is so good, so satisfying, that you can blab about women that don't exist and sex that never happened, and the blabbing makes it all true."

Moira shakes her head in disbelief. I know she thinks I'm a real adolescent, but I'd put a bug in her head. She takes out a cigarette and taps the end of it against her thumbnail. "What did he tell you anyway?" she asks in her low throaty voice.

"That you were a fine woman, that you bucked like a wild horse, and that you drooled a little when you came. That you were better than the girls at The Blue Oyster."

"Well, he was lying."

"Maybe so, Moira. But that doesn't mean it's not true."

After that, Moira is quiet for a long time. I can tell that the only reason she puts up with me is because I'm Jimmy Pearl's friend. But if we don't talk, there doesn't seem much else to do, except watch the afternoon sun rise up above the parlor windows, the dried raindrops on the glass making everything inside look dusty and threadbare. I switch on the lamp with the brown spots scorched into the paper shade so I can see the commodities quotes a little clearer.

"I think I'll put some money in coffee futures. Coffee is bound to go up, don't you think, Moira? Jimmy says people are drinking less booze these days. Capuccinos are the thing. That's why he put in a six thousand dollar Italian espresso maker at The Blue Oyster."

"Jimmy Pearl hasn't seen six thousand together in his life."

"He'll be the first to admit that The Blue Oyster is not doing so well these days. On account of the neighborhood demographics changing."

"Demographics?" Moira looks at me and starts laughing. Then her laughing turns into coughing, until she lights another cigarette. "Do you even know what a demographic is?"

"Sure, it's Jimmy's name for customer. His customers used to be young Italian professionals."

"Gangsters."

"Now they are mostly Dominican."

"Gangsters."

"No, Moira, The Blue Oyster is a neighborhood bar. A homey place, where Lloyd the Slice knows your name, and Bouncer Butko is a rough but friendly guy, and Louella, Kim and Thalia are basically nice girls from small towns trying to make it in the big city."

"You crack me up." This time she doesn't bother to laugh. "I don't even think there is such a thing as The Blue Oyster. I mean, how could an old coot like Jimmy Pearl run some bar a thousand miles away."

"Oh, there's a Blue Oyster all right. It's the pride of Jimmy's life."

"Believe what you want," she sniffs.

Somewhere around five it becomes obvious that neither Moira nor I are going anywhere until we find out what's going on with Jimmy Pearl. She suggests again I go to his room, but something makes me shy away from that. We're jealous of each other's privacy here at the Hotel Winfield, and our little hundred-and-twenty-square-foot room is about all the territory any of us calls his own. The unwritten rule is that when the door is open, people are welcome to come in for a drink or conversation or whatever. But I checked Jimmy's door an hour ago when I went to take a leak, and the door was closed. That's a No Disturb sign at the Hotel Winfield.

"Are you hungry like I am?" I ask Moira.

"No."

"You should eat anyway."

"I'm just going to sit here until Jimmy shows up. You go eat."

"I'll bring you a sandwich."

"Fine. Anything but Velveeta."

Moira and I eat our grilled cheese sandwiches and don't talk much. All I can hear is her crunching potato chips and gurgling down the Diet Coke. It isn't my fault that Jimmy hasn't shown up. But you'd never know it to look at Moira. The pisseder she gets about him not being around, the worse the vibes she's sending my way.

I'd have given anything for Jimmy Pearl's non-stop blabathon about The Blue Oyster. How to run a P&L on every single bottle of liquor to make sure Lloyd isn't getting too generous with his pals. Why coasters are a good investment when your bar surface is solid maple burnished to a silken gloss by time and a million elbows. Liability insurance on Butko. Turning your restrooms into moneymakers with a condom machine in each one—eighty cents profit on every pop.

"If you don't check on him, I will," Moira says around six, just as the parlor is sinking into a dusky gloom.

"Let's give it another hour, and if he doesn't show, we'll both go knock on his door."

"Fine," she says, in a tone which reveals that it's not at all fine with her. "And what are we going to do meanwhile? Jerk our heads around every time we hear footsteps?"

"No, I'm going to continue perusing the *Journal,* and you can smoke three cigarettes. Then we'll go."

Of course we end up doing what Moira said we would. I do

try to concentrate on the Nasdaq listings alphabetically, keeping a mental note of the ups versus the downs, and Moira smokes and coughs, and after I catch her directing hostile glances at me, I start looking straight back at her. Staring at Moira is like staring at the Sphinx, all stone-faced and blank-eyed and bigger than life. She has smoked so many Camels during her life that she's become part of the scenery on the package.

"Okay, let's go," she says finally.

She's breathing hard by the time we get to room 326 at the end of the third floor hallway. "You wouldn't be winded if you didn't smoke so much."

"It's not the smoking. I'm trying not to panic. You'd be worried too if you weren't so insensitive."

When we're finally standing in front of Jimmy Pearl's door, she has raised her fist to rap on the door, but in the end she can't make herself knock.

I tap softly at first. When there's no answer, I knock again, louder. "Jimmy," I say. "These are your best friends in the world come to party with you. Moira is naked and I've got an ounce of *sin semilla.*"

Somehow I'm not surprised that there's no answer. There seems to be an aura of heavy cottony silence around the door, like a heavy, soundless exhalation that goes on and on. It takes a big effort to simply reach for the door knob and turn it slowly. "Are you there, Jimmy?"

I go in first, followed closely by Moira, her raspy breath on the back of my neck. The room is very neat. The skinny bed is pushed up against the corner, a teetering writing table is on the other side, and in the middle of the room, practically taking over the whole space, is a frayed Barca Lounger that he must've picked up at the Salvation Army, because you just don't see those big mothers with the plaid upholstery anymore.

You can't miss him. Sitting up on the bed, leaning against the wall, wearing his white suit and his iridescent blue tie carefully knotted in a Windsor is Jimmy Pearl, his pale blue eyes wide open, his head tilted down slightly, and his jaw drooping toward his collar bone as if he were utterly flabbergasted to see us in his room.

"I knew it," Moira whispers hoarsely. "We should've come to see him sooner."

"When sooner, Moira?" I snap, getting pretty tired now of the woman's eternal dissatisfaction with the ways of the world. "It's not like he died because you weren't around to amuse him."

"We should call 911."

"Sure, Moira, like there's a big hurry." Even as I'm turning to leave, I give the place a quick look. Above the writing table are several framed photographs. Jimmy at twenty with slicked hair and pegged pants standing on the Boardwalk in Atlantic City with three toothy women saying cheese. There's a shot of Jimmy tending bar in front of a wall of liquor bottles and a beveled mirror etched with the big Seagrams 7 logo. And Jimmy with someone who looks like Bing Crosby.

On the table itself is a round metal tray with a bottle of Canadian Club, two squat on-the-rocks tumblers, some cocktail napkins with a progressive picture of the Mona Lisa going from her simpering little smile to a full blown hysterical laugh. Stacked on the side is a pile of matchbooks with the image of a large oyster partially open to reveal a gleaming pearl inside and the words Jimmy's Blue Oyster Lounge, Paramus, NJ Tel. 623-3116. I don't think Moira is looking, because I know she wouldn't approve, but as I'm turning to lead her out of the room, steering her by the elbow around the Barca Lounger, I tuck a couple of the matchbooks and one Mona Lisa paper napkin into my pants pocket.

The voice on the other side of 911 takes my name and address as if I were the one having a life-and-death crisis instead of old Jimmy. I go along; it's the best way to deal with public institutions. He promises to send an ambulance, but not immediately because the victim in question is dead. That is, if I'm certain he's dead. I say yes. Don't touch anything, he says.

Then I drop my last eighty five cents until the first of the month to call the number on the matchbook.

"*Aló, ¿quién habla?*"

"Is this The Blue Oyster?"

"The what . . . ?"

"Jimmy. Pearl. Blue. Oyster." I try to speak clearly and slowly.

"*Ay qué carajo . . .*" The voice trails off just before hanging up.

When I get back to the parlor, Moira is sitting off to one side of the sagging green Naugahide couch off in the darkest corner of the room. I sit down beside her, half expecting she'll move away from me. But she stays put, even though I'm sinking into a hole in the couch that throws me close to her, close enough so that my shoulder is pressing against hers. She doesn't even move her arm. I stay there too. I can feel the rise and fall of her body with every breath, and I can smell the cigarette smoke on her clothes, and I can hear her trying to breathe very lightly so as not to sniffle. I stay there even though the sagging couch spring is digging in and starting to send that hot wire coursing down my butt and all along the back of my leg.

"I called The Blue Oyster," I say. "Just picked up the phone and dialed the number on this matchbook." She takes it, and I let her have it because I've still got the other one. It's nice to have a momento from your friends.

"What did they say?"

"They said they were sorry to hear the news. That they're really going to miss him on account of what a great guy he was, a terrific boss, and a real friend to everyone there. That I should let them know the name of the funeral home so they can send flowers."

"That's sweet of them," she says. "Who did you talk to, Lloyd the Slice?"

"Yeah. He said he was going to invent a drink and name it after Jimmy. The Pearly Gate."

"What else?"

"I could hear the dancers crying in the background."

"And Butko?"

"Oh, he's such a bear of a guy, but you know, he was too choked up to say anything."

"What else?" Moira puts her hand on my arm and clasps her fingers tightly. "Tell me more."

"I don't know what else to tell you, Moira," I say, feeling suddenly that talking is taking too much of an effort. "Things just aren't going to be the same anymore. Everyone knows that."

George Rabasa. Born in Maine of Spanish parents, raised in Mexico City, I bounced back and forth between the two countries during most of my life. Finally, the fates conspired some ten years ago to place me, more or less permanently, in the middle of the exotic Midwest.

I write to honor a small, single talent with which I've been blessed. There weren't many choices. I would have preferred to have been a rock star, a physicist, Mother Teresa, or a fireman.

I also write for self-understanding, transcendence, glory, money. More significantly, I write in order to hang on to the flow of life, to keep the moment from vanishing, to freeze life on paper so that it exists for all time. It's no small thing when you can pull it off.

I meditate, breathe, eat and write in Minneapolis.

My fiction has appeared in StoryQuarterly, Other Voices, Stiller's Pond, Glimmer Train Stories, *and other publications. A collection of short fiction,* Floating, *won The Writer's Voice Capricorn Award, and will be published by Coffeehouse Press in 1996.*

Photo by Gus Gustafson

KATHLEEN MOORE

Mama

This is part of the story of Etta Elizabeth McCauley Furlow who died in St. Paul, Minnesota, on May 21, 1991. The narrative has been organized and rearranged by Kathleen Moore, but the words are Etta's.

❊ ❊ ❊

MAMA WAS SOMETHING else, honey! She never said yes to us when we was kids, not to me anyway. "Mama, can I go to the show?" "NO!" "Mama, can I go to the dance?" "NO!" "Mama, can I . . . ?" "I'll think about it." Well, that was a yes.

Mama was half-Indian. Her father was Chickasaw and he had married a woman out of slavery. Mama told us the story about when she was a little girl living in Tennessee and her mother worked for some white people. Mama's hair was red and very long, way down below her knees, beautiful hair. This white woman had daughters and their hair wasn't pretty like Mama's. One day she caught Mama and shaved her head, cut off all that hair 'cause it was prettier than her daughter's.

Mama stayed with her folks, working on the farm and taking care of her sisters and all, till she was twenty-six. Then she took a steamboat trip up the Mississippi to Cairo, Illinois. Everyone came up the river on the steamers. Cairo was one of the main stations. The Mississippi is one mile wide there. That's where the Ohio and the Mississippi rivers come together. Everything was either going up the Mississippi to St. Louis or out the Ohio going east to Virginia. Roustabouts would unload the grain and cotton from those steamers and put it on barges or it would go by train to the east and west.

Mama met John McCauley on that steamer and married him. I was born on my Daddy's birthday, Halloween, 1909. I was his fortieth birthday present. My Daddy was a fireman on the steamer *Sprague* that was part of the Barrett Lines out of Ohio. He was gone on the river all the time except when it was froze in the winter. Mama didn't like being alone so much so she left him when I was about four years old. I was always running away from Mama to go where my Daddy was. I used to go down to the levee and wait for my Daddy's boat to come in. I think they wrote that song for me, something about "waiting for ships that never come in."

Mama couldn't read or write. On my birth certificate she put her X where it says to sign your name. Mama worked as a cook. There wasn't much black folks, women anyway, could do then but be a cook or a seamstress. She cooked for people on 13th Street in Cairo where only prostitutes lived. Those women weren't allowed to go out of their house. If they got sick, the doctor had to come over, or if they needed clothes a seamstress had to come. My mama did their shopping and cooking. When school was out, I would go to where she was working and she'd have my lunch ready. After school, I'd go there and I could play in the kitchen and the dining room until she got off work. She couldn't leave until she cooked their breakfast, lunch and dinner. After she did the supper dishes and cleaned up, we'd go home. She never let me go out in the street to play or to the playground with the other kids. She didn't want me out there 'cause I'd hop trucks, like the ice wagon, and ride on the back. Hell, the boys did so I did, too.

Mama married my stepfather and she had fifteen more children. 'Course most of them died very young from the influenza or smallpox. Only five of us growed up. I'm the only one left now. I'm the oldest but I'm the only one still living. When we was kids, I had to take care of my little brothers and sisters, get them dressed and get their breakfast. I couldn't leave the house early to play on the way to school. Mama made me wait for the first bell to ring so I had only fifteen minutes to get to school. It was a mile walk so I couldn't play along the way. And after school, I had to get home in fifteen minutes or she'd whip me. I didn't know it then but she was trying to protect me. Then I just thought she was being mean.

I know I was what you call a bad girl 'cause I loved to run away from home and I caused my parents a lot of heartache and fright. But I didn't know that when I was only a child, seven or eight years old. All I knew, I was running away from home. A show would come to town, I'd try to run away with the show. And I'd go down to the Illinois Central station; there was a train that left Cairo at ten-thirty every night and would go to Centralia. The men would open the doors and I'd go on the train and hide up under a seat. I had an uncle that lived in Centralia and I'd go off there to his house.

Sometimes I'd take my little brother and sister with me. I used to hide back up under the front porch and lay real still so Mama and Papa wouldn't find me. Then when they were out looking for me, I could get out and go. I don't know how I kept those babies quiet all that time.

My stepfather was a teamster and he drove the beer wagon for Anheuser-Busch. Early in the morning, he'd take the beer to the saloons and tap the barrel so the men going to work could stop and get their pails filled for lunch. When prohibition came, Papa quit his job. The company wanted him to keep on but Papa did not want to do nothing illegal. That's when Mama and Papa bought the house next to ours and made it a restaurant.

We were busy all the time. Those roustabouts that worked on the barges that came up the river from the South, they would rent rooms somewhere and eat in our restaurant. They got three meals every day for $5.50 a week. I had to get up at six o'clock in the morning and go make a fire in the cook stove and put on the oatmeal. I'd have to sift my mother's flour, she made biscuits every morning. I thought Mama and Papa was so mean. I just knew when I got growed I wasn't never going to get up at six o'clock.

Mama was always doin' for other folks. She would make us kids take a plate of food to someone who was sick or couldn't get out. We'd get home from school and before we could play, she would say, "Take this over to so and so," or "Go chop some wood for so and so." I used to hate that. I always thought when I'm eighteen I'm going to say no when she tells me do that.

Mama was very, very strict. I couldn't date boys in high school. No decent girl went out with a boy. They didn't want their girls getting pregnant. They didn't say pregnant back then. They said, "She's spoiled." "He done spoiled so and so's daughter." If a girl got pregnant, she was put out of school, nobody had anything to do with her. Or she'd be put in reform school. You went to reform school and you had the baby and were kept there. If there were people who wanted to adopt a baby, that's where they would go. Or maybe someone was running a rooming house and needed a housekeeper or somebody to wash dishes, they would go to the reform school and get those girls. Then they could always threaten them, "I'll send you back to that school." So the girls were practically enslaved.

Mama didn't tell me anything about sex. I thought you just got a baby by being a certain age. The older girls would talk about "doing it." I thought they meant the latest dance, "The Eagle Rock." The words to the song were, "Everybody's doin' it, doin' it, doin' it. Everybody's doin' it, the Eagle Rock." I didn't know they meant sex with a boy. I didn't know what that was.

Oh, boy, I'm telling you when I started menstruating, it's a wonder I didn't kill my fool self. They called it getting sick, "Her sickness done come up on her." What was frightening me was I thought I was going to have a baby. I'd hear the big girls talk about not getting a baby so when I heard their home remedies, I thought I'd better take them, too. I caught rain water in a can and put in rusty nails and drank it or drank bluing water.

I wanted the boys to call on me. I wanted to put on rouge and pearls. I wanted high heel shoes. I wanted to court. I wanted all those things. So I ran away again. When I was in high school, I fell in love with this sailor who came up the river. He left and went to East St. Louis so I followed him there. I couldn't find him but I got a job and a place to stay in a boarding house and would have stayed there but Mama and Papa found me and came and got me. Then I didn't run anymore. It seemed I couldn't get away with it.

I thought when I graduated from high school and went away to nursing school, I would be free of Mama's rules. I went to a nursing school in St. Louis, City Hospital #2, that was for blacks. Number 1 was only for whites. But they was just as strict as our parents were. We had to live in the nurses' residence and couldn't stay out past eight o'clock at night. We had services in the morning, sing a song and say a prayer, and then be on duty by seven o'-clock. Your dress had to be nine inches from the floor, long sleeves with cuffs. No lipstick, no perfume, just soap and water. And you had to be single.

I broke the rules a lot. I lost my cap the first week I had it. See, after three months of probation, they "cap" you. I wanted to look pretty so I went and got my hair cut, had it bobbed, but that was against the rules. They took my cap away from me for three months. That's an embarrassing thing, to walk around and be de-capped. A few months before our final exams, they caught me and two other girls smoking and they wouldn't let us graduate.

So there I was back home again with Mama. She sent me to Chicago to take care of her sister who was dying of cancer. I stayed there with my auntie until she died. Then I talked my uncle into letting me stick around. I didn't want to go home. That's like going back to be ten years old again, having to come in at nine o'clock and can't go out to dances. So I stayed in Chicago. I tried to do everything I'd ever heard about. I had a cousin, on my Daddy's side of the family, and she played saxophone in a band. I met Duke Ellington and Louis Armstrong. I went to dances and stayed up all night!

I couldn't get a job as a nurse in Chicago so I did day work. I'd clean houses. I got me a pail and cleaning rags and went around, knocked on doors and asked them if they wanted something done. I could make a dollar and a half a day. That was good money, that was enough to buy some beer that night, go to the show and buy supper. A lot of the black doctors there had been interns in St. Louis and times were rough for them, too. I'd go around to their offices sometimes. Maybe I'd have a quarter and they'd have fifty cents and I'd go to the store and buy some neckbones and some of those Ballard biscuits and some grape jelly, come back and cook it over the Bunsen Burner in their office and we'd have a feast.

I went home in 1936 during a spring highwater. I was worried about Mama and Papa and my sisters. I know Mama, flood or no flood, you just ain't going to get her out! That's when I met my husband. Jim was with the Army Corps of Engineers. They was going up and down the river, dredging it and saving people. I saw this great big hunk over on the corner from Mama's restaurant and asked my sister, "Who is that?" "That's Big Jim. That's Grey Eyes." I said, "Oh, I like that." So my sister got word to him and he came over to the restaurant and ordered some coffee and I got a good look at him. Six foot somethin' and all those muscles. Beautiful grey eyes. He was just what the good Lord made for me.

Mama said I couldn't go out with Jim. A river man? No, indeed. Everybody said, "Oh, you're a nurse and he's just a common laborer. He's not in your class." But we stepped out. It didn't make no difference to me. I didn't give a damn whether he was rich, poor, or what. I just wanted somebody that really cared about me. But my family didn't like that. He's a man on the river and me a nurse. And he went to the pool room and he wasn't a church man and he drank whiskey.

So we ran off. I was twenty-eight and he was thirty-four years old and we running away like children. We went to St. Louis and we just lived together, not married, for about six years. Mama wouldn't speak to me. I couldn't even write to her, couldn't go home on holidays for family celebrations or nothing. Finally, Papa talked me into marrying Jim. Then Mama came and visited me.

Jim was so nice to my mother. Always when Christmas would come and holidays, he'd say, "Etta, you better send Mama some shoes. And see she has a good winter coat." Lord, he just loved her. And when she got down so very, very ill with cancer, he said, "You just go get her and bring her here and let her stay with us." We was living in Chicago then and I was working nights at Cook County Hospital. Sometimes when I got home Mama would wake up and she would cry like a baby, crying "Mama, Mama," crying for her own mother. So I would get in the bed with her and hold her and rock her and I guess she thought it was her own mother and she could go back to sleep. Mama lived with me and Jim for seven or eight months until she died.

This Sunday is Mother's Day, ain't it? May tenth? That's Mama's death day. May tenth of 1959 was Mother's Day. Mama said, "Don't go to church today, Jim. I'm only going to be half a mother today." He didn't know what she meant and when she come and told me I said, "Mama, you're going to be here all day." Well, she was eating her breakfast, you know, like always. There wasn't anything more wrong than usual. I told Jim to go ahead and go to church. She'll be okay. And then at fifteen minutes before noon, she just gave a funny breath and was still.

May tenth. I always set that day aside as special. I got a dress of Mama's that I kept and a purse I gave her and some flowers, they're imitation, that I brought back from her grave. May tenth is a day just for her and me. I lay this dress on the bed and that purse and sit there and say a little prayer. And be thankful that I had her.

Kathleen Moore. July 4, 1994. I'm sitting on the highest rock by Dobbin Creek where it bends through a suburb in Maryland. In this spot, four years ago, I watched my seven year-old cousin, Katy, sit in the creek, her dress already soaked from splashing in the water while I carried her shoes. Katy was the nickname I had always wished was mine and this real Katy was the child I had always wanted to be. She could play baseball with the boys in the morning and have a tea party with her dolls in the afternoon. One day she felt like wearing a dress and the next blue jeans. Katy could get angry or laugh or cry in a split second as the circumstances of the moment warranted. She lived in the present—and the present moment in Dobbin Creek on a sultry summer day was joyful. I watched her make mud pies, and cook them in a sunny spot on a rock, while two elderly women paused on their stroll to smile on her. Pointing to me, Katy said, "My cousin is a good babysitter. She lets me do whatever I want." In that moment I experienced absolute contentment. For that second, the world was perfect and nothing needed to be changed, not even the mud pies.

I write because sitting on a rock just above my head is a spirit who lets me do whatever I want. She lets me sit in the creek and make words from the grains of sand beneath my feet.

Kathleen M. Moore

DAVID BENGTSON

Broken Lines

Performance

THE STEPS AT THE front of the stage are like the folds of skin on a woman's chin. Yet when he climbs them, they support his weight. He follows the line between two floor-boards to the back of the stage where he turns to face the lights. He can see no one in the audience, but he can tell they are out there. How many he doesn't know, but they are there. He has carried a wooden chair with him which he sets down precisely at the spot on the stage where the line he followed on the floor meets the back wall. The dance that he has prepared for this performance demands that he sit here motionless and stare at the audience. There will be no music, no sound effects, no sound whatsoever but the polite rustling that will no doubt escape from the audience.

When the time is right, and he has no idea when that will be, he will stand and follow the same line, one foot in front of the other, feet centered on the line, to the front of the stage where, when the time is right, he will bow and exit to the left or right. He has not practiced this dance. But he has decided that the only performance worth giving is one that the audience will not completely understand.

Moving Violation

He knew he was in trouble when he saw, out of the corner of his eye, the state trooper spin a U-turn on the grass divider. He knew he was in trouble when he saw the needle slumping to 68 after he pulled his foot from the accelerator. And in the mirror, flashing lights.

He's got me, he says.
How fast were you going? she says.
At least 68, in a 55.

So he pulls over. And watches the state trooper step out of his car, slowly adjust the strap on his hat, then approach. The trooper stands behind the open window, leans forward.

Do you know how fast you were going? he asks.
Well, when I looked down, it said 68.
I clocked you at 73. Have you had any other violations in the past six months?
No.
Do you know what the speed limit is on highway 10?
Yes, 55.

And the interrogation continues. No other violations, ever? Well, he'll report the speed as 69. That'll cost ten dollars less. That's the best he can do. And the ticket is issued.

Later, as they are driving, they talk about mistakes, even those that are intentional. She says, how about the Amish quilters? They'll use a different colored square, hidden somewhere, to break up the pattern. This prevents the quilt from being perfect and, therefore, competing with God.

He says, old printers always made sure there was one mistake in their work. Not a misspelled word, nothing noticeable, the numeral 1 rather than an l, the letter i in a slightly different font. And the reason, so that evil had an escape through the flaw.

And who would notice this but one with a trained eye, who knows exactly what to look for. At this, they can't help but smile at each other.

Her Eyes

It happens almost every day. She leaves. Says she'll be back in a while. He knows where she goes. About a quarter of a mile down the hill behind the house is the marsh.

He followed her once. Later, there was an argument. Why do you go there? I don't know. Do you have to go there? No. Will you stop? Don't worry, this won't become a habit, I'll stop. When? I don't know.

And so, she goes. I'll be back in a while, she says.

When she returns, something about her is different. It's not the water still dripping from her hair, not the marsh weeds clinging to her clothes, not the splotches of mud caking on her shoes. It's her face, her eyes, something in her eyes says she's not the same.

The day he followed her, he watched as she walked slowly along the murky edge as though looking for something, then waded out, fully clothed, pulling handfuls of reeds, and finally dove into open water, stayed under for a long time, then surfaced, eyes and nose above water, then swam with long graceful strokes to the reeds, pulled her way through the marsh, and climbed the hill for home.

When he looks into her eyes, he knows that she has been somewhere he will never go, even though he knows the marsh. There is something mysterious, something beautiful in the deep water of her eyes.

Bed Snack

They are standing in the kitchen when he tells her that he has decided to continue his devotion today to yellow foods by having a banana before bed. This, he thinks, will be a fitting finale to the four ears of fresh sweet corn and dish of vanilla pudding he ate for supper.

Smiling, she offers him a stick of butter.

Body and Blood

It is Christ the King Sunday, the last Sunday of the church year. Communion Sunday. They sit five pews from the back on the left side of the center aisle. Others walk in, quietly find their places, sit. No organ prelude yet. Stacked on the altar are the silver trays holding the tiny cups of wine. Under a white linen napkin, the plate of wafers, each one pressed thin, with a cross in relief. Behind the altar the candles are being lighted.

Then he sees it, to his right, something dark, like the flickering shadow from a fire, like the shadow of someone moving into the pew behind him, but when he turns, no one is there. He knows he saw it, though. And it has been here before. He has felt it, but this is the first time he has seen the body, or the darkness where the body was, like a stain in the air where the blood seeped and dried.

Revival Meeting

How often has he driven this narrow stretch from Sauk Centre to Long Prairie? Highway 71. Eighteen miles. Two lanes. At night. Late. Tired. How often has he played with the winding center line? Touched it. Crossed over it. How often has he seen the lights get brighter and felt the urge to turn into them? He thinks about the lights and darkness and the yellow line on the road. Sometimes when the line is broken, he moves closer just to count how many there are in a mile. Sometimes when the line is long and straight, he tries to align the nose of the car with the line, to reel it in.

Sometimes something tells him to turn the wheel. Just a little more. To the left. Toward the lights. Drive into those brief funnels of light. He never does. He never answers the call of light. Never follows it back to the source. But he is afraid that someday he will.

He opens the window. Slaps himself. Turns up the volume. Looks for The Larry King Show somewhere near the end of the dial. Or tries to find one of those revival meetings from somewhere in Georgia or Alabama with a raspy-throated preacher screaming sin and fire and blood and repent to cries of Amen! and wails of organ and choir. One of those meetings that somehow reaches his radio when his car is lined up just right.

Spiritual Fallout

It has happened a few times. Enough times, actually, so that he worries about it. Sometimes during the prayer of the day or the reading of the lesson. Often during the sermon. Usually when the congregation is seated. Always when it's fairly quiet.

When it happens, he digs his fingers into the cushioned pew or the green cover of the hymnal, pushes a fingernail into the gold outline of the cross on the cover, deep enough to leave an indentation, a rut, then follows the line around and around, digging deeper into the crease of the cross, until the urge is gone.

But he knows it will return. And he is never sure when. He's not sure that next Sunday he might not do it. Next Sunday, as the preacher stands before the congregation and front pews filled with confirmands in white robes and red carnations. As he rattles through a sermon about the Holy Spirit, trying to explain how the Holy Spirit is just like the radioactive fallout from Chernobyl. Unseen, powerful.

The preacher is quite serious, but he doesn't realize what he is saying. The congregation doesn't realize. The confirmands are quietly peeling the wrapping paper from the gifts they were given earlier in the service and one by one are finding small commemorative dinner plates left over from the fiftieth anniversary of the church celebrated five years earlier. They don't know that, in English, Chernobyl means "wormwood." The plant of bitterness, the blazing star from heaven that poisoned a third of all the earth's water. The Holy Spirit.

The Holy Spirit that rose from Reactor Number Four in a cloud three miles high. The Holy Spirit of plutonium still inside the cracking tomb of Reactor Number Four. The Holy Spirit of exposure. The Holy Spirit of radioactive milk. The Holy Spirit of leukemia and tumor. The Holy Spirit of Beylorussian children.

He squirms and squeezes the front edge of the cushioned pew. He might do it now. Jump to his feet. And yell something, like "Hogwash!" or something really stupid, like "Everybody duck!" Or break into the first verse of Hank Williams' song:

"Hear the lonesome whippoorwill,"

before two deacons and the church custodian spring onto him faster than anyone dared to spring a few weeks earlier when the man in the pew that the sun hits hard stiffened during the sermon.

"It sounds too blue to fly."

And while they try to quiet him, the preacher covers the microphone with his right hand to keep the outburst muffled from the radio audience, from those who stare beyond the kitchen window to the muddy ruts in the driveway, from those who listen at an open window for the cry of a lone eagle.

First Sunday After Easter

Sometimes he calls it bedside Lutheran or living room Lutheran or radio Lutheran. Today he attends garden Lutheran. Yes, misses church to rake the yard. If he doesn't rake today, it won't get done. That's how he justifies everything these days.

So at 9:30 he's in the iris beds with his bamboo rake, trying to peel away packed leaves. In this old bed, last year's irises are intertwined so that basswood and oak leaves are caught, held tight like sheaves of sacred pages under faded, almost white fingers. To remove the leaves, he first pulls the fingers loose, gently pops them from the rhizomes. Once he does this, the layers, dry then moist, release more willingly to reveal the dark soil and a choir of pale, green voices, the survivors, silent for months.

Two hours and twelve lawn bags later, a deep voice echoes across the backyard. "Throw down your rake and repent, my son!" It is his neighbor, his friend, the minister, calling from the kitchen window. "Don't you know that this is the Sabbath?"

So he drops his rake, falls to his knees, says, Could you bring me some water . . . or maybe a beer?

In cavernous tones, the neighbor continues, "But are you sorry for what you have done?"

He says he is sorry but not so sorry that he will stop raking.

"That's the way it is with all sin," booms the neighbor.

That's the way it is here at garden Lutheran. And in this new bed, the soil, left uncovered for the winter by his own laziness, heaved by frost, has split open, coughed out the mush of most rhizomes planted last fall. Nearby, though, in the brown debris of bellflowers, a few small voices ring, awaiting a good spring rain.

Better or Worse

When he has to strain to read the newspaper at any distance, he knows the time has come to call the eye doctor. She looks at his chart, sees his age, says, I'm surprised you haven't been here sooner. Then she pulls into place the contraption with all of the lenses and begins flipping from one to another asking, Better or worse? Better or worse? Better or worse? As this continues, he is not always sure which is better, which is worse. Sometimes there is no difference between the two.

He leaves with a prescription written on a little white card and a pair of thin adjustable sun goggles to protect his dilated pupils. A week later he has new bifocals. First time for the double lenses. It will take a while to adjust, to figure out where to look. For now, the line separating one lens from the other is what he sees most of the time. Like a blurry horizon. Sometimes, as he looks through the line, he tilts his head slowly from side to side and weaves a bit as though banking and then leveling the wings of a glider. Mostly, his head bobs unnaturally as he tries to identify the best lens to use for those things that happen to be in the middle.

Applause

Today in the paper he reads that a mature maple tree can have from 500,000 to 750,000 leaves. He wonders about the white oaks and basswood.

They have been falling for a few days now. When they started, he stood at the window and counted the ones on the lawn. At the end of the day, he walked outside and picked up each large, leathery leaf, then looked up into the trees to see which other leaves were ready to fall. He knew that the next morning more would be on the ground. And he would walk out to pick them up. He doesn't really mind this kind of maintenance work. Actually, it gives him time to touch each leaf, to run his fingers across the veins, the ridges, the bumps where insects have been, the holes where something has eaten. Each leaf, like a thin hand released too soon by the limb or pulled down by the wind.

He wishes that all of the leaves would drop this way, slowly, one or two at a time. He hates it when they fall in droves, when the wind throws them into crowds furiously applauding their own arrival, their own departure, as they swirl from one yard to another. Simply put, he hates to rake, would rather not, but the neighbors wouldn't tolerate this rebellious attitude. No complaints to his face, of course, but there would be talk. They already talk when they see him early in the fall walking in his yard, bending to pick up each leaf by the stem, to hold it for a moment, then drop it into the white plastic five gallon pickle bucket. And when he has rescued them all, he carries them to the backyard, to the little woods that he has left wild, and empties the bucket.

Reincarnation

Listening to an all news radio station from Chicago, he hears that after Princess Margaret and Lord Snowdon were divorced the wax museum in London immediately recycled his statue into one of George Bush. He's not sure what this means, but he suspects that in the larger scope of things, it must mean something.

Like the shrine over there on the right behind that mobile home. Whenever he drives on this road, he can't help but notice it, about a mile past the sign for Dave's Store. Someone has dug a bathtub into the ground, leaving half of the tub exposed as a simple porcelain shrine for the Virgin Mary. But she leans precariously forward and to the right, as though trying to step out of the tub. He wonders why these people don't keep her propped up, why they don't notice the obvious flaw in their shrine.

He has never been tempted to stop—not even on a foggy night when he wouldn't be seen—and fix this oblique Madonna. But he does wonder what she is trying to get away from. Why is she leaning, as though frozen in the act of escape? Or, is her posture deliberate, a statement by the people who live in this mobile home? Perhaps the statue silently speaks for them by trying to flee her empty, white room.

If he would just pull off onto the shoulder right now, open the door, step out, cross the ditch, and walk through those trees, he'd find a small lake that he has never seen before. A milky haze hovers over the lake as though the spirit of the water has risen. Looking at the fog, he might think about the flock of ducks that he once saw approach a cloud, then veer off, as though the cloud were a solid wall. Or he might remember the World War I story about a battalion of five hundred British soldiers who, to secure their positions for attack, walked into a thick fog that clung to the side of Hill 60 on the Gallipoli Peninsula. Moments later, when the cloud lifted, the men had vanished and were never seen again.

He wouldn't have to walk very close to the lake to know that this scene is there for him to see. But his fear would be that whatever resides within this vapor, within the tiny beads that float in air, is the part of himself that he needs the most. If only he would follow the impulse to pull off, to step out, to walk into those trees. To take those dangerous steps.

Shortest Day, Longest Night

He had thought of setting the alarm for 2:00 a.m. He had thought of getting up and walking outside to look at the full moon, to stand in an open space, maybe down by the lake, for a while, and then make a large circle of footsteps in the snow. To bring along thirteen of those tall white candles, one for each new moon of the coming year, and push them into the packed snow as he walked around the circle, to light them, and then step to the center. He had thought of standing there, at the hub of this wheel of light, at precisely 2:54, the official turning point. He had thought of facing the moon, of somehow celebrating the shortest day, the longest night.

But it is 11:08 the next morning, and he is sitting in the church pew listening to the minister say something about television being a wasteland when he remembers that he didn't set the alarm. And he is afraid that, a year from now, he will have forgotten this idea about the circle and the candles.

The Cows Nearly Make It

He's heading back to town. Ahead of him on the right shoulder, something is moving, something big. He slows down and sees that it's a cow, a Holstein, wait a minute, there's another one in front of it, and another, they're running, 13, 14, 15, 16, he keeps counting, driving slowly. He hits the high beams and sees them stretched out as far as the light reaches, an entire herd of Holsteins hoofing it from their farm to town on the shoulder of Highway 71. He sees 37, 38, 39, 40, 41. In the distance, lights are flashing. 50, 51, 52.

Tomorrow, in the paper, he'll read how the cows wandered off a farm about fourteen miles south of town and were stopped nearing the city limits at 2:40 a.m. A patrol dispatcher will say, "I think we found some of the fastest cows in the state."

As he gets closer, he sees police cars and pickups parked on the other shoulder. 64, 65, 66, 67. Police and others scatter across the highway and ditch, waving their arms and flashlights at the leaders of the herd. 78, 79, 80.

They are two miles from the city limits. Who knows what would have happened if they hadn't been stopped? 81. If they had gotten all the way to town? 82. Two more miles, that's all they had left! 83. And they could have made it! 84.

To the Stones

Maybe you knew you'd end up looking like this, carefully stacked. He says that you are his sculptures. He says that when he listens carefully, you tell him how you should be arranged. One of these pillars he calls Groucho; another, Madonna and Child. Maybe you knew you'd be expected to stay like this forever, not a wall to keep things in or out, not at the edge of a field where others like you are tossed, but here at the edge of his garden where you stand, protecting the irises and dahlias. Oh guardians, oh penetrable walls, wind will invade, snow will cover. The top stone, precarious, may fall. But he will replace it. After all, he says, you are teaching him about balance and order.

Limited Supply

He knows that eventually we all run out of things. Oh, of course there's sugar and gas and clean underwear. And maybe the sex drive. But we also run out of minutes. He wonders how far to push this idea. For example, will he run out of thoughts? Will he run out of words? Will he stop mid-sentence, mouth open, having used up some predetermined quota, unable now to utter another word? Is there any way of predicting the date and time of this occurrence? Is it genetic, environmental? Can it be prevented? He knows about the black-footed ferret and the ivory-billed woodpecker, the red wolf and the cave bear. And this morning on the news he heard that in the wild in Minnesota only six butternut trees can be found that haven't been infected by the fungus that has killed all the rest.

Then he scoffs at his own thoughts. How silly ! But the idea of running out of words does make him think more carefully, for a moment anyway, about what he says. And he holds back the words he knows he should have used.

David Bengtson. I am a teacher who also writes. Much of my energy goes into teaching, and at times there seems to be little left for writing. I envy those who have the discipline to set aside a regular time to write. I've never been able to. I'm also not sure I understand how or why I write.

But I had a dream the other night. I was standing in a room fur-nished with only a table and three chairs. The table was covered with a checkered cloth and set for a meal. I decided to sit at the table for a few minutes and see what might happen. Suddenly two men in white coveralls wheeled an upright piano and bench into the room. They lifted the cover and left. Silence. The stale smell of smoke. I walked to the piano and cautiously sat. My right hand slowly moved to the keys and began to play the melody line from "All the Gold in California Is in a Bank in the Middle of Beverly Hills in Somebody Else's Name." Then my left hand joined in, and before I knew it, I was so engaged in playing the song and surprised that I could that I didn't realize the room had begun to fill with people, that there were more tables now, more chairs. That I was on a stage colored by bright lights. That there was a small combo behind me. That the audience was applauding wildly. That they wanted more. So I grabbed the microphone, stepped away from the piano, unbuttoned my shirt to the waist, and broke into a rousing version of "Diggin' Up Bones."

During my performance I began to wake up and realized that what had awakened me was the radio alarm—tuned, of course, to KEYL, central Minnesota's country giant. Playing quietly was Randy Travis singing the chorus of "Diggin' Up Bones." So, does this mean anything? Does this have anything to do with writing?

I've received a Prize for Poetry from the Academy of American Poets and a Loft McKnight Award for Creative Prose. My wife, Mar-ilyn, and I have two daughters, Cory and Kjersten. For the past twenty-six years we have lived in Long Prairie, where I teach English at the high school.

I do love to sing. I love to sing those soulful country ballads with strong melodies and simple lyrics, like that Hank Williams song, I'm So Lonesome I Could Cry.

David Bengtson

Photo by Mary B. Lieberman

CLAIRE VAN BREEMEN DOWNES

Lena's Book

REACHING BACK ACROSS the war years for memories always seems like reaching beyond a deep chasm into a world so different that it puzzles me to chart the way from there to here. Those years before the war, I felt snugly blanketed by family, surrounded and protected. I'm remembering, for instance, the coldest winter of the Depression and the furnace broken. We sat, those evenings, close around the kitchen stove with our schoolbooks or handwork, going off at last into the shivering darkness after a bedtime treat—popcorn, perhaps, or cocoa and cinnamon toast. That's the way I remember my family, a circle of warmth against the cold and the dark. And if that safe shelter was more perception than reality, perhaps there are times when seeming safety is enough.

The world before the war seemed to me not only secure, but eternal—as though we would always live in the small sleepy town with the tiny green campus where my brothers and sisters went to college, and we would always drive out on Sundays over the graveled country roads cutting through the red clay hills to the little Friends chapel, Tansy Hill Church, where my father was the lay minister.

Only a handful of farm families kept the church alive, and I suppose that nowadays, when the roads are better and it's easier to get into town, no one bothers with the old place. It stood on a hill, as churches should, but was Quaker-plain to downright ugliness. Simplicity can be beauty, but it requires a purity of line and a loving attention to workmanship that this forlorn box lacked. It had, of course, no plumbing and no electricity, but neither did even the most prosperous of the farms thereabout.

And some of the farms were truly prosperous, those that had at least some rich bottom land and also boasted frugal, industrious farmers. The Janssons were that. They were careful managers, and Alma Jansson set a good table. Her rich, plentiful Swedish cooking always delighted me—as did the fact that when it was our turn to eat there, I was free, after a stint of drying dishes, of course, to spend my afternoon sprawled on the ancient black leather settee, with old books from the glass-fronted shelves in the parlor.

The Millers' farm was a good place, too. They were fairly new to the community and were modernizing their place rapidly, getting some of the latest machinery and using new methods. When the war came, their son Mike was drafted early and his dad had a hard time holding the place together. But before the war the food on the table was good and Mike was very handsome and so old—twenty, at least—that a thirteen-year-old could idol-worship without involvement. Mike's sister Millie was just about my age and there was no end of interesting things to be doing on a Sunday afternoon, until suddenly it was time for supper. And after that, we were off to the evening service at the church.

For the night meeting, except for a few Sundays in summer, the lamps had to be lit. For the most part they were old-fashioned oil lamps, with their soft mellow glow, but I remember, too, the astounding brilliance of the new patent lamp that hung over the center aisle. It was a bit scary, with the pumping before you started it and the fragile mantel that looked to be woven of spun

glass and glowed brighter than an electric bulb when it was lit.
But it certainly made light enough to read by.

Usually Sunday evening meeting was short and simple and
before I knew it I was nodding to sleep in the car on the drive
back to College Place. Once, though, evening meeting was not
short and simple at all, but that comes later in my story.

Which brings us, I suppose, to the Blacks, Allard and Lena
and their four daughters, who lived about a mile the other side of
the church from the Janssons. The small, frame, basementless
house, scarcely more than a cabin, clung rather tenuously to the
hillside. Inside, the rooms weren't plastered and covered with
wallpaper, as I was used to, but were finished with a thick shiny
builder's paper nailed to the uprights with tiny brads. The collection of family photos, enlarged and hand-colored and set in wide
oval frames, hung defiantly against the bleak background.

Theirs was one of the poorer farms, just steep, eroded clay
hills, not half so fertile as the acres of the Busbys, Lena's parents,
who lived on east a few miles. No doubt some of the lack of pro-
ductivity lay in the farmer himself, for Allard, though nice looking and soft-spoken, was nobody's idea of a go-getter. He plodded
along at his own pace and when he wanted to stop and go into
town, he went. And Lena was always happy to cram her battered
hat on her bird's-nest hair and go along—round, small head bob-
bing on her thin, long-necked body like an apple on a stick. She
did love to be gadding. But not the hardest grubbing could have
made that marginal farm pay, and Allard, with no son to help him
in the fields, had to work alone.

There had been a son, the first of their children, but he had
died as an infant, and after that came only daughters. Maybe that
was a part of why Lena was obsessed with men. Mostly, at least so
far as the preacher's family was ever allowed to know, her obsession took the form of trying to get her daughters married. Her
methods were crude, and quite early in our years of duty at Tansy

Hill, our parents learned to leave my teen-aged brothers home when it was our turn to dine with the Blacks.

One Sunday Allard came to church with a swollen jaw and bruised cheek. He volunteered no explanation, nor did Lena, and the girls just looked too rabbity-eyed scared for words. Alma Jansson told us the story, though, at dinner—remembering, as she looked at me, to expurgate details. So it's only an edited version that I have to offer.

There had been a social at the schoolhouse Friday night and, during the course of the evening, Rose Ellen Black, next to the oldest of the sisters and not yet seventeen, turned up missing, and so did Tim Clancy, son of a new family in the community. Lena got all upset—"As though she hadn't put the child up to it herself!" Alma snorted—and sent Allard out to hunt for the pair. They found them, down in the little grove at the foot of the schoolyard, and that's when the ruckus began. Someone, probably a Clancy, said something sneering about the situation, and Allard, shouting, "You can't say that about my daughter!" waded in. Apparently everybody then chose up sides and rolled up their sleeves. It was a memorable melée indeed, talked of for years.

It must have been clear to most of the adults at Tansy Hill, long before, that Lena—in a time and place that talked of marriage and children, but never of sex—spent most of her time thinking of sex and, within the limits of her concepts of the world, of ways to use sex to gain economic power, or at least a meal ticket. So her book should have come as no surprise, really.

Perhaps the surprise was not the subject-matter, but the weight of the endeavor itself. Certainly, Lena seemed only nominally literate. Not astounding, when you remembered that she had married before even finishing eighth grade at the one-room schoolhouse down the road. But as I think back on that family and its inheritance, I don't think that it was from Allard that the two younger girls got the enthusiasm for learning that eventually carried them beyond the reach of their mother's machinations.

Jody, the youngest, the one that looked most like her mother, dark-haired and wiry, was really a sharp student—though at twelve and thirteen, I couldn't appreciate that, because she was just enough younger to fall unquestionably into the category of bratty twerp. Ellie, my favorite and the one closest to my age, was not so quick to learn as Jody, but had a tenacious determination that made up for any slowness. Their mother may well have been the source of their capability, for Lena, too, had abilities, though hers had been thwarted so long and were so twisted by her starkly sexual philosophy that they could be of no comfort to her, nor bring her the respect and applause she craved.

Very likely she started the book to get just that respect and applause. When Mother, later, was trying to explain to me a sudden midweek meeting out at Tansy Hill, she grew embarrassed (she always did around such subjects) and said that Lena had written a book that shouldn't have been written—that some unidentified someone had shown Lena some unidentified book that used crude and explicit language. Whether it was unredeemed pornography or merely a somber naturalistic novel, I have no way of knowing, nor do I know the route by which either of the above might get to Tansy Hill. But Lena, so it was said, looked through it, said, "Pooh! I can do better than that!" and got busy with tablet and pencil. There were those who said she had indeed outdone her model, at least in the number of four-letter words and sexual rowdiness.

How large her manuscript had grown, whether she had somehow access to a typewriter or whether it was still in her half-formed scrawl, who it was that read it, who spilled the secret—all those were questions I did not think to ask in proper time of anyone who might reasonably know. At the moment of the happening, no one would have answered me, of course, for I was considered too young to be allowed any knowledge of the business. And so all of the small events went on without my partaking in them or understanding their meaning, and before long we were leaving

College Park and the war was beginning. Later, when I grew curious about the whole odd episode, I was too many miles and years away to hope to learn the truth.

Presumably, the manuscript was brought out as evidence on that Wednesday night when Lena came before the church elders. Someone, having seen the writing or heard of its content, had demanded the inquisition. That was why in the early spring of our final year in College Park, my parents reluctantly prepared for the formal meeting of the church fathers in assembly, and why my mother tried to tell me about it without telling me anything that she thought might smudge my innocence. What Lena may have said in her own defense on that occasion I do not know. It is, in any case, irrelevant. As with all inquisitions, Lena's discipline was inevitable, as was the burning of the book.

The book went into someone's cookstove, I suspect. No formal, public rites were considered necessary. Lena, however, was required to make public confession on that night when the Sunday evening service was different from any other. That I saw with my own eyes.

There was a special point in the service at which she was given the opportunity to rise and address the congregation. She moved awkwardly to the front of the room, her thin shoulders twitching. Behind the round glasses, her near-sighted brown eyes were red-rimmed. Her round face, too small-seeming atop her long withered neck and tall frame, appeared even more ravaged and wrinkled than usual, though she had not neglected powder and the habitual bright, defiant spots of her rouge. The frizzy dark hair bushed out from under her navy-blue hat. She began to speak, in ugly gasps that were more like sobs. The sentences came out in little bits.

"I'm sorry I wrote that book. It—it was a bad book, and I'm sorry. I didn't know—how evil it was to do that—and I can't think—why—I wanted to write—such things. I'll never do so again. Please—please, all of you. Forgive—" And the confession ended in tears, Lena removing her glasses and pressing to her eyes the linen hankie she had been twisting into a rag as she spoke. She stumbled to her pew and sat down.

Silence lay upon us all. Was the silence forgiving or condemning? I do not know. I have heard since of a church practice called *shunning*, and this was not that, but certainly it was a *shaming*. As though I were four instead of fourteen, I squirmed in my seat, uneasy, the germ of mutiny and rebellion waking within me. And then my father lifted his hand as though in benediction and began to sing:

> "Just as I am, Thou wilt receive,
> Wilt welcome, pardon, cleanse, relieve . . . "

The book was burned. Lena Black was cleansed and pardoned of her sin and accepted into her congregation once more. Her tears subsided; a trembling smile began.

But my mutinous spirit was only lulled. As years went by, it became ever more wakeful, and I learned to look back on that night sadly, as on a betrayal. It was not that I felt Lena's book had any hope of literary excellence; it was not that I even liked Lena. But her book was her attempt to say something about life. It was hers, and she was robbed of it. She, who had so little, could not keep even that scrawled attempt at immortality, could not keep even a touch of pride in her accomplishment. The world lost no masterpiece, but the people gathered in that room—yes, my parents, too, and even I—lost some part of our humanity, some touch of compassion, some sense of enduring justice.

Claire van Breemen Downes. *My father believed us pilgrims and strangers, merely passing through this world. We passed through a lot of it. Moving about the Midwest, I adopted each new place fiercely, making it my home town, however temporary. Eventually we reached*

*Colorado, then Florida, where I finished college. A year's teaching in
rural Florida sent me eagerly to graduate school at Tallahassee, where
I completed a master's degree in English literature and met another
transplanted northerner, Alan Downes. Though the first years of our
marriage were as nomadic as my childhood, we have been settled in
St. Cloud since 1969. (I still marvel that all five of our children finished high school in this same town, the youngest moving from
kindergarten through twelfth grade right here.) I retired from the
English Department of St. Cloud State University in 1988, wanting
time to organize manuscripts and complete a novel.*

    My poetry has appeared in The Great River Review, Tampa Re-
view, Christian Century, Nostoc, Sing Heavenly Muse, *and elsewhere. Small essays have appeared in* Minnesota Literature.

    *I have always considered myself a writer, even when the obvious
order of my day was washing diapers or grading freshman themes. I
write to explain things to myself, for writing is not only committed
public engagement, but a private attempt to bear the unbearable and
explain the inexplicable.*

JEAN V. HUSBY

The Lullaby
(1896)

R AGNHILD KNEW THAT, unlike her mother, her father
never regretted his decision to emigrate from Norway. In
fact, Olaf Hanson felt the hand of his Lutheran God directing his life. Here in western Minnesota the prairie sod asked
only to be turned and worked, whereas the rocky, mountainous
land of Norway had battled him all the way. Each year the fertile
loam of his quarter section of land yielded bigger and better crops
of oats, barley, flax. A fine herd of Holsteins grazed along the wil-
low-lined river. He had built a barn and replaced the crude log
cabin with a new white clapboard house.

Ragnhild, at sixteen, was proud of her father, his farm, the
new house. She helped make decisions during the building—
about room size, the location of doors and windows, even the
choice of wood for the mantelpiece. Her uninterested mother was
not willing to take part in the planning, and gradually Ragnhild
took her place. In one instance only did Brit rouse herself to make
a decision. She chose wallpaper for the parlor, a pattern of big red
roses. Ragnhild hated those roses. Yet, the very fact that her
mother had asserted herself to voice a preference in the matter
gave Ragnhild hope that her mother would become less distanced
from all that was taking place around her, and so she said nothing.

In their life on the farm the positions of Ragnhild and her fifteen year-old sister Gudrud were well defined. An unspoken law
decreed that Gudrud assume the place of the son Olaf had lost.
She worked the farm with her father, was as adept as he at driving
their team of work horses to plow, harrow, disc, rake, plant. In
1896 an early spring woke the land with sunny days and warm
showers and by mid-June Gudrud and Olaf were cutting sweet-
smelling hay.

As in Norway, so in Minnesota, the women milked the cows.
Twice daily Brit and Gudrud drove the lumbering creatures into
the barn for milking. Ragnhild was never asked to help with this
ritual. She was expected to stay inside to do the housework, to
cook and wash and clean. Her household tasks gave her much
time with her mother and could have produced a closeness between the two, but they did not. Brit kept her own counsel. Contained within herself, she reached out to no one, not to Olaf or
Ragnhild or Gudrud.

Britha was a small, rather forbidding woman, her reddish
brown hair pulled back severely from a center part and gathered
into a bun at the nape of her neck. She went about her daily
work on the farm doing what was required of her without any attempt to make life pleasant or joyful for the family or herself. She
was never idle; it was as if work was the panacea for all that troubled her.

Ragnhild remembered her mother when she had a twinkle in
her eye, that year they emigrated from Norway, a tenderness in
her demeanor which had drawn the children to her. Now those
light blue eyes were dull. She seemed indifferent to what went on
about her. Her compulsive need to use her hands constantly man-
ifested itself; wherever she went, if she were not carrying pails of
feed for the chickens, or produce from the garden, or buckets of
milk, Brit would remove her knitting from a large pocket in her
apron and knit as she walked. She made scarves, mittens, sweaters
in drab greys and tans. The neighbors joked about her, speculated

that she even knit underwear for Olaf. The sound of her knitting needles became synonymous with the woman, Britha.

One day Ragnhild overheard three women discussing her mother. They were using the Norwegian word *gamle* to describe her as an old-country person, one who is unable or unwilling to change, to become American.

"Olaf needs a son," the oldest of the three stated. "Gudrud works with him like a man, but he should have a son."

"It must be eleven, twelve years now since they came here," another added, "and no more children in all that time." She herself had nine. "How does Britha do it?"

The third woman surmised, "One of these days Olaf will look around for a willing woman. It's a wonder he hasn't already."

"Losing that child when they came to this country has affected her." The oldest lady pointed to her head.

Ragnhild, listening, felt pain for her mother. She recalled the day when her desperately ill brother, Arne, had been taken from them at the Port of Entry. That day, at the age of five, she had suffered with her mother in the bewilderment of what was happening. Now, the sixteen year-old farm girl understood everything the women were saying.

Several weeks after Ragnhild overheard that conversation, she and Gudrud came home from school earlier than usual. Their farm was on the edge of town, a mile and a half from the school. In the snowy winter they must follow the wagon road; spring and fall offered a short cut around the fields and through the pasture to their house. On this particular spring day Gudrud dallied by the last place in town to watch old Mr. Harstad dig a drainage ditch at the side of the road. Ragnhild hurried on the path toward home. When she reached the farmhouse she quietly let herself in, not really knowing why she was being so quiet.

From her parents' room came strains of music. Ragnhild was puzzled. Could Mor be singing? Still wearing her wraps, her school books under her arm, Ragnhild tiptoed toward the music as if pulled by an invisible thread. Her mother, who never sang, was singing. *"Bya, bya, liten gutt,"* sitting in her rocking chair in front of a window softly crooning the lullaby to a bundle of clothes she cradled tenderly in her arms. *"Bya, bya, liten gutt,"* over and over and then humming on and on. She rocked back and forth, moving with the tune. Ragnhild melted deeper into the hall. Into her consciousness flooded memories of the hold on the ship *Hekla.* She was listening to the sounds of her mother trying to soothe Arne. She could smell the stinking hold, hear the gratings and groanings of the ship, as she lay against the rough wall on the lower bunk. She remembered crawling across Mor and Arne and looking into the glazed eyes of the whimpering child. *"Bya, bya, liten gutt."* The rocking mother, aware of nothing but the "child" in her arms, sang on and on.

To Ragnhild, with a rush, came the words of the local woman talking about her mother, "Losing that child has affected her." Was she right? Is Mor's mind affected? Is she still grieving for Arne? Is it possible Arne is still alive, that he didn't die that day at Castle Garden? Softly Ragnhild slipped into the kitchen and, without removing her blue wool coat, sat down at the oilcloth-covered table. She gazed blindly out the window—and heard her mother's pleading voice, those many years ago, when they had to leave Arne at Castle Garden, "Please, Olaf, please let us stay here and take care of Arne. I must feed him." And then she heard the silence of her father.

From that moment on she began to watch her mother more closely, to see her more clearly, to feel a need to protect her, the impulse to help Britha slowly shaping her life.

Again and again she encouraged her mother to learn English. Patiently, she let Britha know that she understood living here in Willow Water, that there was no urgent need to learn the new language; half the inhabitants were Norwegians who spoke their native tongue. But, she carefully explained, these immigrants *want* to become American. "Do you not want to be American?" she asked. Brit did not answer. Ragnhild tried to make fun of it, this language thing, by noting that even the *Setesdalen* were losing their brogues. Brit did not laugh. Ragnhild told herself not to be so impatient, reminded herself that she had teachers at school to help her while Brit had no one, except her family. "This is a *cup*, Mother." "This is a *plate*." "We are going to *church*." Brit simply ignored her English-speaking daughter, pulled out her knitting and let the clack, clack of the needles take over.

Ragnhild and Gudrud did indeed go to church—and in English. The Lutheran Church itself was divided by language, offering one service each week in Norwegian, one in English. Olaf yearned to go to the English service with his daughters, for he had made steady progress in learning his adopted tongue, but in this matter he must consider the wishes of his wife. His religion taught that one must do nothing to cause another to lose his faith. If he did not take Brit to church she would quit going and he would have sinned. Anticipated guilt dictated his actions. So, Brit and Olaf continued worshipping with a dwindling group of old-country parishioners clinging to familiar ways. Each Sunday Olaf, with his erect bearing (he had served two years in the Army of Norway), would walk up the center aisle, his right hand on the elbow of his shawl-clad wife. They would seat themselves in the fifth pew from the front directly out from the pulpit, to be able to look directly at Reverend Langemoe.

The community of Willow Water looked up to the Reverend Langemoe. He was articulate, well-read, the best educated man in town. They called him Reverend, not the more informal Pastor. A tall man, big-boned, a commanding presence; he exuded authority. There was something aristocratic about him which demanded deference. Yet the people liked him, for his trustworthiness, and they knew he cared about them.

Ragnhild's clear soprano voice found her a place in the church choir, and Gudrud, not wanting to sit alone in church, joined too. Early in the spring of 1895 Reverend Langemoe had asked Ragnhild to lead a children's choir. Someone was needed to teach the young ones to sing the hymns in English. He offered, as her helper and organist, his daughter, Livia, and so began a friendship that was to last a lifetime. The two girls would spend hours together, Liv informally teaching her friend to play the organ. When winter came, the coldness of the church nave drove them to the parsonage where they continued their music together at the Langemoe's piano.

Ragnhild envied her friend that piano, coveted it. She asked her father if there were any possibility they might buy one for their house. "Perhaps, sometime," was his half-yes reply. Indeed, Olaf liked the idea of being rich enough to own a musical instrument. Ragnhild's musical talent came from him, of this he was sure. If it were not for Brit, he would offer his deep bass voice to the choir. Yes, some day he would buy a piano. As for Ragnhild, she spent more and more of her time at the parsonage.

On a blustery day in March the two girls were playing duets when Liv's father entered the room, ostensibly searching for a notebook. Instead of leaving when he could not find it, he folded himself down into a chair to watch and listen. The girls stopped playing and looked at him. "Yes, Father?" Liv questioned.

He rose and approached the piano. "Ragnhild, I've been thinking about your family." He leaned an arm across the corner of the piano-top. "What can we do to get your mother to be part of the congregation?"

Ragnhild's face flushed.

"She comes only to the Norwegian services with your father," he continued. "She doesn't have anything to do with any of the ladies. She should be coming to Aid." He paused. "Why doesn't she come?"

"She doesn't speak English." Ragnhild stated what they both knew.

"Some of the women would speak to her in Norwegian."

"But the program is in English, Reverend Langemoe."

"Yes, that's true. Still, we must do something to try to get her to come."

"I can try," the girl answered, but added honestly, "I don't think she will."

Over the next few weeks variations of this same conversation took place between the clergyman and Ragnhild. Then, one day, when Liv was not in the room, Ragnhild braved the situation and spoke her thoughts to this man she had learned to know and trust. "I think Mor is very unhappy. I found her singing one day . . . . " She went on to tell him about the day she found Brit holding the bundle of clothes, rocking and singing the lullaby. "I think if my mother could find out what happened to Arne at Castle Garden, she would be happier. I really think she believes that he is out there somewhere. But it is so strange. She thinks of him as a baby. He would be thirteen years old by now." She was silent for a while and then added, "I think she is not sure that he died that day—and it keeps her unhappy."

Although Langemoe knew the story of the child left at the Port of Entry, the idea that they had not tried to find out about him had not occurred to him. Now he realized how deeply the girl had considered her mother. He sat for a few minutes looking out the window at the yellow-green of the early spring leaves. He must verify what he suspected and asked, "Has your father tried to find out what happened?"

Ragnhild shook her head. She looked at her hands and waited for him to speak.

"It wouldn't hurt to try to find out for sure. Maybe we should try." He tapped one foot and continued to look at the spring landscape. "I'm going to Crookston next week. I'll make inquiries about how to go about it." He turned to face Ragnhild. "And then we shall speak to your father."

He made the three day trip to Crookston, the County Seat. The County Attorney told him to write to the Immigration Service in Washington, D.C.

On his return to Willow Water, the conscientious Minister suggested again to Ragnhild that they should involve her father. She refused, fearing he might put a stop to the process.

The clergyman carefully crafted a letter. "I am writing on behalf of a parishioner, Miss Ragnhild Hanson." He stated the problem. "She would like to know if your records show that her brother, Arne Hanson, then aged two years old, died at Castle Garden, the New York Port of Entry, on May 15, 1885." He went on to give the authorities all the information Ragnhild could give him of the family's departure from Norway and arrival in the United States.

Then, yet once more, he encouraged Ragnhild to tell her parents what they had done, that the letter had been written. Only after the letter had been posted did Ragnhild follow his advice and tell them.

With uncharacteristic excitement Brit asked, "When will we hear? Will the Government write to you, a girl of sixteen? How long will it take? It was good of Reverend Langemoe to help you."

"Ragnhild, you shouldn't bother the Reverend with our troubles." Olaf's voice was gruff. "I am disappointed in you." His voice rose. "You should not have done it! I don't like it at all!" He slammed the door as he stormed out of the kitchen.

No more was said of the matter, although it hovered in all their minds. Ragnhild attempted to pray, but could not. For what should she pray? *Do I want to know Arne is living out there somewhere, no one knows where? That would be worse than knowing he is dead. What is Mor thinking?* Brit seemed to Ragnhild to be more unapproachable than ever. *Perhaps she thinks talking about it would not please Father—and she is right there,* Ragnhild reasoned with herself. *Father doesn't want other people consulted about matters which he thinks should stay in the family and he hates speculation about anything.* Weeks passed. Her hopes of getting definite information, whatever that might be, began to fade. Perhaps Far was right and she should not have troubled Reverend Langemoe. Perhaps it is better not to know.

Fall moved closer to winter. The girls concentrated on their studies.

On a crisp, cold Friday in November, Liv approached Ragnhild at school to give her a message. Liv's father would like to talk to Ragnhild "at his study in the church tomorrow morning."

"At the church?" Ragnhild questioned this unusual request.

"That's what he asked me to tell you," Liv replied matter-of-factly. "I don't know why."

The Minister's Study at the Norwegian Lutheran Church was in front of the nave, a small room off to the right side of the or-nate wooden Gothic altar. To get there, one must go through the wide-open worship space. On that afternoon in November a dis-quieting sense of foreboding surrounded the girl as she walked quietly over the wooden floorboards through the cold, empty room, up the steps and along the altar rail. She looked up at the familiar painting on the altar wall of Christ leaving the tomb, the two Roman soldiers lying at either side of an opening to a cave, holding their shields before their eyes. The rich brown of the sol-dier's tunics, their hard helmets, and Christ all white and shining. She knocked at the door.

"Come in."

The man sitting behind his desk, in his black suit and white clerical collar was *The Minister*, not her friend's father. Ragnhild felt an awe in the presence of the official clergy. She stood there.

"Please be seated, Ragnhild." Reverend Langemoe pushed back his chair a few inches, opened his top desk drawer and re-moved a long important-looking envelope, placed it in front of him on his desk. "The Immigration Service answered our letter." He put on his metal-rimmed glasses and looked at Ragnhild. She sat forward on her chair. Her grey mittens fell to the floor. The minister's serious tone stifled the smile which had started to ap-pear on her young face. "It is not what we were hoping for." He took the letter out of the envelope, spread it on the desk before him. "Now, Ragnhild, God's ways are not our ways. You know that. Sometimes the answers to our prayers are not to our liking. He works in mysterious ways." He went on in this vein while Ragnhild waited. Finally he said, "I will read part of it to you." He lifted the white paper up in front of him. "Here it says, 'I regret to inform you that I can be of no help in verifying the death of Arne Hanson. The immigrant records were moved from Castle Garden to the new facility on Ellis Island. Last year there was a fire at Ellis Island and all the records for the Port of New York for the years from 1855 to 1890 were destroyed.'" Reverend Langemoe took off his glasses, laid them alongside the letter, then raised his eyes to search the face of the girl in front of him.

A deep silence enveloped the two.

"How will I tell Mor and Father?" Ragnhild's question was anguished. "You," and she considered the competent authoritarian figure before her. "No, I should tell them. Father would not . . . " and her voice trailed off, "but Mor . . . "

"You will find a way, Ragnhild. The Lord will help you. You must pray for guidance." He sat there for a minute, then picked up the letter, folded it and slipped it back into the envelope. He handed it to her across the desk. "Here, take the letter with you and show it to your father. Shall we have a word of prayer together?"

Ragnhild's footsteps dragged as she walked the path around the field toward home. She picked up a stick and struck dry leaves from the grasses and low-lying plants as she walked, not in anger, but rather giving a rhythm to her thoughts. When she reached the pasture she threw down the stick and stopped for a while before letting herself through the fence gate. Her smooth sixteen year-old forehead was furrowed in a pattern it would assume many, many years later in old age. Suddenly, her chin jutted out and she pursed her lips as if saying to herself, "Well, that's what I have to do." She kicked some pebbles with the toe of her high-topped shoe and walked on with an air of determination.

The noon meal was always a hearty one on the farm and the family took time to eat it. On this Saturday in November the meal seemed interminable to Ragnhild, yet she wanted to lengthen it. When the family had finished the last morsel of their bread pudding, she pulled the letter from her pocket.

"You heard from the Immigration Service," Olaf stated in surprise.

Brit became agitated. "Tell me, tell me." She plucked at her daughter's shoulder.

Gudrud jumped up to stand behind Ragnhild. "Well, read it, Ragnhild. Read it."

"You have to sit down, Gudrud." Ragnhild became quite formal. "I will tell you, in Norwegian for Mor's sake, what it says." She took a deep breath, glanced once at her father, then looking directly into her mother's eyes began slowly. "Mor, the letter says that Arne died that day at Castle Garden." She paused. "There was a Lutheran Chaplain there to serve all the Scandinavian immigrants. He said prayers over Arne when they buried him." Ragnhild held the letter in her lap. They all sat still as if frozen in position. "That's all the letter says," Ragnhild concluded limply.

Brit said nothing. She pushed back her chair and rose from the table, took off her big-pocketed apron and hung it on a hook on the wall, put on her heavy grey sweater that hung there. The family watched as she opened the door to the back porch. They heard the slam of the outside door as Brit let herself out into the cool November air. From where he sat Olaf could see his wife as she veered off the road and headed across the meadow in the direction of the willows and the river.

Ragnhild longed for her father to go after Mor, to speak, to touch, but she knew he would not.

Olaf picked up his battered brown felt hat from the floor

where he had dropped it before the meal and pushed back his chair. It grated on the floor. "Gudrud, come. We have work to do."

Solemnly Ragnhild handed her father the letter. He folded it in half and palmed it into his back pocket without looking at it.

Jean V. Husby. *I grew up in the farming community of McIntosh in northwestern Minnesota. Its Scandinavian people, who perpetuated their old-country traditions, made an indelible impression on my life. After I married I lived in Kansas City, Missouri, where I helped raise a family, began to write stories, worked as a musician, earned a university degree. I now live (write, garden, make music) on Maple Hill within sight of Lake Superior in Grand Marais.*

"The Lullaby" is one of a number of stories I have written, am writing, about the people of the fictional town of Willow Water in western Minnesota.

Other articles, short stories, book reviews, a column on theater, journal entries, a poem, have been published in newspapers and small press publications. An article I wrote on hunger was distributed nationally.

Writing is an integral part of my life. When I'm not actively working on a piece the ideas roll around in my head until they demand to be put down on paper, at which point I quit procrastinating and get to work.

DAN HUNTSPERGER

Pandemonium, Bird Song, and the Great Unknown

O N A LATE SEPTEMBER afternoon I sat in the backyard jotting down notes and arranging into coherent order my journals and observations from thirty-odd years of camping trips. My work progressed slowly because I was happily distracted by the nearby activities of others. In the flower garden to my left, a convocation of dragonflies hovered and swept in restless flight. Most had reddish-brown bodies, but some were of a grayish cast. Their favorite places to light were the dry, breeze-swayed tops of plants that had passed beyond summer maturity into the early stages of decay. I heard the steady chant of crickets, punctuated by frequent dissonant calls from a sizeable flock of starlings, whose members, mincing and waddling over our tired lawn, harvested an unplanned crop of weed seeds. My wife, Audrey, and our youngest son, Tom, were planting tulip bulbs in front, and Tom's enthusiastic pup Max wriggled his tawny body into the thick of everything.

Earlier I had helped Audrey dig compost for their project, enjoying the musty smell of humus when I turned it over with the garden fork. Audrey pointed out a tiny olive-green bird flitting through the overhead limbs of our gnarled, unkempt bur oak. We couldn't tell whether it was a warbler or a kinglet—so swift were its movements. I lost sight of the vibrant little creature when I momentarily brushed a cloud of gnats from my eyes. Later, many small insects, resembling a scattering of misplaced punctuation marks, dropped on my notebook paper as I wrote. The gnats and the other winged midgets were certainly a part of the bird's sustenance, and I speculated on how many of those diminutive insects the bird needed to eat if he wished to fuel a flight to Memphis. A hundred? Surely more than that. Several thousand? Small wonder that we couldn't fix the migrant bird's form in our vision for more than a few moments. Its nervous, seemingly random, activity was tied directly to its survival.

A monarch butterfly, sweeping gracefully on a sudden gust of wind, arced over the house. It descended to eye level, stopped briefly to sample a bloom on a clump of phlox, flirted for a moment with an unopened red rose, and then once more lifted over the roof and away. Shortly after the monarch disappeared, the wind bounced a curved, light brown leaf along the roof eaves, and at first, not looking at it directly, I mistook it for the butterfly. Bird and cricket sounds were drowned out temporarily by the deafening racket of a chain-saw one house down and across the street. The owner was removing a large, weathered limb from an aging silver-leafed poplar in his yard. Later, a power lawn mower droned monotonously through the grass. I closed my notebooks and carried them into the house.

Audrey and Tom made spaghetti that evening, and I agreed to do dishes. We dined before dusk. Max fell asleep under the dinner table. He had run around and around the house after his master for the sheer joy of it, had chewed on chunks of old compost and fish tails from the pile, had dogged our footsteps between the vegetable garden in back and the new tulip bed in front, and had attempted to walk through a small rose bush rather than around it. That last misguided act had scratched his tender young belly, and he cried for a few moments, but the tiny mishap was a small price to pay for his delightful day's outing.

When I started to clear the table, Audrey and Tom, envisioning the spring tulips, had already pushed their empty plates aside
and were studying the brilliant illustrations in the nursery catalog
one more time. As I looked at them and the sleeping puppy, I
shared their contentment, knowing that such simple pleasures as
we had enjoyed on this gentle day constituted the very marrow of
the good life.

After the dishes were finished, I glanced out the western windows for some faint vestiges of sunset, but the houses and trees
across the street blocked it from view. I caught a hint of saffron
and pink sky glowing over the top of my neighbor's garage and
through the branches of his twin oaks. The black scars on the
poplar bark, and the intertwined greens, grays, and browns of the
oaks, elms, and poplars had been clearly defined by the daylight,
but in minutes all the leaves, trunks, and limbs would be uni-
formly black against the pale horizon of early night.

Even as I savored the fading day, a neighbor youth backed his
car out the driveway. With tires screeching and the radio blasting
rock, he pointed the rusting Mercury Comet south, and burnt
rubber all the way down the block. The car's muffler, if it had one,
had long been breached. His speed served no practical purpose,
since our street ended at the block's end, where he would have to
turn either east or west. Something or somebody would certainly
come tumbling down before the last discordant notes from the
old Comet rattled a prelude to its final resting place in the junk
yard.

I smiled to myself, thinking how our small station wagon had
started to sound noisy lately. I had no wish to exit from our con-
fining suburban street with such obstreperous racket, and I
thought smugly, "Older, wiser men want quiet automobiles."
"Old and wise"—what satisfaction it gives us to link those words
together after we reach the age of sixty or thereabouts, though except for the fact of having survived, we generally have small ex-
cuse for such self-congratulation. Oh yes, in the manner of a tod-

dler learning that touching a hot stove is an extremely unpleasant one-time encounter, we do profit from some shared experiences of adulthood. But with few exceptions it is safe to say that: (A) an intelligent, admirable, and spirited youth will mature into an admirable, spirited, and intelligent old man, and that (B) a harsh, asinine, and insufferable young blockhead will grow into an asinine, offensive, and grumbling *old* blockhead. Such modifications as occur in their beings result mainly from the deterioration of their physical parts, so that as Type A ages he will find restrictions imposed on the pleasures he enjoys with friends and loved ones, but thankfully, for the very same reasons, Type B will do much less harm.

In moments the belligerent, localized clamor of the neighbor boy's Comet had blended in with the distant hum of highway traffic. In my own youth, I generally walked away my frustrations. I remember a long-ago summer night when I paced down the farm driveway under the stars. Warm air caressed me, but with a hint of coolness from the moisture-laden currents that slid up from ditches and the creek bottom. No industrial smoke or city lights dimmed the splendor of the stars. Crickets sang in the tall unmowed grass, and from the alfalfa field to the west, some wild creature, probably a fox, screamed fitfully. I also turned west on the main graveled road, walking steadily down it, choosing a hardened wheel track as the easiest place to walk. I heard a freight train whistle and the sound of the Canadian National freight hungrily swallowing track between Warroad and Baudette. I knew it was there, even though it sounded much closer, because the nearest track ran there. I heard a small scuffling sound from the gravel at the road's edge just ahead of me, and I remember stopping stock still for a moment, but hearing only the fading sounds of the train and the beating of my heart.

❋ ❋ ❋

Audrey and I left the land and came to the city when she was nineteen and I was twenty. Initially, we adjusted to our new surroundings with the pliability of youth. Audrey, optimistic by nature, who loves people instinctively, and small children especially, would have adjusted well to any situation that wasn't overtly hostile. For myself, after the first novelty of city life wore off, I often thought wistfully of winding creeks, small green fields, and timbered horizons. More and more I felt that the quality of life, short of unpeopled wilderness, increases in inverse ratio to the number of inhabitants per square mile. The camping trips, the return visits to the land, the reminiscing of old farm neighbors and friends, the annual check of inventory on the adjoining forested sand ridge—whitetail deer, whip-poor-wills, blueberries, cicadas, owls, cuckoos, bear tracks, ovenbirds—these things were for me near necessity if I wished to remain a lucid and productive member of urban society.

In the two decades before I reached retirement age, my clerical job had become computerized. The daily workload, force-fed electronically, frequently offered stress situations worthy of an executive's desk on mahogany row, but its day-to-day tedium rivaled the experience of any corn-treading, muzzled ox.

In contrast to my own recurring dissatisfaction with my means of livelihood, a refreshing feature of every camping vacation was the chance to watch wild living beings fit with neat perfection into their unique ecological niches. On twilight walks I sometimes glimpsed a great horned owl gliding across my path and into the dark branches of the jack pines. I knew that my brother predator, born with uncanny sight and hearing, would shortly deal death to some frightened skittering creature of the night. The horned owl is superbly equipped to kill everything from skunks, ducks, and rabbits to mice, voles, and bird nestlings, and it does so. Like all predators, from the African lion to the garden toad, it is as indifferent to moralizing scruples as a moss-covered rock.

There is in all of non-human nature a certain submission to efficient amoral power that is awesome to consider. We humans usually let others kill our meat, although many of us lead lives of quiet aggression in our efforts to subsist. However, if we overstep certain bounds, remorse and self-loathing await us. Even the dullest of human beings has some perception of right and wrong, and only the worst of us completely ignore the inner promptings of our better selves. We can scarcely help comparing the complexities of our moral choices with the apparent stark simplicity of the hunters and the hunted in the animal kingdom.

One time, while cleaning out my unsightly garage, I found a nest of small, naked mouse babies in some forgotten debris. Knowing that they would grow into destructive, germ-carrying adults shortly, and that some of them would find their way into our house, I gritted my teeth and killed them. Only then did I observe the mother running back and forth feverishly in the vicinity of her young ones' nest, and plaintively squeaking her sorrow. How deep was her grief? Only a reflexive act, some scientist-naturalists might say. And when we grieve for the death of a human child, is that only a reflexive act? It doesn't do to get overly sentimental about these things. Nonetheless, my conscience bothered me.

I regard the mother mouse's apparent grief and the horned owl's dispassionate consignment of its victims to oblivion with equal wonder. The coldest and most detached scientist at one end of the intellectual spectrum, or the empathetic poet-storyteller at the other end can only guess at the world perceived by his fellow creatures. But the poet-storyteller comes closest to the mark, as when Leigh Hunt describes the fish:

> " . . . swift, small-needing, vague yet clear,
> A cold, sweet, silver life, wrapped in round waves,
> Quickened with touches of transporting fear."

From before the time of Aesop, we have taken a kind of comfort in observing the behavior of animals and birds; nor have we hesitated to project our ethical principles and lapses on them. Although oral storytellers have become nearly extinct, our creature cousins still march across the printed pages of folklore, stories, and poetry. Foxes and buzzards, hyenas and bluebirds, sharks and honeybees, eagles and moles—all, unknowing, enrich our lives. And the word *animated*, it is good to remember, is simply an adjective form of *animal*.

One of the most desirable aspects of camping is the absence of urban noise. Our year-round home is at its most peaceful in winter, but even when Audrey and I are quietly reading, our mechanical indoor servants are hardly ever silent—the furnace motor drones, the refrigerator hums monotonously, and our cuckoo clock ticks urgently. And in the outdoors the traffic sounds from nearby thoroughfares never cease. On less happy occasions the telephone rings several times an hour, interrupting a television program already resonating with loud fake laughter and commercials. The answered telephone, likely as not, will present us with a sales pitch or an appeal for funds, delivered by a stranger who can't pronounce our last name properly and who brazenly calls us by our first names.

When summer comes, we walk out eagerly into a world of greenery and sunlight, but our ears are assailed by airplanes and helicopters overhead, automobile traffic sounds from near and far, power lawn mowers, power hedge trimmers and garden tillers, chain and power saws, and boom boxes that live up to their names too well. On such days, when the sound of bird song has been effectively blocked out, I'll turn to Audrey and say, "It's too confounded noisy down here." (Why do I say "down here" after more than forty years of not living "up there?" I am partly thinking of our camp in the woods, but also, if we've spent our entire youth in one place how we never lose our identification with it, even though the ground we trod daily is now marked with the paths of strangers. There is irony in this nearly unconscious attachment to the remembered center of a childhood universe, like a useless decayed umbilical cord that has never been removed.)

When the hubbub becomes overpowering, I think longingly of the basic discourses and music of nature: the exultant, energized voices of children in speech or song, the majestic bass roll of thunder, a lover's whisper, the gentle persistent soughing of the wind as it moves through a stand of jack pines, ice booming on the frozen winter lake, crickets calling in the heart of summer, rain cascading onto the ground in its dynamic progression from a hiss to a roar, the infinitely subtle sigh of drifting snow, a blue jay's sassy autumn shout, and the white-throated sparrow's lovely melting whistle.

In the north, the white-throated sparrow sometimes sings long before the spring dawn, while a brilliant full moon casts shadows of the dusky, pointed evergreens on the forest floor. His call drifts out from the shades of the conifers with a poignant grace that matches the moonlight. The mockingbird has a far more extensive repertoire, and the nightingale has had the praise of poets since the days of ancient Greece, but our own captivating native sparrow fits his music to his surroundings with a charm unsurpassed by other songsters. We humans, with our intricate language, multitudinous vocabulary, and nearly infinite variety of facial expressions, voice inflections, gestures, and body postures, cannot express our nostalgia, regret, longing, or hope so readily as this small bird with his few precious notes.

The very earliest experience of any kind that I can clearly recall is hearing a meadowlark sing. I couldn't have been more than three years-old at the time, and I sat happily on the grass beside a grownup whose face memory will no longer present to me. The meadowlark sat on a crude wooden fence post, part of a fence line that separated our barnyard from a green field of alfalfa. He sang beautifully because that was the only way he could sing. I remember thinking that I could easily touch the bird, but I made no effort to do so.

Shortly thereafter my parents gave me a thick stack of Arm & Hammer bird cards that they had saved for several years. The bird cards were 3" x 2", and they could be collected gradually with each purchase of Arm & Hammer Baking Soda, or one could acquire a full set of thirty cards by sending the company six cents in coin or stamps. New sets were issued periodically. Each card had a color picture of a bird on the front, with its name underneath. The back side had the bird's scientific name and a brief, pithy description of its general character, habits and range. My parents and older members of the family taught me the names of all of them before I had learned to read well. I found it an easy task to transfer my delight from the cardboard images to the real feathered creatures that sang and flew throughout my boyhood domain—pasture woods, the creek, and the farmyard. I thought that I would learn to talk with them (children don't much bother with the "how" of such matters), and I envisioned them perched on my shoulder, following me, flying overhead, as many birds as there were bird cards, while I carried the firewood in each evening to fill the box in the storeroom behind the kitchen stove.

When I was almost nine, I discovered a fascinating pastime for summer evenings. A small log building, which we called the Pig House, stood in the home pasture between the barn and the banks of the creek. Here we often kept litters of little pigs to be fattened and sheltered before we moved them to a larger enclosure. Using the crevices between the logs for a foothold, I found it easy to climb up onto the roof. Lying quietly there about ten feet above the ground level, I enjoyed the sight and sound of the numerous barn swallows. They filled the air with their twitterings as they glided gracefully across the darkening twilight sky, catching untold numbers of barnyard insects in their flight. In my imagination I flew with them, blithely free and no longer earthbound.

When we heard the wild geese calling on their migratory flights, we hurried outdoors to see them. Sometimes they were too far away for us to distinguish anything but their silhouettes. At other times they flew so low that we could see their white cheeks contrasting with the black of their outstretched necks and heads.

Here in the metropolitan suburbs, the wild geese have become tame, occasionally to the point of being a nuisance, but I still thrill to their calls, which, even now, seem to proclaim freedom and adventure. And here, as in the north woods, spring and early summer are the prime times for bird song. Before the snow has melted, the killdeer calls off in the distance. The cardinal sits atop the tallest trees and sings so loudly and assertively that we can hear him through closed windows and doors. Later, when most of our nesting birds have already arrived, the brown thrasher comes with his varied and beautiful repertoire. The catbird takes the second chair to the brown thrasher, but he is no mean musician either. Robins are such common birds that we take their beautiful song for granted, and an April twilight without robin song is an imperfect entity. In April when I was a boy, our usually placid creek, swollen with the melted snows of spring, murmured its watery way at the foot of our house, the robin's song joining it to make unparalleled harmony. Today, when the robin sings in early spring, my memory fills in the accompanying sound of running water.

Although the jubilation of early spring is the high point of the year, there is song for every season. The northern oriole serenades us with his cheery whistle in early summer. When the family is raised, they leave the nesting area for a midsummer tour, but they come back in early fall with a few more whistled choruses from the males, a last farewell before their trip south. The blue jays are birds for all seasons. They have a great many calls, some of a conversational nature, but most are renowned more for dramatic impact than musicality. These neighborhood extroverts tattle on every stray cat and mob any supposed miscreant, whether furred or feathered, but they undergo a complete personality change during their period of domestic duty. The blue jay is the very model of quiet, unobtrusive behavior as it disappears silently into the tree that holds the family nest. Blue jays really come into their own in autumn. Then, when the air is cool and the forest floor covered with acorns and leaves, they shout and scream their zest for life. An autumn morning is to blue jay call as spring twilight is to robin song.

When winter comes, the frozen tree limbs groan as the cold winds blow through the barren woodlands, and humans bundle up against the chill. The black-capped chickadee calls out its name merrily on such days. If I fill the bird feeder in the front yard, one or more of them will sing thanks before and after; and sometimes, if I'm patient and lucky, one will come down and feed from my hand. Later, especially on sunny winter days, it sings its sleepy, tender two-note song, the higher note always first, and the second lower note strongly accented, sometimes doubled. By contrast, the busy nuthatches' calls sound like uninhibited nasal laughs. It is difficult not to give these two winter birds—cheerful, industrious, and trusting—positive human attributes. They make the best of neighbors.

Modern scientists who specialize in animal behavior have made intensive studies of bird communication. The two most commonly accepted explanations for bird song are that it is a way birds broadcast territorial claims to other males, and that it is their way of appealing to females to join the singer. Having paid due homage to science, I admit that I much prefer Izaak Walton's seventeenth century comments on the bird song of his native England:

> How do the Blackbird and Thrassel with their melodious voices bid welcome to the cheerful spring, and in their fixed mouths warble forth such ditties as no art or instrument can reach to!

Nay, the smaller birds also do the like in their particular seasons, as namely the Laverock, the Titlark, the little Linnet, and the honest Robin, that loves mankind both alive and dead.

But the Nightingale, another of my airy creatures, breathes such sweet loud music out of her little instrumental throat, that it might make mankind to think miracles are not ceased. He that at midnight, when the very laborer sleeps securely, should hear, as I have very often, the clear airs, the sweet descants, the natural rising and falling, the doubling and redoubling of her voice, might well be lifted above earth, and say, "Lord, what music hast thou provided for the saints in heaven, when thou affordest bad men such music on earth!"

I'm not an early riser by nature, but more than once I've left my fellow campers in their tents, so that I might watch the birds and hear them sing in the hour or so before dawn. They may be observed flying and calling above and through the ghostly clumps of white birch and the unkempt, brooding jack pines—their salute to the coming of light evident around every bend of the trail and in every patch of woods. The birds' joyous celebration of the rising sun is as exuberant as it was in my boyhood days, but I know now that their relationship to man is a highly circumscribed emissary arrangement, for we can only surmise the emotional and perceptive parameters of their identities. Their brief winged lives, untainted by a foreknowledge of death, are possibly richer and more untrammeled than a century of human days.

Robert Burns spoke basic truth when he said in his "Ode to a Mouse": "An' forward, tho' I canna see, I guess an' fear!" We know, without referring to actuarial tables, that our days on earth will eventually end, but we can never reckon the future between now and then with any likelihood of success, for plan how we will, practice prudence, test the winds, and add the figures, there will be factors, people, weather, that we never guessed. In an age of burgeoning technology and spiritual malaise, we wistfully search our encroaching horizons for signs of eternity, but we remain prisoners of time. If we could live as our fellow sentient creatures, the birds, seem to live, conscious only of *this* moment, would it not be as good as immortality?

※ ※ ※

One of the current catch sentences is the brusque advice, "Get real!" and it isn't bad advice either. Insulated spiritually by the fantasy worlds of the mass media, and physically by air-conditioned homes and automobiles, we tend to forget a commonplace fact of life: All basic wealth comes from the land. Computers and other electronic hardware may tabulate and record that wealth and its by-products with admirable speed, but they can never produce it. We have been mining our basic wealth at an ever more feverish pace as the twentieth century draws to a close. We have, in a manner that medieval alchemists might envy, transmuted that wealth into a dizzying variety of commercially viable products. In America particularly, and in the Western world generally, these products are usually artifacts that are totally unnecessary for the shared human requirements of food, clothing, and shelter. Since the end of World War II, we have produced more innovations in our command of technological know-how than any one human can absorb. From computers to laser beams to gene-spliced bacteria to surrogate birth mothers, we have proved ourselves to be the supreme manipulators. But in spite of our brilliantly contrived additions to the initial primitive tools, we still have with us the immemorial problems of murder, disease, power madness, indiscriminate lust, poverty, dishonesty, encompassing greed, and general lack of vision, just as surely as they had existed before Socrates or Jesus walked the earth. We have manipulated better than we have loved, consumed better than we have given, and ignored better than we have perceived.

One result of our indifferent carelessness and greed has been the deterioration and disappearance of many rural and wild tracts. While the birth*rate* grows in much of the world, we Americans behave as if there were no birth*right* worth preserving for future generations. All but the most poverty stricken in our country buy and discard consumer goods as if there were no tomorrow, and, sad to say, this is the aspect of our culture that much of the world yearns to emulate. We have been blessed with freedom and wealth, but thoughtless, irresponsible freedom is a recipe for chaos. When a dead leaf is released from a tree, it is, in a sense, free. But without volition of its own, it becomes a hostage to every kicking foot and every wind that blows.

The emperors of Rome, fearing disapproval and uprisings from alert, discontented citizens, kept them pacified with bread and circuses. Modern technology and marketing techniques have changed the situation only in kind. Twentieth century rulers of democratic countries have found that the masses will remain relatively quiescent if they can afford television and pizza. Too often we substitute freedom of choice for a numb frenzy that rules our days. Largely ignoring the freshly hued miracle of early morning, we join our peers in a mad bumper-to-bumper stampede down the concrete freeways: Red light, green light, entrance ramp, exit ramp, and a bumper sticker on an ancient truck that reads, "Are we rich yet?" Our work world, when we get there, likely as not is governed largely by computers, video screens, and unresponsive management personnel whom we scarcely know. Separated from reality and one another, subdued by stress, and chiefly motivated by the thirst for gain, we perform our duties.

At the end of the day, or the end of the week, we hurry to that other unreal air-conditioned world of the shopping center where we find piped-in music, specious splendor and, behind the allure of innumerable shop facades, row upon row of things: Frostless refrigerators, cozy comforters, 35 mm cameras, VCR's, stone-washed jeans, Nintendo games, waterbeds, microwave ovens, coffeemakers, camcorders, CD's, ceiling fans, instant cash, and a sign that says, "Have your cholesterol level checked here! FREE blood pressure readings." Ah, the wonder of it all, and if only we choose to buy the right things this time, we will be properly compensated for our daily drudgery. With our chosen purchases beside us, we hasten home where the television screen, in full living color, is waiting to present more images and messages to keep us rushing down the concrete freeways . . .

We must seek to break away from this compulsive round. As campers on the earth, we have a pressing need to approach the remote places and solitude *some* of the time, if only to rouse us from the unreal world that we have been conditioned to accept. Stand on a country road at twilight and hear one solitary automobile far away toward the distant town. Watch a golden sunrise over a wilderness lake and smell the morning air. Attend a small country church service and come away without scoffing. Walk by a grove of trees and listen to the first rush of wind in the leaves while the dark clouds pile high and a thunderstorm prepares to cool the countryside after a hot, sultry summer's day. Will my grandchildren and their children be able to enjoy such simple and infinitely pleasant things as these? The time of one man is short, and I suppose I'll never know. But if this green planet is trampled dry and becomes merely the crowded thoroughfare for a tawdry caravan of sickly, denatured men and women with manufactured playthings, I'll be glad to have left.

Dan Huntsperger. Since retiring a decade ago, I've concentrated on important things—family, friends, nature, books and writing. Other than enjoying my grandchildren, my happiest accomplishment during this peaceful time has been the completion of a 340-page memoir, Early Light.

My industrious parents raised seven children on their 200-acre farm, which included timber, bog, and creek bottom. I was born in their log house with a neighboring midwife in attendance. We lived just south of Lake of the Woods, with our cattle grazing and barefoot children playing along the winding banks of Zippel Creek. We were far from cities, or even any large towns, and our backwoods fields and clearings retained a pioneer flavor until the feverish era of World War II jolted us from our isolation forever. Early Light *celebrates the joys and sorrows of country life in the Minnesota border region during those years framed by the two world wars, with special emphasis on the 1930's.*

The essay included in this anthology is a slightly altered chapter from Early Light. *Several excerpts appeared in the regional magazine,* Loonfeather, *and other portions were published in two COMPAS anthologies, for which I used the pen name, Howard Hadley. Writing the memoir has been more pleasure than labor. Since its completion I have devised other fictional sketches and stories about the same countryside. With many filled wastebaskets to demonstrate, I can testify that for me at least, writing good fiction is vastly more demanding than writing good memoir.*

MARJORIE DORNER

Look at Me

THE GIRLS IN THE next booth were chatting in that high-pitched, breathless style of teenagers, their voices rising and falling, their words punctuated with frequent gales of laughter. He wasn't really listening to what they said, just hearing the sounds as background while he waited for Molly. Some men might have found the sounds annoying, but they reminded him of his own daughters, off now at separate colleges, and the noise soothed him like music.

From time to time, he would glance over at the girls, taking in the outrageously sloppy clothes, the thick, laced-up boots, smiling a little at the earnest way the two heads—one blond and one dark—tipped toward each other while they talked. They wore their hair in an identical style, long and crimped at the sides and back with bangs jutting forward and lofted into stiff fans above their foreheads, almost like cantilevered bridges. He knew that they built these structures with gallons of mousse and spray—he had frequently complained about the price of the lotions and potions he had been forced to finance for his own girls—but he was filled with admiration anyway.

In fact, the older he got, the more impressed he was becoming with how things in general were done. It often struck him as odd, his own capacity for being impressed, because he would have guessed that it should be the opposite—that he would get more jaded as he got older. But it hadn't worked out that way. He knew plenty of men who were "handy," who could build things, fix things, take a car engine apart and put it back together better than it was originally, men who would sit around at Shorty's after work gesturing with their blackened hands and waxing wise about the insides of a generator. But he, Joe Matthews, was not such a man. The way machines worked, the mysteries of electricity, the miracle of his car starting at all on a morning when the temperature was twenty-nine degrees below zero, all filled him with appreciative awe.

He was often struck by the irony that he now owned an automobile dealership and, while he could be persuasive about the advantages of various option packages, he had almost no idea of what caused the independently suspended wheels to step over bumps as they did or even why the windows went up and down when he pressed a button. Maybe he was a good salesman, he sometimes thought, because he shared the customers' childlike delight in such gadgetry. In any case, owning the joint meant he could hire guys who knew about the inside stuff. It also meant that he could walk down the street on a nice, early-spring Saturday to have lunch with his wife without having to worry what the boss was thinking.

Molly didn't work on Saturdays. She'd been with the store long enough now to choose her own schedule, and she liked, as she said, to "have Saturdays for me." Today she was coming into town to get a new perm and had suggested that they get together for lunch first at Huck 'n Tom's, their favorite riverfront cafe. As usual, Molly was a little late and he was staking out a booth for them, having already sent away the waitress who had pounced almost as soon as he sat down, inquiring in her chirpy voice if she could help him. Joe had long since given up being irritated by his wife's tardiness; he was perfectly reconciled to it now, and besides she was never horribly late, never made people miss movies or have to reheat meals. Ten, fifteen minutes, tops.

"Look at that," one of the girls in the next booth, the blond one, hissed to her friend, gesturing with her head toward the front of the cafe. Joe found himself reacting along with the brunette, turning to locate the point the blonde was staring at, and he found himself looking at Molly coming through the door, her head already turning from side to side in a searching motion.

Off to his right, Joe heard the darker girl's response. "Oh, God!" she groaned in a stagey exaggeration of horror. "That's the best argument for dying young I've seen all week."

At first Joe was simply stunned. He looked back at the girls, confirming that their eyes were fixed on his wife, on nothing else. Then he felt a hot wave of anger surging up from his stomach, flooding his face, racing to the top of his bald head. His only thought was that he wanted to leap up, grab those girls by their cantilevered bangs, and smash their heads together until blood splashed onto their half-eaten BLT's.

Molly had found him by now, was crossing to the booth where he was sitting. He was trying to get control of his face, didn't dare to look up at his wife as she slid onto the bench opposite him. To his right, he could hear half-embarrassed giggles, excited whispers.

"What's the matter?" Molly said. No greeting. Just that instant recognition that he was not himself. "You're looking pretty cranky."

Her voice, once light and girlish, had lowered in pitch over the years, so gradually, of course, that Joe hadn't noticed until one day, when she was about forty, he'd heard her on the phone in the kitchen; it had struck him then that she sounded like Kathleen Turner. She had always been direct and firm in her speech, just a little louder in public places than he'd been raised to believe a woman should be, and their daughters had patterned their own way of talking after her, so that now Joe found it normal, ordinary.

"It's nothing much," he answered, stealing a quick glance at her, knowing he could never under any circumstances—not under torture—tell her what the brats in the next booth had said. "Just a hectic morning at work."

"Well, loosen your tie and forget about it," she said, laughing. "Why'd you wear that tie, anyway? It goes better with the grey suit." She'd pulled a menu toward her and had already opened it.

"I don't know," he answered absently, wondering if the color was draining back out of his scalp. "I was thinking about Amy this morning. Maybe that's why I picked it." Their younger daughter had given him the tie last Christmas and he knew this reference was enough for Molly to know what he meant.

"I think it's all right that she hasn't picked a major yet, don't you?" Molly said. They'd been discussing this "problem" on and off since Amy's last phone call. "Why should kids have to carve into marble at twenty what they want to do for the rest of their lives? Just because Peter knew almost from birth that he wanted to be a chemist doesn't mean the girls have to follow suit."

When she spoke *to* the children, Molly used the affectionate nicknames she had invented for them when they were babies— "Sweetie," "Pumpkin," "Puddy"—but when she talked about them, even to him, she was often formal—"Peter," not "Pete"; "Bethany," not "Beth."

"I'm not worried about Amy," he said. "That's not it. Amy will be fine."

"I suppose you already picked out what you're going to eat," Molly said, rattling the stiff menu in her hands.

"Sure," he said. "The shrimp's on special."

He couldn't stop himself from thinking about the girls so close to them. How dare they? What was so hot about *them* that they could be so cruel about another human being? Molly's preoccupation with the menu gave him a chance to look hard at the pair. They noticed him watching them and the blonde blushed, turned her face to the wall. But not before he'd had a chance to assess her looks and to stare appraisingly at the features of the brunette, whose shoulders were heaving with suppressed giggles. They both had the pinched, unformed look of modern kids. The blonde's eyes were too close together and the brunette had a blotchy complexion.

They were snatching their things together now, leaving their meals unfinished. They made a lot of noise getting up, sweeping into their jackets. Then they scurried toward the cash register, walking close together, leaning in toward each other in one prolonged nudge. Joe eyed them coldly, deliberately trying to assess them as objects of sexual desire. Under the tattered jeans and baggy shirts, there were, almost certainly, bony knees, sharp elbows, jutting hip bones—very little in the way of breasts or behinds. Thinking about those bodies pressed against his own in a close embrace made the arthritis in his shoulders twinge.

It was not that he *never* had sexual thoughts about younger women, that he was "past it all," as he'd sometimes heard people say of men as young as fifty. In fact, lately, he'd felt strong stirrings whenever he was around his son's fiancee. It had begun as soon as he first found out that the relationship between "the kids" was a sexual one. It was Molly who had clued him in last year when he'd said something about Sarah's roommates. "Oh, her name is still on the lease, I suppose," Molly had said, a little edge in her voice, "but, of course, she's living with Peter." After that, whenever he saw Sarah, he imagined Peter having sex with her, speculated what her long, ample body would look like without the jeans and ski sweaters she often wore. Soon, he was imagining having sex with her himself. He didn't feel guilty about this at all, regarded it as a harmless fantasy—nobody's business but his own.

"Your mother called this morning," Molly was saying.

"Oh?" he said, turning the salt shaker in his hands. "What about?"

"Just to tell us we don't have to pick her up for church tomorrow. Some of her card playing cronies are taking her to early Mass so they can gamble for the rest of the day."

"Oh, it's not *gambling*," he snorted, watching through the window as the two girls walked past the cafe and disappeared, carrying with them his fervent wish that they would fall under a bus.

"You don't know how much those gals lose to each other," Molly said with a laugh. "I'm just glad the cops don't raid people's living rooms. But I suppose it all pretty much evens out over the months."

Now that the teenagers were completely out of sight, Joe lifted his gaze to look directly at his wife, trying at last to see her as the girls did, to see her objectively. *Did* she look bad? When he'd first caught sight of her coming into the cafe, he had felt what he usually did when he saw her after a few hours of separation—a little upsurge of gladness, a feeling of well-being as if his brain had said to him in a calm reassuring voice, "Well, that's all right, then. Everything's fine." But he had not consciously registered what she looked like today, as opposed to other days.

Molly was bent over the menu again, her hair falling loosely to her jaw line on either side of her face. Her hair wasn't looking good today—definitely not good. In the past few years, she'd been having a color treatment she said was called "weaving"—paler streaks blended in to brighten her natural color and to mask the grey. But now that the old perm was "almost dead," as she called it, the swatches of darker roots were obvious, and the paler ends looked broken and dry. With her head bent over this way, the flesh along her jaw sagged, puddling up under her chin. She was wearing a knit jogging suit, one of her old ones, faded from many washings and just generally ratty looking. She looked up at him now and he saw that she was wearing her old glasses, the ones with the owlish frames, and that they had slid down the bridge of her nose. Her eyes behind the thick lenses looked huge, blurry.

"Why are you staring at me like that?" she said, a little frown forming between her pale eyebrows.

"Was I staring?" he said, feeling himself blush. "Preoccupied, I guess. Why aren't you wearing your contacts?"

"I'm getting a perm, remember?" she answered, as if he would immediately understand this explanation. When he continued to look blank, she went on. "The fumes bother my eyes. And besides, I don't want to risk having perm juice leaking into my eyes while I'm wearing my contacts."

"Oh," he said. "I see. And I suppose you wore the jogging suit just in case some of the perm juice gets on your clothes."

"Exactly. This outfit is pretty gross already, so I don't have to mind what else happens to it." And she gave him a contented smile, completely unselfconscious, before dropping her gaze onto the menu again.

Joe was remembering what Molly had looked like when he first knew her. They had met in college when he was a junior and she was a freshman. It was at one of the first anti-war rallies where he had been dragged by another girl he was dating then. Joe himself didn't have much of an opinion about the Vietnam War except that he, personally, didn't want to go to it. And one of the speakers was Molly O'Reilly. She was tall, brighter in every way than most of the girls he knew; not just smarter—though she was that, too, he learned—but literally brighter in all her colors: strawberry blond hair; pale skin that looked lit from the inside and turned deep pink when she was emotional about anything; blue, blue eyes behind wire-rimmed glasses. He had dated girls prettier than Molly, but in retrospect he came to think of all of them as 25 watt bulbs compared to her 100 watts.

The chirpy waitress was descending on them now, her practiced smile in place.

"Are you ready to order?" she said, holding a pencil above the top sheet of her order pad.

Molly looked up at the girl, pushed her glasses up on her nose, and smiled—the sincere, open smile she gave everyone.

"I'm afraid I need a little more time," she said. "We've been chatting too much, I guess."

Joe felt a flash of irritation at his wife as he saw the waitress's smile freeze in place and heard her say the ominous words, "Okay, then. I'll be back in a few minutes." From many, many lunches spent in restaurants, Joe had learned that sending servers away without ordering was a mistake; he suspected that they had a firm rule that customers who did this must be ignored for at least fifteen minutes thereafter. As the waitress turned to leave, he glared at Molly, half-aware that his anger had more to do with the teenagers' insult than with being kept waiting for food he wasn't very interested in anyway, but he couldn't help himself. Why was she so disorganized? Why couldn't she dress up a little to have lunch in a public place where his customers and co-workers were likely to see her?

"Oh, these glasses!" Molly said as she turned her attention to the menu again. "They're just useless for reading now. I guess my eyes have changed since I got this prescription." She pulled the big glasses off her face, put them onto the table, and brought the menu closer to her eyes.

Being angry with his wife always scared Joe a little. And he knew he was over-reacting now to something he would normally shrug off good-naturedly. So he made himself think about something else, turned his mind back to those college days when they'd begun dating. At first, Joe had not known quite what to make of the chatty, intense young woman he'd contacted by asking everyone he knew who she was and what dorm she lived in. Raised with only brothers around him and his rather prim, emotionally reticent mother as his sole model for feminine behavior, he was not prepared for Molly.

She wore all her feelings on the outside. When he took her to the movies, she would throw her arms up as if to fend off blows

305 —

whenever something bad seemed about to happen to one of the characters; she would say, "Oh, no!" right out loud after the bad things *did* happen; and she would cry rather noisily at sad endings or touching scenes. If he got her small presents or did something nice for her, her big eyes would instantly fill up with tears. At first, this had alarmed him deeply; only after a year of being with her almost daily did he believe her when she said, "I'm happy. I'm crying because I'm so happy."

"Oh, I forgot to tell you," Molly said now, glancing up again. "Your mother wants to know if we have any ideas about what she can get Bethany for graduation."

"We don't even have any idea about what *we* should get her," Joe said with a little chuckle.

"That's what I told her," Molly sighed. "She's just getting antsy, that's all. And it *is* less than two months off. The only thing I've managed to do so far is to get the motel rooms reserved. I'm so glad Amy's school gets out a little earlier. She would be just sick if she had to miss her sister's commencement. Do you think we should offer to pay for the extra room for Peter and Sarah?"

"And maybe we should book a flight for them, too?" he said. "Chicago is such a *long* way off, after all."

"Don't be silly," she said mildly, ignoring his sarcasm. "You know perfectly well they're driving up. I'm just worried about their expenses."

"He's earning his own money now, Molly. He *has* been earning it for more than three years. No need to keep slipping him twenties when I'm not looking."

She made a face at him, wrinkling her nose and pursing her full mouth.

"And no more talking now until you've decided what you're going to order," he said, gesturing at her menu. But he said it gently because he was feeling somewhat better.

"It seems so odd to think of Bethany graduating from college," she said dreamily. "I didn't mind so much with Peter, but, gosh, it seems just yesterday that I was pregnant with Beth." And she lowered her eyes again to read.

Joe looked around the cramped little cafe, but he was hardly registering what he saw. Molly's words had triggered a new train of thought, and he was remembering her pregnancies. Wasn't it strange that people were always writing articles about how pregnancy affected a woman's emotions and moods, but nobody ever wrote about how it affected the husbands? Were other men like him, he wondered, or had his reactions been unique? Women talked to each other about it—he'd overheard some of this conversation over the years with a mixture of fascination and embarrassment—but men were pretty tight-lipped about that sort of stuff.

He had always found the early stages of Molly's pregnancies very sexy, could hardly keep his hands off her when her breasts began to swell and her skin took on that sweet texture and taste. The later stages scared him silly and he would never have been able to tell a living soul about the waves of revulsion that would sometimes sweep over him when he saw her distended abdomen, the stretched skin, the belly-button turned inside out. He had felt ashamed of himself and, at the same time, grateful as hell that the doctors advised against sex in the last weeks.

After each of the kids was born, he would watch Molly's body with a keen fascination, how it changed and shifted in shape. Her breasts would stay like globes, seeming even more rounded as her middle shrank. After Peter, her stomach went back to the flat, firm plane he had loved to touch when they were first married. After the girls, it stayed rounded, a soft little mound whose contours he admired most when she was lying on her back in bed and he would trace with his fingers down the length of her body. Lately, he'd noticed how her hips had spread, how when she stepped out of the shower and lifted her arms above her head to wrap her hair in a towel, her body from behind looked like a pear, a gorgeous ripe pear.

Now he moved his gaze back to his wife there across from him in the narrow booth. Without her glasses and with the menu lifted up to her face so she could peer near-sightedly at the list of food which was the same as it always was, her looks had decidedly improved. She would probably just order the special in the end, after all the delay and fuss. The thought made him smile. A patch of sunlight from the windows had fallen onto the plastic surface between them, spotlighting the left side of her head. Joe loosened his tie, sat back to wait for her. He was feeling good again, his equilibrium almost completely restored.

He had to admit that, most of the time now, he was happy. He didn't think about it much, didn't examine it. For about three years, when he was in his late thirties, he'd done a lot of thinking, had felt restless and a vague discontent all the time. They were living in Chicago then; Beth and Amy were still in grade school. He had hated the city, felt exhausted almost every day from fighting traffic, hustling to make sales quotas, paying bills. And his hair was starting to fall out. Every time he took a shower, there were big wads of it, like soft brillo pads, in the drain. He would examine his head in the steamy mirror, turning it from side to side, lowering his chin and raising his eyes to get a look at the crown where streaks of pink flesh were beginning to show through his damp hair. It just depressed the hell out of him. He knew, even at the time, that he was being silly, that it shouldn't matter so much, but whenever he caught sight of himself unexpectedly in a store window, he felt like somebody had smacked him one.

And the little blonde who had answered the phones in the showroom in those days, the one who looked at him out of the corners of her eyes when she said, "It's for you, Mr. Matthews," had begun to interest him. Something in that breathless voice made him feel he had a full head of hair. They had lunch together a few times, but nothing else ever came of it. Molly had started the painting classes in adult education about that time and had insisted on using him as a model for her nude sketches. "I'm too embarrassed to look at those kids they use in the studio," she would say. "I won't sketch your face, I promise. Nobody will know except the two of us." At first, he just flatly said, "No!" But she kept after him, teasing, cajoling. So at last, when the kids were in bed at night, he would strip and allow Molly to pose him, sometimes standing, sometimes lying on their bed, and both of them would giggle while she did it.

He got a kick out of the serious way she would bend over her sketch pad, lifting her eyes to him as if he were not himself, not her husband, but a stranger or even an object, an abstract shape that she admired. But often, her face would soften, a little smile would break through her concentration; then she would get up, come to him, and stroke his naked flesh, kiss his shoulders, cradle his head against her soft breasts. After a while, he forgot all about his hair.

Remembering those nights now in this cafe in his old home town where Molly, big-city girl though she was, had adjusted cheerfully to the slower pace, he felt sudden moisture welling up in his eyes. He groped with his feet under the table until, finding one sneaker-clad foot, he took it gently between his sensible brown shoes. She looked up quickly in surprise. Through the prism of his tears, her face looked soft and young, her pale hair like a diamond-studded halo around it.

"What's the matter," she said, her hand moving toward him across the patch of sunlight.

"Nothing," he whispered, smiling broadly at her. "I'm just happy. It makes me happy to look at you."

Marjorie Dorner. *I had the good luck to be born into a family of oral-tradition storytellers who also read to me, so early and so much that I could read before I went to school. By ten, I had begun to write stories of my own. So telling, reading, and writing seemed all one to me, almost from the beginning. Raised on a Wisconsin dairy farm among a crowd of siblings, cousins, uncles and aunts, I had the* *drama of human relationships presented to me almost exclusively in terms of family. My fiction has naturally focused on family, particularly on families rooted to place—to the land. Raising my own two daughters, who are now adults, has only made that focus clearer. In my four mystery/suspense novels, I have concentrated on how the intrusion of violence or terror affects ordinary people and their families. One,* Family Closets, *is set among deeply enmeshed Midwestern farm families. And* Winter Roads, Summer Fields, *an interconnected series of short stories, is set among the same people.*

My present writing interests include efforts to shape and order some experiences of people in mid-life. I've completed four stories in a collection titled Available Light *and I'm planning a literary novel about a group of women confronting their 50's. That family and Midwestern places will be heavily featured should surprise no one.*

Freeze Frame, *one of four published mysteries, is a 1991 winner of the Minnesota Book Award for mystery, and* Winter Roads, Summer Fields *a 1993 winner for fiction.*

Photo by BSU

WILL WEAVER

Blaze of Glory

A YOUNG DOCTOR SCRIBBLED the prescription; he had a beard and his pen scraped loudly in the small room where Dolores Johnson waited with her husband, Herb. Herb sat in his undershorts on the examining table. Clearly he could put his clothes back on now, Dolores observed; under the bright fluorescent light he looked white and sagging and chilly. Oddly she thought of "Caves of Mystery" (or was it "Mystery Caves"?) in South Dakota, a tourist attraction where she and Herb had stopped on their honeymoon more than forty years ago—its damp and humped stalagmites, its single light bulbs hung room by room.

"Cardizem, Herb," the doctor said, ripping the prescription sheet from its pad and spinning on his chair toward Herb. "You've taken it before, right?"

Herb glanced at Dolores, then turned away to reach for his pants.

Doctor Field leaned back. He wore blue jeans and tennis shoes, the kind of doctor who was proud of his ability to speak to the common man. "How old are you, Herb?" His eyes briefly scanned Herb's chart.

"Seventy-one," Herb muttered, zipping and reaching for his shirt.

"And I presume you've had a good sex life?"

Herb paused with one arm in his shirt, one arm out. Dolores looked quickly away, toward the wall, to the bright red and yellow poster of the human heart—its valves and ventricles, its chambers, its arteries; the artist had added little road signs such as "Free direction" and "One Way" and "Detour—Under Repair."

"You could say that," Herb answered gruffly. Clothes rustled.

Dolores looked back to find Herb angrily mis-buttoning his shirt.

The doctor continued. "What I mean, Herb, is that the side effects—impotency—are why some men don't like Cardizem."

Herb refused to look at him, and kept dressing.

There was silence in the room. "Does Cardizem make you impotent, Herb?" the doctor asked. He glanced at his wristwatch again.

Herb muttered something, jerked at his shirt and began to redo the buttons.

"Are you impotent now, Herb?"

Herb remained focused on his shirt buttons; the doctor turned to Dolores, who blushed scarlet and shook her head no. Herb looked up to glare at her this time.

"This tells me that you probably didn't complete the last prescription," the doctor said, "which is why you're having arrhythmia again, Herb."

Herb reached past the doctor for his socks and shoes.

The doctor drummed his fingers once. "Think of it this way, Herb," he said, standing, holding out the prescription, speaking in that overly familiar, too-loud manner which someone, somewhere was teaching young doctors nowadays, "you've got two choices. It's either your pecker or your ticker."

Dolores, holding the prescription (she had been the one to reach for it), stood in the hallway while Herb finished dressing. In truth she was waiting for the young doctor, intent on giving him a piece of her mind (he had smiled, clapped Herb on the back, nodded to Dolores and slipped away before either of them could speak). Now in another examining room he spoke loudly to someone about urinary matters, about kidney stones.

Dolores turned away, refocused herself; it was a skill that Herb did not have.

"Are you all right in there?" she said through the door.

"I can still dress myself," Herb growled.

There was some rustling, the clink of a belt buckle. Then silence for a long time. She thought of the heart poster; she guessed he was looking at it.

"Should I go on down to the pharmacy?" she asked. "Get the . . . pills?"

Shoes clunked and then Herb opened the door. He was fully dressed now, in his bright orange Pendleton wool shirt and his town pants, a leather belt tucking up his girth, a man with pale blue eyes and a full head of platinum hair, someone she would still choose.

His eyes lightened briefly at her look, then lowered their gaze to her hands. To the prescription. He reached for it. "I've still got some left from last time," he said with false brusqueness. "I'll get this refilled next week sometime."

For a long moment they held the little square of paper between them. In his blue pupils she saw a flicker, a tiny gray shadow of fear. She let go.

❊ ❊ ❊

And on Monday she let go of her job.

Gave notice.

Retired.

For twenty-seven years Dolores had been head clerk at the local Electric Coop, but a recent *Reader's Digest* article entitled

"The Golden Age of Travel" and now a flare-up of Herb's ar-rhythmia convinced her it was time to go. "Retired" was a word she had always reserved for really old people—shuffleboard play-ers, canasta types, corn-kernel bingo enthusiasts—yet Dolores herself, a straight, trim woman with lightly tinted brown hair, was indisputably sixty-four, and Herb already seventy-one. As well, Herb had a brother in Southern California, and Dolores a sister in Florida, both of whose children they had seen grow up only in Christmas snapshots. That plus the discounts for AARP mem-bers—as high as twenty percent—all were in the same article, which ended with this sentence: "What are you waiting for?"

The days surrounding her departure from the office (she still couldn't call it "retirement") buzzed with energy. The reception, the stream of cards and letters, the solicitations to join Garden Club and Women Aglow (both of which she put off for now), the calls from her sister—it was almost too much. Even Herb seemed livelier, though he still muttered about the young doctor with the beard.

On the first Monday of her new life Dolores laid out the old Rand McNally on the kitchen table. It was important to be deci-sive. To make plans. She turned first to the United States map and slowly penciled a line toward California, then across to Texas. Herb said nothing.

As she worked Herb paced back and forth behind her, rattling the nutcracker and bowl, comparing window thermometer read-ings. Finally he said, testily, "Those maps are twenty years old. The roads have changed completely. You can't plan a trip with old maps."

Dolores got up and drove downtown. She brought home a bright, hefty twenty-dollar road atlas. Herb, as it turned out, was substantially correct about new roads, but his smugness served to soften his resolve on another, coincidental matter. "There's an ad in the paper," Dolores said, holding up a new *Herald*. "Clean used eighteen foot Winnebago one owner," she read. And looked up at Herb.

A week later, thanks to Dolores' Coop profit-sharing check, the motorhome was theirs. The Winnebago was part of an estate sale; the son and executor, a man balding already in his forties, came by with the keys. "At least they had one good trip," he said gravely. He held the keys out to Herb.

"Any chance they had a spare set?" Herb asked.

The following four weeks Herb spent servicing, fine-tuning the motorhome. Tires, battery, thermostat, brakelines—he left no mechanical part unworried. He insisted they sleep in it at least once before they left, which they did. The bedroom was cramped, with a low ceiling, but the mattress passable. "It feels like camping. Without the tent," Herb said. Luckily deer season came along and sent him to the woods, which allowed Dolores to finish packing.

Finally, on November twelfth, they left Lake Center at 6:45 in the morning with the temperature at nineteen degrees and 11,041 miles on the odometer. Herb sat strapped in the rider's seat, exhausted from hunting, his cheeks windburnt, his eyes red-veined but open wide. He waved to Lake Center cars he recognized, which included nearly all of them, while Dolores concentrated on her driving .

They passed the lake itself, the community college, and, finally, the city limits sign. A thrill tingled through Dolores, and she leaned forward in the seat. Ahead on the open road the weather was typical for November, gray with light snow, and though Herb drifted off to sleep almost immediately, she examined everything that passed: a wooly cluster of damp and steaming cattle; a green checker-board Christmas tree plantation; a single arched curl of snow that drooped from the powerline; a gleaming crow along the shoulder picking at a dead raccoon. She drove, mile after mile, with a slowly increasing assurance, with rising excitement, with something near to joy. At the Minnesota-South Dakota border the skies lightened and the sun suddenly blossomed in a brilliant, frosty corona. "Look!" she cried out to Herb, "look!"

Herb jerked awake and flung up an imaginary rifle. "Where?" he shouted. "Where?"

❆ ❆ ❆

After that Herb woke up fully and began to worry about the furnace. About the water pipes. About the birdfeeder. He was certain the Bartlett boy would not put out thistle seed and suet, that all the birds which whistled and chirped in his yard would go across the street to Walter Anderson's feeder.

"They've been coming for years to our yard," Dolores said. "And Joey Bartlett is an A student."

"A's don't mean what they used to," Herb muttered.

With Dolores driving they rolled on. Herb took a turn at the wheel that afternoon, but Dolores found it hard to relax. His driving had been less certain the last year, and today the motorhome tended to ride the center line. And what if?—but she did not let herself think about that. Rather, she calculated miles, hours and driving time so that her shift would take them through Sioux City, the first major city on their route.

"Say," Herb said, turning his gaze to a billboard. "Mystery Caverns. Didn't we visit those on our honeymoon?"

The billboard was faded but still stood straight.

"Yes, we did," she said.

Herb squinted. "Closed for the winter," he read, swiveling his head at the sign. Then he turned to look at her. "Too bad." She smiled, touched his arm.

❆ ❆ ❆

Dolores kept the motorhome rolling south and west. Herb was a retired highway engineer, and he provided a state-by-state analysis of the road conditions: the seams in the asphalt, the pothole ratio per mile, the general layout of curves and overpasses. Dolores drove.

Through Nebraska, so large it ought to have divided into two states.

Through Colorado and the bright, sharp edges of the Rockies.

Through Utah, which had surprising natural beauty; Dolores had always thought it a desert state.

Through Nevada and its pale purple mineral hills, its bright casino oases.

Through frightening Donner Pass, and down into California.

❈ ❈ ❈

They stayed a short week with Herb's brother in San Bernadino in an overly developed tract with identical ramblers and rock and cacti lawns. Barry was an aerospace engineer, or so they had been told via Muffy's Christmas letter every year. In truth Barry was swingshift foreman at a tool and die plant that did occasional work for Boeing. This was let slip by Muffy, who talked incessantly, as if someone switched her on in the morning and left her on all day. That, plus their two Schnauzers, which nipped at Herb's ankles whenever he passed, kept Herb and Dolores in their motorhome for longer and longer periods of each day. To Dolores, Barry and Herb appeared to be from two different families. The brothers spent their afternoons playing gin rummy, slapping down their cards, venturing conversational gambits such as, "How you can stand those winters in Minnesota is beyond me."

"Me, I couldn't take not having a lawn. A real lawn, with grass."

❊ ❊ ❊

A full week sooner than planned, Herb and Dolores were back on the road. "Well, that's over with," Herb said, even as they were waving goodbye to Barry and Muffy. Dolores felt her eyes well up, but refocused herself.

"So now what?" she said.

"Head east, I guess," Herb replied. "No hurry now." Dolores managed a half-smile.

An hour later, San Bernadino in the dust behind, they were as happy and talkative as two escaped parakeets.

Occasionally Herb looked over his shoulder and muttered, "Aerospace engineer."

"Help me with the map, dear," Dolores murmured.

❊ ❊ ❊

Heading to Arizona and beyond, they took secondary highways and stopped at tourist traps. Dolores bought small turquoise jewelry items and salt-and-pepper shakers; Herb a silver belt buckle and an agate string tie. They turned in wherever they wished for an afternoon nap, and slept easily as eighteen wheelers rumbled past. One day they covered only eighty-two miles. Often they did not know, even by midday, where they would park their RV that evening, where they would sleep that night—which carefree attitude, as all Minnesotans would agree, sooner or later meant trouble.

Arriving after dark on the outskirts of Albuquerque, and following notes taken from an uncertain AARP 800 operator, Dolores finally saw the sign for "Fresh Aire" RV Park. She checked her jottings; it was supposed to be "Bel Aire" or perhaps "Mel's Aire," but "Fresh Aire," set well off the highway and ringed by a hedge and tall wooden fence, looked quiet, orderly and private. She turned in and parked.

In the morning Herb was first to awaken and crack the shade. Dolores dozed.

"We're dead," Herb said.

"What's that?" she mumbled. There was a long silence, during which she fell back asleep.

"We crashed somewhere and we're dead."

Dolores sat up with a start; she peered out the window. A regular RV park, yes, with rows of campers and some nice trees and central commons area with showers and small grocery store, people here and there chatting and walking their dogs, nothing out of the ordinary. Except that the people were naked. All of them. Buck-naked. Jay-naked. AARP-naked. A whole campground of white-haired naked people.

"I kept looking for wings," Herb would say later—but at the moment he and Dolores both shrank lower in the window.

"Welcome, neighbor!" a round-bellied man from next door called out to them.

Herb narrowed the shade. "Good morning," he croaked.

The man's wife appeared, a sturdy, well-tanned woman wearing only reading glasses on a neck chain. Herb swallowed; his Adam's apple squeaked. "Heard you come in late," the woman said pleasantly. "Coffee's on over here." With that the two of them began to set up folding chairs and a table no more than eight feet away.

"We might sleep a little longer," Dolores managed to say.

"Whenever you're ready," the woman added cheerfully, and settled into a sunny chair.

Herb and Dolores retreated to the center of the motorhome. They stared at each other. "What are we going to do?" Dolores whispered.

Herb stroked his jaw. Looked out once again.

They did nothing at all for several minutes. Every once in awhile one of them would peek out the window again to make sure they weren't dreaming. Or dead.

It was Herb, finally, who took charge. He looked straight at Dolores. "We are, I believe," he said, "in Rome."

❉ ❉ ❉

The first cup of coffee was a bit tricky but the couple from Indiana, Ray and Arlene Davis, were the nicest, most normal folks one could hope to meet. The four of them sat in a half circle of lawn chairs facing into the sunlight.

"Freshen that up for you?" Ray said to Herb, bringing around the thermos.

"Sure," Herb said; he sneaked a glance at Dolores.

"Just a splash," Dolores murmured, keeping her eyes on the cup as Ray stood before her and poured. She noticed that the Davises had draped bath towels over their lawn chairs before sitting down; she wished she had thought of that. After an hour, the plastic webbing of her own chair felt like a waffle iron across her bare butt, yet she decided against getting up and moving around. Shifting about she managed to sit there naked in the southern sunlight with complete strangers and talk about children and relatives and the open road and interesting wildlife and car accidents until Arlene began to lay out four paper plates for lunch.

"Let me help—," Dolores said, hopping up. She had forgotten she was naked but the lawn chair had not: it stuck to her. It hung right on her.

Herb laughed and kept laughing.

"Let me get that—" Ray Davis said gallantly, and hopped up to peel off the chair.

"Why, thank you, Ray—," Dolores said. She was certain she was blushing on unknown areas of her body, but she also had an arched eyebrow for Herb—whose smile faded.

"Now how can I help?" Dolores said, pressing quickly ahead, assisting Arlene with the picnic table, bringing pickles and fruit from their own refrigerator. In the fisheye mirror of their Winnebago she caught sight of herself, a white round woman with a red plaid butt. Well, red plaid her butt might be yet round she was not—in fact she was in better trim than Arlene Davis or any other woman she had seen so far at "Fresh Aire," and she was certain that Herb and Ray Davis, too, were aware of that fact. She ignored the mirror and went right to the picnic table and stood there in full daylight and made egg salad sandwiches.

By midday both Herb and Dolores had loosened up enough to stroll, by themselves, into the commons area. Rubber thongs slapped on the shuffleboard court, and horseshoes clanged on steel posts. "I used to throw some good iron," Herb said, and made a ringer on his first toss. The matter of Herb's afternoon nap never came up, for that day there was nude swimming in the little pool, nude cribbage in the shade, and nude potluck for supper.

❊ ❊ ❊

That evening, back at their little Winnebago, Herb opened the door. Heat washed over them like the breath of a sauna.

"Whoa!" Herb said, leaning away from the blast. They had forgotten to open the windows fully. He squinted up at the sun. "The heat is different down here."

They went inside nonetheless and they sat down heavily and with simultaneous sighs. Herb mopped his forehead. Sweat began to trickle on both of them. They stared at each other. "Too hot for pajamas tonight, I guess," he said.

Dolores laughed. Herb joined her, but their tiredness quickly silenced them. Dolores found two towels and they mopped at themselves. Afterward they sat there in silence again. Dolores looked down at herself. "Odd," she said, glancing about the motorhome. "All day outside I've paraded around naked."

Herb watched her.

"But now that I'm here, inside, I feel like I ought to have clothes on."

Herb's eyes moved over her body.

"Do you know what I mean?" she asked, softly, looking straight at him.

Herb swallowed. "Come over here," he said.

She let her eyes move over his body. His shoulders carried pink epaulets of sunburn.

"Here," he said, pointing to their mattress.

She smiled.

"Hurry—," he added, his voice suddenly throaty.

Dolores sat there a few seconds longer, living in, inhabiting the shimmering space of this moment.

Will Weaver. *One beginning of my fiction writing harks back to when I was a no-good youngster on the farm in northern Minnesota. Goofing off with guns and gopher traps was more exciting than school assignments, but one spring day a book report loomed. No time to read a whole book, I made one up: plot, title, author, the works. Mrs. Henderson, my eighth grade teacher, penned a red 'A' and wrote on my report, "Willie, this sounds like a wonderful book. I'll be sure to look for it in the library."*

When I was twenty-something and living in California I first began writing sketches centered on my own life. Mainly I looked back to the farm: red barn and white silo; the purple, November fields; deer hunting; the taste of summer lake water in my nose; my mother heading off to work in town; my father's steel traps.

As a thirty-something fellow in the Stanford University Writing Program, I learned how difficult it was to write simply and clearly. After finishing at Stanford I returned home to Minnesota, all the way to the family farm where I wrote about California and travels in Europe. However, that writing was not worth much, and soon I didn't write at all; I was too busy mending real fences, milking real cows.

Now at age forty-four I teach writing at Bemidji State University, live on an unpaved street in this pleasant small city, and go to the land often. My life turns mainly toward my two children (eleven and fifteen years old), my students and my writing. I have written three books: Red Earth, White Earth *(1986),* A Gravestone Made of Wheat & Other Stories *(1989), and a novel for young adults,* Striking Out *(1993). "Blaze of Glory" is an excerpt from a new short story.*

RICHARD BRODERICK

Falling Out Of The Sky

A Memoir

" . . . how everything turns away/Quite leisurely from the disaster;
the ploughman may/ Have heard the splash, the forsaken cry,/
But for him it was not an important failure . . . "

W.H. Auden

FOR ME, THIS story begins with an image worthy of Brueghel.

My brother Kevin and I are harrowing my grandparents' front yard. It is an overcast afternoon, Palm Sunday, 1963. Spring is in the air. The ice is off the big lake behind the double lot shared by my house and my grandparents' place, and the hardwood trees lining the streets of my hometown are beginning to show a fringe of green.

For the better part of an hour, we have been aerating the matted topsoil with tools that look like rakes with curved tines that come to flattened points. We work in a rhythmic cycle of silence and conversation. At 17, Kevin is three years older, a few inches taller, his arms, shoulders and chest taut from years of working out.

Today we are friends, which we usually are, except for the times when my family's treacherous tides of alliances and feuds pit us against each other, usually as allies of another family member. But today we are on good terms and I enjoy listening to his scathing commentary about our task, our maternal grandparents, mutual acquaintances, my father. Above all, my father.

My father is a big man, six feet tall, shoulders and arms still powerful from the years he spent on the New York docks working his way through high school and college; at 49 he remains a gifted athlete, a former Golden Glove boxer, no one to tangle with.

He has a personality to match his physical presence, overpowering, charismatic, by turns extroverted and self-pitying, able to leave us in tears with his clowning and wit but just as likely to lash out at one of us at any time, for any reason. And when he does it is with his hands or his belt; he does not believe in sparing the rod.

Yet he is no ogre; if he were, it would make things simpler. At times he can smother me with affection, make my ears burn with self-consciousness and pride when he introduces me at his office as "my son, the genius." At other times, he can bark at me, even strike me for the most trivial reasons. As with most children, only more so, my feelings about him are a hopeless confusion of love, fear, dependence, resentment, idolatry, hatred. At times I can even wish him dead because it is impossible to conceive of anything like that happening to him. He is, despite my mother's outspoken personality, the undisputed center of the family, the sun around which we, his planets, revolve.

Unfortunately Kevin has never been one of his favorites. Of the siblings it is fair to say he is at the bottom of the pecking order. There are four qualities my father demands of us, that define his idea of maleness—intelligence, athleticism, verbal facility, the ability to defend yourself and your honor with your fists—the most important of which is academic excellence. In this area, Kevin is a disaster, a basket case. He and I share memories—painful for him because of the humiliation, painful for me because I am forced to watch my older brother be humiliated—of doing homework across from each other at the dining room table, my father, during one of those periods when he has decided to apply himself to Kevin's grades, standing over him, quite literally trying to knock sense into his head.

But now into our closed circle of family dynamics comes an omen, an arrow fired from the future. We do not know, cannot know, that on this day everything we have come to think of as normal life, of life itself, is about to dissolve, has already begun to recede into the past.

About three we look up from our work to see my father's bronze Chevy Impala turn into the driveway that separates my house from my grandparents'. My oldest brother, Eddie, is in front with my father: they are returning from Mt. Tabor where my father—compulsive about home repair—has been getting some woodworking done by a part-time craftsman. My father is sitting on the passenger side, the view of his face partially shadowed by the roof. Even so, I can see he wears a strange, unreadable expression. Is he angry? In pain? Impossible to tell. Even stranger is to see Eddie driving. Fiercely territorial about his car, my father almost never turns the wheel over to anyone else, especially Eddie, with his hot-rodding disregard for highway safety.

"What's he pissed about?" Kevin grumps.

"Dunno," I say. "He's always pissed about something." Strictly speaking, this is not true; my father is highly variable, by turns angry, peevish, buoyant, often riotously funny, and I am not even miffed at him today. It is just something to say, a show of solidarity with Kevin.

The car passes, continues its descent to the bottom of the driveway, then disappears into the garage tucked in the back of the house. My brother and I continue our work.

❊ ❊ ❊

It will be several hours before we discover the meaning of the odd tableaux earlier in the day.

The evening meal at my house is usually a happening of one kind or another, most often a free-for-all of put-down repartée led by my father, often culminating in a violent outburst when the put-downs begin to strike him too close to home. Then it is bellows of, "We're going to have a new regime around here!" and "We're going to start showing some respect!"

But tonight is different. At dinner, in the room he himself has paneled with knotty pine, my father is almost silent, deeply preoccupied. My mother keeps up a chirp of conversation, but her efforts seem forced. This, too, is a departure and so makes me, makes all four of us boys, tense, as does anything out of the ordinary about him, for don't we all spend a lot of time reading his signs, trying to predict his moods?

After eating, I slip away from the table, relieved that nothing has happened despite the odd atmosphere, and go outside to work with Kevin on the yard.

It is a little past dusk when our attention is attracted by a commotion at the front of my house. The door opens, slams shut. Eddie rushes out into the yard, comes back inside; there is the sound of raised voices from the dining room. Nothing is more of a draw for us boys than the prospect of witnessing a violent confrontation in which we are not directly involved, so Kevin and I hurry over to see what's happening. We don't say it, but both of us are thinking the same things: maybe another fist fight between Eddie and my father. Or maybe a shouting argument between my parents! My mother and father rarely have words in front of us, but on those occasions when they do . . .

But we are disappointed. What we come upon is, at first, inexplicable. And when its meaning does present itself, it is so strange that I don't know what to think, and so end up thinking and feeling very little.

In the dining room, behind the table which has been pushed aside to make room, my father is on the floor, his shoulders and head cradled by my mother who is kneeling in front of the closet.

A chair has been tipped over, adding to the antic quality of the scene. My father has a peculiar look on his face; glassy-eyed, staring at nothing. Strange sounds are issuing from my mother's voice, a kind of mewling that only after a few moments do I realize is a steady issue of reassuring words delivered *soto voce* toward her husband, who seems in no way sensible of them or anything else. Stranger still, Eddie is on one knee facing my father, a posture both imploring and oddly threatening. He, too, is talking to, or rather at, my father. But what does this all mean?

I have never seen these three people act this way before in my whole life and my first instinct is to think that maybe this *is* an act of some kind, a weird comic performance I have not been let in on. I step further into the room, and that is when my mother spots Kevin and me. "Go outside," she says, her voice pleading, desperate. "Everything's all right. Your father doesn't feel well, that's all. Go outside. Please!" So we return to the dusk, the first of a series of dull chilling realizations beginning to break inside me.

"What do you think's going on?" I ask Kevin. In the light of the street lamp I can see him shrug, wag his head from side to side.

"I don't know," he says glumly. But then, he tends to be glum, doesn't he?

❉ ❉ ❉

At fourteen I am pretty much a normal kid, backward in some ways, in others ways—like academics—advanced but not to a degree that might excite comment. I am very much concerned with fitting in.

Still, there are certain oddities. There's an intensity about me that I can sometimes see reflected in the face of playmates who occasionally seem evasive or non-committal about some game I've thought up. I am crazy about sports, especially baseball, and spend hour after hour on summer evenings tossing a tennis ball against the garage and fielding it on the rebound, all the while carrying on the play-by-play of an imaginary game in my head. Yet I suffer such severe performance anxiety that, even though I am a fine sandlot ball player, I fail all three times I try out for Little League.

Other things: I am very emotional, self-conscious, sensitive, though I do my best to hide these qualities, especially from a family in which any strong feeling is taken as a sign of vulnerability, where everything you say or do can and will be used against you. I can fall into deep melancholy or soar with elation for no particular reason. I have an instinctive sympathy for the underdog—when we play cowboys and Indians in the woods that ring my hometown, I usually want to be an Indian. Right now, my fervent religiosity is being tempered by a burgeoning but no less fervent interest in sex. In times past, however, as a Catholic school kid or an altar boy serving high mass, I often felt myself in the literal presence of God. I am a firm believer in the Beyond and the Hereafter. I do not know the words yet, but I have had powerful experiences of transcendence and immanence.

Fortunately, I don't need to keep all my enthusiasms under wraps. In the shadow of my father's respect for the practical benefits of education and my mother's love of language and books, I am able to indulge my reading habit without fear of ridicule.

Early on in life, I spend hours poring over the *Inferno* section of Dore's edition of *The Divine Comedy*, attracted less by the prurience of naked bodies than by the eerie feeling that Dante's damned souls are as alive, or even more so, than many people I know.

In third grade—just about the time you would expect it to happen—I develop a passion for the Hardy Boys, devouring each new edition to the series the instant my father brings it home to me. In the hours I spend with Frank and Tom Hardy and their apple-cheeked chum, Chip, I learn important lessons in dramatic compression, suspense, plotting and narrative. Even the garish dust jackets of the books, with their illustrations of young boys not much older than I peering breathlessly through the floorboards of an abandoned mill or rounding a stormy cape in a small boat on an impossibly dark and wind-swept night, teach me things about the importance of imagery, the need to draw the audience in, make them part of the action. And so by the time I desperately need the knowledge, I am already fully aware of literature's power to confer consolation and escape.

The center of my life, its touchstone, is my family. The Brodericks, according to the myth promulgated largely by my father, are the same but different from other families, "normal" yet superior. We are the toughest, funniest, smartest, most athletic family in town, as well as being Irish and Catholic—to us, ennobling traits. A natural aristocracy, with my father as chief baron. Anybody picks a fight with one of us picks a fight with all of us.

The price of membership in this elite, however, is high. Like most families, we learn to keep a lid on it. But perhaps unlike most families, we are volatile people, conflicted, ultimately fragile yet caught up in a code of behavior unintentionally designed to magnify the intensity of our feelings. As a collective, we are ready to blow. All it needs is the spark.

❊ ❊ ❊

Kevin and I are still outside working when we see the flashing lights of an approaching ambulance.

Till now, ambulances, fire trucks, police cars, these are dire fixtures in other people's lives. So it is with curiosity giving way to puzzlement that we watch as the ambulance turns into *our* driveway, pulling to a stop with that tempo of deliberate haste I will soon come to associate with professionals responding to an emergency.

We scramble over to see what's happening. At this point, I am still so oblivious I don't even feel alarmed. There is official hustle and bustle at the front door, then my father is wheeled out and placed in the back of the ambulance and taken away.

Later and over the course of several days, and in bits and

pieces of information that never quite add up in my head, I come to learn that the reason my father looked so preoccupied in the car that day was that he'd had a seizure on the floor of the wood-working shop. And then another after dinner—the explanation behind the strange scene that evening in the dining room.

And he has had these seizures because he has a problem—an inflammation in his brain, is how it's explained to me—that has something to do with a black mole he had removed from his arm some time in the past. And now he is in the hospital and can't move the right side of his body and can only speak in a mumble and the reason I don't sort any of this out at first, the reason the details are a little hazy to me is that—incredibly—I don't feel I really have to know. I am not hysterical or even afraid. He's my father. He's going to be all right. Whatever happens to be wrong with him at the moment, he's going to recover. After all. He's my father.

But instead of getting better, over the course of the next five and a half months he withers away. The malignant brain tumor—a metastatic offshoot of melanoma—that comes close to killing him within two weeks of the initial seizure (there were several more during the course of the summer) will be momentarily held at bay by steroids, just now being introduced to fight cancer. He will regain his speech, feeling in his right side. The price will be a slow and undignified rather than a quick death. The steroids will drain him of strength and cause him to bloat with edema. The muscular physique of which he has been sometimes ridiculously proud will waste away. He will lose what hair he has left, grow weak, peevish, infantile.

In the process, something strange will happen. I come to pity him. The man I once feared and loved and raged against inside my head, I feel sorry for. My father.

Of all the events of that summer detailing his downward progression—and our role change—two stand out. The first is just a fleeting image. At a lakeside beach in New York State my father shuffles down to the water to wade for a few minutes. On the way back to the beach umbrella he needs to sit under because he's not supposed to be in direct sunlight, he spots a couple of pretty young women sunbathing. By now his muscle tone is gone, his legs and arms are hairless spindles, his stomach sags. Nonetheless, I see him look sidelong at the women and try to suck in his gut. I look away, quickly.

The other occurs a few weeks later. My father is in the back yard, sitting under an umbrella by the lake. Michael, my youngest brother, and a neighbor kid named Artie Frank have climbed to a tree house atop a 60 foot oak growing on a small spit of land directly across from our house.

Somehow Michael manages to lose his balance and falls to earth. My father, despite all his former pride in being the protector of his family, can only call out fretfully as others run to see if Michael is all right. Miraculously, he survives the fall, and my father sinks back into the lounge chair, exhausted by the excitement.

But even though I come to pity him, I will not come to accept that he is going to die. Not until the very last day of his life. That afternoon, unusually warm for mid-September, he is in the downstairs bedroom where he's been moved because he can no longer climb the stairs. A few days earlier, the bone in his right forearm, made brittle by steroids, broke, and his arm is in a cast. He is semiconscious, responding in grunts and gasps, his eyes glazed.

I am sitting on the couch just outside the bedroom and I can hear the labored wheeze of his breathing. I am suddenly very tired and for the first time I allow myself to think the unthinkable. I hope he dies soon, I say to myself, not with bitterness or pity but with a great feeling of detachment. For his sake, let him die.

That night, about two in the morning, he does.

❊ ❊ ❊

The first two days after his death, I am in an odd, dissociated state. I feel almost as if nothing has really happened. I feel—nothing.

But during the second night of the wake this unnatural composure begins to waver, then cracks altogether. Standing over the casket, I break down and begin wailing. I have to be dragged away.

Back home I am lying on my bed when waves of sobbing suddenly overtake me. This anguish seems to be coming up from someplace deeper inside me than I ever knew existed, and after a few minutes I begin to get scared. I'm never going to be able to stop crying. I'm going to go on sobbing like this until I can't breathe anymore, until my heart gives out and the big black jaws I can feel closing around me snap shut and swallow me whole. I am not just fighting for composure now, I'm facing personal extinction, my own physical destruction. I panic and the panic has the effect of shutting down the sobbing, like a wellhead explosion blowing out an oil fire. I crawl back from the edge of the Abyss.

Since then I have sometimes wondered what would have happened if I hadn't, if I had given in to that darkness. Would I ever have returned? Would it have been better, in the long run, not to fight the feelings of rage and abandonment, to have lost control? Would I, like some imaginary space traveler, gone in one side of that black hole and emerged somewhere else in the universe, in another dimension, or time, when—having flown apart—I would have knit myself back together in a saner, more reconciled pattern?

I will, of course, never know. Instead of losing it, I end up struggling for years and years. At fourteen, without the spiritual or emotional resources to reckon with it, I suddenly have to grapple with the fact of human mortality.

✳ ✳ ✳

For reasons I don't entirely understand, certain kinds of radical loss—coming at certain times in our development—can have the effect of stripping life of its meaning; this is what people really mean when they say, "I can't go on without you."

Without the centripetal force of my father's presence, my family slowly falls apart. My mother struggles valiantly to hold things together, but at 41, with six kids ranging in age from 19 to 18 months, and no career to speak of, there isn't much she can do. It's beyond her. Six months after the funeral, Eddie—a brittle diabetic afflicted with guilt over his troubled relationship with my father—will suffer a total mental collapse from which he won't recover for nearly five years. Kevin, still luckless and seething with pent-up anger, will soon leave school and marry his high school girlfriend. A few years later she will run off with someone and take their two children with her. My brother Michael will get into trouble with the law, eventually lose himself in a wilderness of drug and alcohol abuse from which he has never really emerged.

I act out, too, but in different ways. With everything I believe in shaken or shattered, I go on to reject virtually all of it. I carry immense pain and anger inside me, an acute sense of alienation from my peers and an equally strong sense of my superiority: after all, *they* haven't suffered what I suffered. I declare myself an atheist—unconsciously trying to kill God in revenge for killing my father.

And I begin to read, wildly, everything that might offer me some clue to what I am trying to figure out while at the same time feeding my sense of alienated superiority. Each night I retreat into my room, close the door on the chaos of my family life, and read until three or four in the morning. I read Camus and Sartre and Nietzsche but also Plato and Aristotle and Aquinas. I read Greek tragedy and Shakespeare, Checkov, Ibsen and O'Neill. I read novels, Hemingway and Fitzgerald and Wolfe, Turgenev, Dostoyevski, Zola, and Flaubert. I haven't a clue what much of this means, but I absorb it anyway, as if through my skin, at a level that is not quite conscious and therefore all the more indelible.

I also decide, without really understanding what my decision entails, to become a writer. At first I'm attracted to the idea because it seems like an heroic way of life. Only over time will I discover it is also a way of imposing coherence and meaning into experience, of constructing an inner life and a sense of self. By a terrible irony, my loss—the most painful in my life—somehow transforms itself into a source of creative energy, a momentum that carries me forward and backward in time.

Yes, I would have traded all of it in advance to have been able to grant my father a normal life span. But that is not, and never was, within my power. I also know, again in ways I can't explain, that what powers I do possess somehow derive from the impact of his death.

But this is just one of the many mysteries awaiting me the day Kevin and I, like figures in a medieval painting, pause over our harrows and ponder once again the irresolvable mystery that is my father.

Richard Broderick. *Most Americans have a mental image of New Jersey as a state deep in oil refineries and crumbling cities, but in truth most of the state is quite bucolic. Certainly the community where I grew up was a green and pleasant place, with wooded hills and several small lakes, the largest of which lapped my backyard.*

Until I was 14, my life was largely idyllic. Summers I spent swimming or playing ball or roaming the woods with friends. My family was large, intense, active, funny, and extremely interesting—sometimes too much so. I had the good fortune of growing up in close contact with both sets of grandparents and a big clan of cousins, uncles, aunts.

All of that—all—came to an abrupt halt with my father's death. For me, it was at once the end of childhood and the beginning of something else, a journey, I suppose, that I will never finish.

Photo by Andra Van Kempen

BILL MEISSNER

Fathers

The Tug of War

M Y FATHER WAS a lawn mower. His scent was not fresh but pungent, and his lines were straight, even, the grass always cut in columns so straight you could measure the horizon by them. You could keep time by him, too—his steady gait as he walked up the stairway, the few floorboards he hadn't fixed creaking faintly under his weight. You could keep time by him, standing in the doorway, drumming his fingers on the molding, looking not at me but off into a corner of my bedroom, then announcing that we were going to mow the lawn.

I never understood the logic behind lawn mowing in those days. I just knew that it always happened at the wrong time. He had the uncanny knack—or maybe it was more like a conscious plan—to begin the lawn mowing detail on Friday evenings after dinner, when I was just about to go out. I knew a '52 Rambler waited outside for me to drive; my buddies from high school scanned the street for me as they leaned against the pillars of their porches, carving their initials in the wood. And there were girls, their long legs stepping out of the north shore of the lake, girls towelling their bare glistening shoulders dry in the dusk as they stood at the edge of the beach. These thoughts were calling me, and I found myself leaning toward them in my white t-shirt, and always, at that moment, my father was standing there: a thick brick wall suddenly blocking my open window.

His voice grated against the plaster of the room: "I want to get it done before the weekend."

My shrug must have bothered him as I stared at the parallel striped pattern on my bedspread. I suppose there was a look of irritation on my face, too, but because he wasn't staring right at me but at the tiny, spreading cracks in the plaster in the corner of my room, he probably didn't see it.

I usually countered his lawnmowing orders with something like, "I was just going out."

"Well, you're not," he'd retort, his words chiseled, stony.

As he stood there, I thought of that old mower: its tan enamel oil-stained, its underside a dark green, plastered with the wet grass. I thought of that mower: at times, its hollow bar seemed to pull at me as I paced the half-acre behind our house. Other times, when I was nearly finished, the whole mower seemed to gain weight and it slowed me down as I pushed at it to go faster.

❀ ❀ ❀

That Friday evening, the impasse reached, we each stood in our silences a moment; my silence was thick and dark, like a pool of oil. His silence must have been like a father's net: all the knots too tight and wanting to loosen a little, but afraid. He turned his stocky body and walked slowly down the stairway, knowing full well that I'd follow him, which I always did. I might take my tee-shirt off, wad it up into a ball and throw it to the floor first, but I'd follow him.

He was wearing his undershirt and workpants, and as I

walked behind him, I began to see my life in the future. I thought about how every step I took on that creaking stairway was like another genuflection, another nod of agreement to his plan, another cower to his rule. I saw a quick vision of myself someday, in an undershirt and workpants, walking down some creaking stairway toward a paint-chipped tool shed.

So when I got to the base of the stairs and watched his wide silhouette cross the window shades toward the shed in the back yard, I grabbed my keys from the end table, stepped out the door, turned the opposite direction and ran toward my car.

The Rambler's door opened easily for me, its hinges oiled. It was my car, it always had been. My father had bought it for me at an Army surplus auction for my sixteenth birthday. I gave it a tune-up and repainted it, covering its Army green with a layer of metallic red so the car had some semblance of coolness for a seventeen year-old. When I turned the key, the car started quickly. Backing out past his tan Chrysler parked on the grass, I saw him come around the corner with the lawn mower and just stop there. But he didn't look up—just kept his eyes fixed on the ground in front of him, as if he'd just come onto a patch of bristling weeds made of iron, weeds he knew his sputtering mower could never cut.

"Blade's too dull," I'd often complain to him after I'd mow. I noticed that the weeds and long grass simply bent over beneath it, then sprung back up again in a few days. "Can't we get this thing sharpened or something?"

"That blade's fine," he'd always respond. "You just have to slow down a little when you mow." Then he'd put one foot on the flat top of the Briggs and Stratton motor, a motor that never quit on him, he often told me, not once. A motor that started on first pull in spring even after sitting in the shed for a long, cold winter.

❉ ❉ ❉

That night I backed into the street, and drove away without looking at him. *He can keep his damn mower,* I thought. *He can mow all night, for all I care. He can mow every lawn in town.* I drove alone for a half hour along the deserted county roads near the lake; the sun had set and the glow of my headlights seemed to be leading me where I needed to go. I rolled down the window, turned up the radio volume and let the rock 'n roll songs blare through the distorted speakers and into the countryside, each song an anthem for my freedom.

Then I saw a pair of lights flare up behind me. I expected the car to pass me as it gained on me quickly, but it didn't. As the car got closer, I recognized its silhouetted shape. It was the Chrysler, and inside, my father was that form, hunched toward the steering wheel. He stayed behind me, flashing his brights. I took my foot off the brake pedal and my Rambler coasted to the gravel shoulder of the road and he eased his car close to mine. I clicked the ignition off. For a few seconds, I felt short of breath, as if I had just run the mile in gym class, and I could hear, through the dash, the hot engine of the Rambler ticking as it cooled. He stepped out of the car and like some state trooper walked slowly toward me, following the white line at the edge of the asphalt road. As he reached my rear fender, I started the car and floored it without even thinking. My old Rambler wasn't used to such acceleration, and the six cylinders stuttered beneath the hood a moment, the car hesitating, and then it took off like I knew it could, spinning up a cloud of gravel dust around my father.

I knew the Chrysler had guts, and that beast could do nearly a hundred and ten on the open stretch of asphalt where my father took me once, but I didn't care. I didn't know where I was going; I was just trying to lose my father, lose him, leave him far behind with his world of orders and lawn mowers and straight columns.

In the rear view mirror I saw his headlights closing the gap of darkness behind me. In seconds his headlights edged within inches of my bumper, and I began to sweat as I glanced into the rear view mirror, then back at my speedometer, which read 85, then into the mirror again. I was desperate, and I knew that after what I'd just done there could be no slowing, no turning back. The Rambler didn't seem to have any power left; still, I kept pushing hard on the floored accelerator until I felt as though I might break through the floorboards and up to my knee.

It was then that I noticed another set of headlights behind me, and, a few seconds later, a red cherry light stung my eyes.

I gasped and yanked my foot off the accelerator, as my father must have done at the same moment, because our cars, as if they were doing a dance, coasted gradually to a stop, keeping the same, even distance between them.

I stepped out of my car and walked on shaky legs back to my father, who stood on the shoulder of the road next to the cop.

"What's goin' on here, Dwight?" Rollie asked my father. He was a county cop we'd known around town for years, and my father was a member of the Knights of Columbus with him.

My father looked guilty, the shadows carving deep creases in his skin. Then, as Rollie pointed the flashlight upward, I saw my father's face become suddenly fragile, apologetic.

"Nothing," my father replied, his voice suddenly calm, controlled. "The boy here," he said, then paused, faltering a moment, "the boy's having carbuerator trouble with his car. I tried to fix it, told him to take it out for a run on the road. Told him I'd follow him in case the car killed."

"You had to go *that* damn fast to test it?" Rollie puffed. "Sure looked like some kind of race to me."

I could feel the arteries in my neck throbbing from the adrenaline. I knew that with a speeding ticket—at this speed, at least—I'd lose my license, which I'd had for only a year. My father knew that too.

"Well, you see, the car only killed at higher speeds," my father said. "Runs like a top on city streets, though." He managed a chuckle.

Rollie shook his head as he shined his flashlight at our licenses, making them both appear thin and translucent. "I don't know who the heck to ticket here, the lead car or the one who was following." He paused a few seconds, rubbing his double chin as if to find a solution. "So I'm not going to give neither of you one." He shifted his stare toward my father. "Just take this as a warning. You can't be out racing like a couple of teenagers. You better take care of this boy, and clear up the problem on that Rambler some other way. This ain't the Bonneville Salt Flats, you know."

❋ ❋ ❋

After the squad car drove away, my father didn't say anything, just tipped his head back, looked at the opaque sky as if he was recognizing something, and then laughed a quick, sharp laugh.

At that moment I felt that maybe everything was okay. "Thanks, Dad," I said, trying to sound confident, though my nerves were tangled and sparking like crossed distributor wires. "I mean, for bailing me out."

He turned toward me and opened his big palm. "Give me the keys," he said, his voice flat, like a piece of tin.

"Huh?"

"Give me the damn keys. You're walking home." He took a step closer to me and spoke through gritted teeth. "You're walking until you're eighteen."

I lifted the keys, attached to a leather strap, from my pocket, lowered them into his palm, and he clenched them. But I didn't let them go, feeling a sudden rush of anger. And thinking about the ten long miles back to town, I still held on to my end of the leather strap.

In those few seconds, as we both pulled on the keys, I could feel the whole world pulling on us like a tug of war—the whole world pulling us together, pulling us apart at the same time.

Then the strangest thing happened. He seemed to release his grip and he let them go, and the keys jingled into my fist. He closed his eyes with an expression I didn't quite understand. In the dim light I tried to read his face, but I just couldn't figure it out. That was the thing about my father—I was always on the verge of understanding him, but I never quite could.

He pivoted toward the Chrysler, opened the driver's side, paused, leaned on the wide tan door and looked at me, as if he were about to say something. Then he slipped behind the wheel.

I thought for a moment of the tan lawn mower he must have left in the middle of our front lawn. I pictured it in a field: stained with oil, low on gas, sputtering, my father trying to cut a straight path through the long weeds and not really knowing how.

That night, the layer of clouds was thick, impenetrable, and no stars or moon appeared as we drove toward the horizon on that county road. When I glanced in the rear view mirror, the asphalt road was pitch black.

I turned the radio down and followed closely behind my father's car as our lights cut a column through the darkness. At one point, his Chrysler seemed to hesitate a little, and I concentrated on keeping an even distance between our two cars. Not too far back, not too close. All the while, I couldn't help but focus on the taillights, and wonder just how long I'd follow them, and how far, their steady red eyes neither angry nor forgiving, but simply watching me all the way back to town.

One Egg at a Time

My father's large, bony hand was not perfect. Nor were his knuckles, protruding more with each year of work in a factory assembly line. His hand was not perfect, the veins beginning to show through the translucence of skin like hesitant, uncertain highways.

Late that Saturday morning, my father stood in front of an aluminum pan at the old Philco stove, slowly making my breakfast. I slumped in a chair at the kitchen table in my rumpled teeshirt, yawning, waiting for him. I was somehow irritated with his actions, wanted him to hurry up with the breakfast so I could leave the house and meet my buddies. Steam from the coffee pot, brewing since six a.m., rose, and the scent swirled, faintly pungent, in my nostrils, and my father, balding and overweight in his white undershirt and brown trousers, cracked an egg against the porcelain surface of the old Philco stove.

It didn't occur to me then that the egg is a perfect shape. But it occurs to me now: An egg has its own beauty, its own inner strength; if you ever hold an egg lengthwise between your thumb and index finger, you'll never be able to crush it. Not even the strongest person can crack an egg while holding it by its ends, the lines of the egg too exact and streamlined and strong.

When my father cracked the egg, he turned it on its side, where he knew it was weaker, its shell thinnest. Everything has its vulnerable side; he knew that. He knew that, especially after years of bringing up a son, of telling me the rules he knew I might not obey. After all, I was seventeen, and on the verge of something I didn't understand. Somehow he knew I'd ignore those rules about driving too fast, chugging slippery cans of beer in the car with my buddies, staying out past my curfew. He wasn't surprised that I'd get caught by the coach, sneaking Kools behind the brick wall of the high school. Somehow he knew that I'd throw stones at distant windows that were out of my range and that I'd hit them anyway.

But he never let on what he knew that late Saturday morning, my mother gone to the laundromat, when he made me those eggs. He didn't lecture me, even though I came home two hours past curfew and slept until eleven, even though I knew he was up at his usual six a. m., angry and feeling the slow ache of a son pulling away from him. Instead, he just did what the moment called for: cracked an egg on the side of a stove and let the yolk pour carefully into the pan without breaking. It irritated me that he always had to be so methodical. But he told me once that the eggs would fry better that way, that some things were better if you dealt with them slowly, one thing at a time. I remember feeling impatient that morning, but mostly my head was swirling with images from the night before: the loud squeal of the rock guitars at the school dance, the smooth oval faces of girls and the metallic taste of the sweaty cans of beer behind the Woolen Mills. Then my thoughts jumped ahead to next week's football game, to what clothes I'd wear that afternoon and when I'd meet my buddy Tommy at the soda fountain where we'd hang out, sipping cherry Cokes and listening to the click and bing of the pinball machines. My head filled with every thought except what was happening at that moment: my father, leaning toward that stove, lifting the lid on the pan to check the single egg, which began to sizzle in the butter as the burner heated.

❊ ❊ ❊

We didn't talk while he made my breakfast that morning. While the egg cooked, he glanced up at the bare plaster walls of the room that rose to meet the high ceiling. Then he walked over with the percolator of coffee, offered me some by raising it slightly in the air. I declined with a shake of my head and nodded at the milk instead. Milk: the drink of a boy. He poured me a tall glass, the white foam of bubbles silently bursting at the top of the glass, then poured himself another cup of coffee, black, carried it to the stove and glanced under the silver lid of the pan at the spattering egg, which was almost done. I remember seeing him pull his arm back quickly as the hot grease splattered against the skin of his wrist.

I could hear the vague murmur of the old Zenith television in the den, the barking of Mrs. Fenske's dog next door, chained in the yard where it wore a circle of dirt, and, in the pause between them, the call of one distant crow through the open screen door. Then I drowned out those sounds with the rock song still in my head from the night before—*The Animals* chanting, "We gotta get out of this place, if it's the last thing we ever do."

One egg finished, he turned his stocky body from the stove, carried the pan toward me, tipped the pan, and the egg slid onto my china plate.

"How's that look?" he said.

"Okay," I said, biting off a yawn.

"Does it look okay?" he said, looking into my eyes that tried not to meet his.

"Yeah," I muttered, wondering why he had to repeat.

And that was it. A first morning conversation, a one-sided moment of giving and taking.

I began eating that egg and in the silence of the eating, between the murmurs of the T.V. and the barks of the dog and the distant call of one crow, I heard the next egg crack—a quick, simple sound that seemed to echo off the high, bare plaster walls of the kitchen. And that sound, which might have been music, simply irritated me. *Sheeze,* I thought, *why does he always fry them one at a time? Can't he just hurry up for once in his life?*

My father, cracking the eggs one by one, tossing the shells into the brown garbage bag placed next to his feet. My father, taking his time, paying attention to details, probably noticing the beauty of each egg before he cracked it, its shape and proportion and balance, a marvel of nature. My father, probably wondering about what might have hatched from that particular egg if it were not taken from the chicken. And then there was me. All I wanted was to stand up from the table. All I wanted was to push on an accelerator and feel the speed press me into the upholstry, and go where I wanted to go, and to get there right away.

❊ ❊ ❊

A decade later, I stood at his gravesite in a clearing among tall pine trees. I stood there looking at his flag-draped coffin and listened to the sound of one distant crow. I stared as they lowered the coffin into the grave with chains and those few seconds lasted too long—at that moment I wished everything would pass and I could be in the future somewhere, wished I could be anywhere but right there, right now. At that moment, I realized I should have stretched out some of the other moments, not forgotten them so quickly. I should have slowed things down, savored their taste. I tried to focus on the sound of one distant crow, its soothing cawing. I tried to picture, for an instant, its nest, a neatly woven collection of straw and string with a few speckled eggs in it. Then the crack of the VFW rifle salute shattered my thoughts.

❊ ❊ ❊

"Finished?" my father said, eyeing my china plate where I'd just eaten the first egg. Our uncomfortableness makes us say lots of things for no other reason than we thought we should say them.

"Yeah," was my quick response.

Then he leaned over me, tilting the frying pan, and the second egg, still sizzling slightly, slid onto my plate.

I didn't understand that those few minutes might have been as close to perfect as any moment of my youth. My father's hands weren't perfect, but that moment was. And I just sat there, my elbows denting the plastic tablecloth, anxious to get going. I simply let the moment roll past me, in its oval shape, and then it was gone.

I hunched over that second egg, my fork clicking on the plate, chugged my glass of milk, then pushed myself away from the table and stood up.

"Where are you going?" he asked, his back to me as he faced the sink. He turned the faucet on and the cold water hissed as it rinsed the hot frying pan.

"Don't know. Just out."

He turned toward me. "How was that second egg?" he asked, his broad face trying to brighten a little.

"Okay," I replied automatically, walking toward the wooden screen door. I thought, in the back of my mind, that I should have said more, but I didn't. And I knew now that he might have wanted to say more, too. He might have wanted to put his leaden palm on my shoulder, but instead he just stood there, facing me, paunchy in his white undershirt, arms at his sides. Nothing could stop me from going where I had to go, nothing could stop me from stepping across that small, dirt-patched yard and into my future.

I pushed hard against the screen door that morning, then paused for an instant in the doorway, and inside that pause I might have listened to the silence in the kitchen behind me. Or I might have listened to the sounds outside: the barking of a chained dog, the caw of some distant crow. Instead, I only heard the door crack shut behind me as I hurried toward my waiting car.

Bill Meissner. *My book of short stories,* Hitting into the Wind, *was published in 1994 by Random House. Three books of my poetry have also been published:* Learning to Breathe Underwater, The Sleepwalker's Son *(both from Ohio U. Press) and* Twin Sons of Different Mirrors *(Milkweed Editions). I grew up in Iowa and*

Wisconsin, and am now Director of Creative Writing at St. Cloud State University.

I can best describe my process of writing/inspiration by using analogies to sound and light. Sometimes significant images or memories are like tuning forks perpetually humming inside me. All I have to do is listen. Other times, an idea emerges as a small crack of light that's shining through from my unconscious mind. It develops into a story. The writer's job is to expand that narrow space of light into a window, to crawl in, and then to climb back out with an armful of words and, ultimately, share that story with the reader.

MARGI PREUS

Off the Deep End

T HE LAST DAY Don spent in the attic was kaffee klatsch day. He awoke from a dream in which he was trapped in the basement of Our Savior's Lutheran Church. The house always smelled like that place whenever Melanie stoked up the thirty cup coffee percolator.

Don flung off the quilt made out of old silk ties, rolled off the mattress that was his bed, shook off his dream, picked up his scissors and got back to work. There was not a moment to lose.

The day he'd gone up to the attic had started like every day since he'd retired. He got up, ate breakfast, read the paper, and followed Melanie around the house, just, Melanie thought, like Oscar used to. He did not resemble Oscar in his looks; Don did not have velvety ears or sad brown eyes like Oscar. He had thinning hair and a thickening waist. He still wore the same style glasses he'd worn in high school. He still, even though he was retired and could wear any one of a dozen velour leisure shirts he'd been given, wore a white dress shirt which emanated a slightly sour smell left over from years of anxiety on the job. Not much of an outdoor person, he was not a warm, nutty brown color like Oscar, but had pale skin, so white as to be almost translucent.

He had followed Melanie almost to the top of the stairs when she turned to face him, so that he was obliged to stop, awkwardly, one step below her.

He looked to her like a man in a black and white advertisement in some of those old *National Geographics* still stored for no reason in the attic. "Don, you look like an old advertisement in an old magazine," she said.

Don blinked at her. Her friends, years ago, had said he "looked just like Clark Gable." Had he really, or was it just that he'd had a mustache?

She continued up the stairs. Don followed. She felt like she would slug him, send him tumbling down the stairs. She was angry with him for following directly behind her up the stairs, for wearing that rancid old shirt, for shaving his mustache, for just being who he was.

"You're getting underfoot, Don," she said, "like Oscar, remember him?"

"That guy that came to rout out the drains?"

"No, our beloved pet."

"Oh, right, *that* Oscar."

As usual, Mel thought, he was missing the point.

"You're always around, yet you never talk to me. We never have a conversation."

"Was Oscar a gerbil, then?"

"Donald, I'm talking to you."

"Yes, and I'm talking to you, too," he said.

"Maybe you need a hobby or something. A hobby," she said, "I think that's an excellent idea."

"Wait a minute. A turtle, right? Oscar was a turtle?"

Just to see if he'd follow, Melanie kept going. Since there were no more stairs except the pull-down attic stairs, she pulled them down and started up.

Don followed.

"We should go on vacation," she said, at the top of the stairs.

"We *are* on vacation!" he said, halfway up.

She raised an eyebrow. "*You're* on vacation," she said, wiping the dust off an old trunk. "I'm doing what I've done for the last 450 years."

"A cat!" said Don, sitting down on the trunk. "That's it. I know he was a cat."

"Okay, don't get a hobby!" Melanie cried. "Let's not go on vacation! Don't do anything! Just don't follow me around anymore!" Mel turned to go and Don stayed seated, a little afraid to follow her just now. He heard her heels clacking on the wooden stairs and then the distinctive sound of the pull-down stair pulling up, the snap of the springs, the clatter of the staircase folding up and the pop of the door closing.

There was a long, dark silence after the door closed. Don sat on that trunk in the dark (Mel had asked him to hang a lamp—he hadn't) and listened to a branch dragging on the roof (hadn't been trimmed). He could hear the steady drip of the downstairs faucet (hadn't been fixed). He was even aware of the downstairs clock not ticking (hadn't been wound). But other than those primitive senses, his was a completely empty head.

Slowly, thoughts came to fill it, gradually coming into a kind of vague focus. He realized that he could hear the kitchen faucet dripping, for one thing. How could that be? He discovered that a heating duct near him seemed to amplify sound coming from the kitchen. That was interesting.

He wasn't sure, but he guessed that Melanie was mad at him. Gone off the deep end, as he used to say about her. She had also stopped sleeping with him awhile back. He hadn't asked why; he figured it was one of those secrets married people had and he shouldn't pry.

He was on a roll now. He was thinking. He thought about re-form—his own reform. He could be a better person. Yes, it was possible! He could change light bulbs with more frequency, for instance. He'd scrub out those garbage cans, first thing in the morning.

He found himself addressing God, whom he hadn't spoken to in years. "If you get me out of this," he said, "I promise to get the car washed, inside and out."

He was awakened the next morning by a pale, thin light leaking in the dormer window. He paged through some old *National Geographics*. He thought more deep thoughts about God, contemplated man's inhumanity to man, moved on to what he knew about theories of planetary collisions and then on to coffee, bacon and toast. These final thoughts may have been prompted by the smell of these items being perked, fried and toasted downstairs.

His stomach rumbled. He thought about Native American vision quests, about fasting. He imagined himself on a high hill overlooking a broad plain. Ponderosa pines bent in the wind; below him he could see the dust lift up and spin across the range. Buffalo roamed. Antelope played. Melanie broke a glass downstairs.

"I know you're thinking about me!" she called up. "I'm wearing nothing but a black garter belt and a holster."

A holster? Had she said that? He imagined her downstairs rounding up doggies. "Yippee ie ti yi!" he yelled back.

"I'm going to the dentist," Melanie yelled up. "Do you want me to get you anything? An appointment? A lollipop? Novocaine?"

"Hey—wait!" Don started to yell, but he heard the front door slam.

"Okay," he yelled down to the empty house, "I'll stay here then." And he did.

He kept himself entertained. He took to thinking. He even started enjoying it. Eventually, he started rummaging around in boxes, finding moth-eaten sweaters and old ski socks with holes in the heels. He found a box of Melanie's clothes that had gone out of style and he tried a few things on. Why not? he thought (he was thinking now!) But that wasn't as interesting as he'd hoped and he put most of the things back. He slept; he ate casseroles Mel left at the foot of the stairs. He spent a fair amount of time with those *National Geographics.*

Sometimes he pressed his ear to the heating duct and listened to what was going on downstairs. This morning he heard Melanie's quiet movements: she was dusting down the stairs between the carpet runner and the wall; he heard the soft cloth thump, thump, thump down the stairs. Now she was going into the kitchen; he even heard the click of her heels on the linoleum crossing to the coffee pot.

She would be pouring herself a cup of coffee; the sun would be coming through the kitchen window so it framed the table. Her apron was blue, with splotches of purple, the room done in quick, sure brush strokes. She leaned back against the counter and brushed a hair from her face. Her face glowed pink from the sun, her eyes were made translucent from it, her apron reflected it the way a pond might, on a summer's evening. The light shimmered like a mirage on the kitchen table; it spilled over and onto the floor and ran across her shoes so they looked wet.

Don wished he were there, sitting at the table just so he could see it. It was a scene Don had observed a thousand times and never appreciated. It was like being at the Chicago Art Institute and walking by the Impressionists without looking. Which he had also done.

❄ ❄ ❄

That night he woke to moonlight shining in through the little dormer window, glancing off of something in an opened box of

Christmas wrap. It sparkled and shimmered, as if it were beckoning to him. He sat up in bed; still it twinkled. It might only be, he thought, a bit of shiny ribbon or silvery wrapping paper, and he laid back down. But then he saw a little spot of light on the ceiling above him, like a note made of moonlight, and he sat up again. "On the other hand," he thought, "it might be a forgotten Christmas gift, a gold watch, a diamond tie tack."

So he crawled over to the box and peered in, gingerly moving the paper around until he discovered the source of light. It was a pair of stainless steel scissors.

He held the scissors out in the palm of his hand and looked at them in the light of the moon. They were cool and heavy. They were beautiful. Then he looked at the stack of *National Geographics* right next to him, shining in the moonlight, beautiful also.

He began to cut. The only sound was that of the scissors slicing away in the quiet room, the soft turning of the glossy pages, the clunking of the scissors as he set them down. He admired the pictures he cut, and even the corners and edges, which came off in the shimmering shapes of crescent moons, pyramids, and winding rivers. The next day he found some gluesticks and tape in that box of wrapping paper and he glued and taped the pictures down. When he completed the work, he inspected it for flaws, smoothed any ridges or bumpy edges, held it out to take one last look, and threw it out the window.

❊ ❊ ❊

Melanie picked up the phone and dialed. She heard Tim's voice saying hello and she said hello back before she realized it was his answering machine. "This is your mother," she said. "Your father has locked himself in the attic." That wasn't exactly true, but it was hard to explain these things to a machine. "He yells things at me. 'Yippee ie ti yi.' He yelled that at me." Then she whispered, "I think he's been wearing my clothes. Not out or anything," she added quickly, "just trying them on. He's gone off the deep end. I think we'll have to put him in a nursing home." Then she hung up.

"Well that's done," she thought and she poured herself a cup of coffee and sat down at the kitchen table. She felt that she had sat at this table alone only three times in her life. Once when her children were small, the day they went off to kindergarten, once again when they went off to college and once more now that Don had gone off to the attic.

She listened to the traffic hum, to the branch she'd asked Don to trim dragging on the roof like a pirate's peg leg. She looked out at the snow gently falling. Suddenly, something much larger and more colorful than a snowflake fluttered past the window.

Maybe the shingles were falling off the roof. What next! She put on her hat and coat and went to retrieve the thing from the neighbor's yard. It wasn't a shingle. It looked, at first glance, like a grade school art project, but then she found herself not just seeing each individual picture, but gazing at the thing as a whole. It was a kind of jungle scene created, not simply of cut-out pictures of jungles, but with scraps of pictures of all kinds of things: a city skyline, a Buddhist shrine, a snowy pinnacle. There were all shades of lush and succulent greens, made up of automobile interiors, astro-turf, elm trees like the ones that once grew on the boulevard out front, green leaves composed of green words, maps, seaweed, frogs; verdant jungle foliage created from a field of soybeans, a John Deere tractor, Peggy Fleming's skating outfit. Perched in a tree was a toucan made up of pictures of Guatemalan fabric. The fur of an ocelot was made from russet potatoes, the tufts of his ears, shriner cap tassles, and his eye, the burning desert sun.

Without thinking very much about it, Melanie took the collage to the basement, laid it on the work bench and painted it with shellac. While it dried she built a frame—something she never would have guessed she knew how to do—out of pieces of trim Don had forgotten to mount in the downstairs bathroom. Then she hung it in her room, where it was the first thing she saw in the morning and the last thing she saw at night.

❊ ❊ ❊

Don made more collages, and as each one was finished he threw it out the window. There was a desert, the Arctic; he started work on a mountain range.

Then he found the photos. They were in big boxes with metal edges shoved under the eaves. There were pictures of the twins as babies, toddlers, children, teens; pictures of Don and Mel, even pictures of Oscar. So Oscar was a dog—he knew that—a smooth little brown sausage-shaped weiner dog.

At first he stared at each one, then he leafed through them rapidly. Like the flash of a camera, he remembered picking those warm little babies up out of their crib and kissing the tops of their fuzzy heads. He remembered wanting to squeeze them tight, too tight. He remembered going into their room the night he finished building the fall-out shelter. He stroked their cheeks and wept, afraid for them and the world they would grow up in.

Now the nuclear thing didn't seem so imminent. Well, it hardly mattered, the world was falling apart anyway—morals, pollution, acid rain, decaying cultures, vanishing species, disappearing rainforests. It was disintegrating on its own.

His relationship with his sons disintegrated too. Having children wasn't what he'd expected. Before they were born, he imagined himself holding the little guy (then all of a sudden there were *two* of them) on his lap and reading him the newspaper. When he tried it the first time, one of the twins tore out the crossword puzzle and ate it and the other one rattled the pages so hard he fell through, banged his nose on the floor and cried.

By the time they grew old enough to appreciate the newspaper, Don's lap simply wasn't an option anymore, and the three of them fought over the sports page.

He started cutting. And, pasting his children's faces down, putting his hands on their faces, his fingers pressing down on their foreheads or chins or even noses, made him feel connected to them again. The smooth, glossy photographic paper was like young skin and he felt as if he were touching them and in a more intimate way than he had since changing their diapers.

❄ ❄ ❄

Mel drove over the mountain range as she was pulling out of the driveway. She slammed on the brakes, jumped out of the car and carried the thing into the kitchen table, fussing over it as if it were a kitten she'd run over instead of a crumpled piece of paper. She wiped it clean and glued the edges down, and when she had repaired it as well as she could, she took a good look at it.

It was a mountain range. It looked a little as if someone had driven up the side of it with a truck with monster tires, but under that, it was, like the collages before it, breath-taking. Dramatic mountains swept up to meet the sky which was several shades of deepening purples, created from, Melanie could see when she looked closely, an Eskimo girl's anorak, Gorbachev's birthmark, a chiffon scarf, a glass of burgundy. A waterfall composed of snow and sky, elk antlers and astronaut suits tumbling and foaming down the mountainside and finally crashing onto boulders that weren't boulders at all, but people's faces. Her children's faces. Then she saw the faces were everywhere—the faces of birds, flower petals, parts of rivers' snow. They were mountain goats clinging to the cliffs. What did it mean?

❄ ❄ ❄

Don heard the pull-down stairs pulling down with a snap, clatter and pop. Then voices at the bottom of the stairs calling up, "Dad! Dad!"

He went over to the door and looked down at two grown men's faces looking up at him. They looked as old as he imagined himself to look. He smiled, waved. "Hi!" he said pleasantly.

"How are you doing?" Todd said.

"Fine," Don said. He turned and went back to his work.

They didn't come up.

He could hear the troops forming downstairs, going through maneuvers, manning their battle stations. He heard the huddle at the kitchen table, strategizing, discussing him. Words floated up: "senile," "Alzheimers." They discussed his mental health, the condition of his arteries, his finances. Don worked frantically, feeling, as he had never felt before, a wild, intense sense of urgency, feeling time slipping away from him. He felt frantic to reconstruct the world with what was left of it.

Melanie sat at the table with the boys, watching them devour a coffee cake and listening to them talk about their father in terms that made her hair stand on end. She knew the nursing home was her idea, but that was before the art projects. She wished they would just go home so she could sit at the table alone again.

She heard Don walking around upstairs. Pacing probably, like a writer searching for the *mot juste* in his garret in Paris. Starving, but passionate. Young, he wore a silk scarf he found in this attic room, a scarf once owned by Melanie, one, in fact, she had wanted to throw out, but Don had said, "Are you crazy? That's 100% silk, made by genuine worms." He was probably growing a mustache.

"Tomorrow," said Tim.

"No, not tomorrow," said Melanie. "The girls are coming over for coffee."

Don kept at his work, fell asleep, had disturbing dreams and woke, starting in to work again.

He heard the ladies come in, singly or in groups of two or three, their voices rising and falling, the twittering of their laughter like songbirds out of practice. Now they were in the kitchen; he heard the clatter of coffee cups on saucers, the tinging of spoons against china, the contented sighs after each had eaten one and several half-slices of cake. Now they were full and happy; the steam from their collective cups of coffee created coronas around their heads.

Their voices rose up through the heating duct, then a burst of laughter like a covey of birds exploding from a bush—so that Don practically fell backwards from it. Their perfumes mingled—lilac and nutmeg and cardamon drifted up the duct and into Don's nostrils. He felt weak. Suddenly, he longed to be there: the rich smell of coffee brewing, the percolator gurgling contentedly in the background, to be surrounded by these women with their round, rosy cheeks, their dresses, blue and red, striped and checked, a circus tent of color, perfumed and charmed, their hair shining, these women waving their hands so their rings and watches flashed in the sun, making their happy little full-of-cake sounds like puppies when they're nursing.

Then he heard the first pop. Downstairs, Melanie heard the slow clatter of the stairs unfolding and they both heard the final snap of the stairs, unfolded.

Today was the best bet, the twins had decided, while Mel was distracted. Besides, they had to get back to work. The boys started up, but backed down quickly when a bowling ball bumped down the stairs.

"What was that?" said Mrs. Iverson.

"Oh, probably one of my shoes falling down the stairs," said Mel.

The ladies nodded and clucked, wondering about Melanie's shoe size.

Then they heard the pattering of a can's worth of tennis balls, the clatter of a handful of golf balls, the thunk of a partially deflated football, a motorcycle helmet rolling and a couple of ping pong balls pinging down the stairs. When the balls ran out, Don sent down things with wheels: a toy dump truck tumbled down, came to a screeching halt at the foot of the stairs and dumped a load of shredded newspaper and mouse droppings on the hall carpet. Then a baby buggy with a broken axle bounced down the stairs, and finally, Don's old golf bag, the clubs inside rattling menacingly.

It was the golf bag that finally got the ladies to their feet. They had sat quietly at the table through the bumping, the clattering, chattering, tinging and clunking, but finally they could contain their curiosity no longer and jumped up and ran up the stairs to the second floor just in time to see the golf clubs launch like missiles from the bag.

The ladies quickly pressed themselves along the walls with Tim and Todd and watched as a T.V. cart, a luggage carrier, and finally five pounds of rocks drummed down the stairs.

"Hey! That's my agate collection!" said Tim.

After that there was a long silence during which Mrs. Sorenson looked at Mrs. Jensen; Mrs. Jensen looked at Mrs. Mortenson; Mrs. Mortenson looked at Todd; Todd looked at Tim and Tim put on the motorcycle helmet and started up the stairs armed with a golf club.

The others followed. They went up the stairs in single file, Todd and Tim to capture their father, the ladies to see what they could see. But when they were finally assembled in the attic it was not Don they confronted, but themselves. The ladies and the twins formed a semi-circle facing a semi-circle of themselves. Don had created life-sized replicas of each of them out of pieces of pictures and photographs. Shoes were created out of the ceiling of the Sistine chapel and duck decoys. Mrs. Jensen's unnaturally red hair was a volcano, Mrs. Sorenson's nose a banana, an amazing likeness. One of the ladies had King Kamehameha's ears, another the lips of a Chuckchi hunter, another a Salvadoran child's sad eyes. Mrs. Thompson wore the fur of a nutria on her head for hair, and Todd's mustache was actually a picture of Oscar.

"It's more like me than I am," said Mrs. Mortenson. It's what they were all thinking. Mrs. Jensen liked the dress on the cut-out better than her own. Her floral print dress had been created from pictures of flowers, sections of gardens, lilac bushes, rhododendrons and azaleas, and when she touched it she thought it gave off the perfume of hibiscus.

There was no cut-out of Melanie. Melanie wasn't there anyway. She was sitting alone at the kitchen table, head in hands, feeling horrified, humiliated, embarrassed, and strangely elated. She hadn't felt this way since the day she was married. There was a tapping sound on the window and she looked out. It was Don, hanging upside down, with his foot tied to a rope made out of what looked like old silk ties. He smiled and his silver tooth flashed. Mel ran out and cut Don down with a knife still thick with frosting. He crumpled into the peonies.

"Don? Don?" she said, not so much asking if he were all right, but asking, is it Don or someone I don't know? He stood up and hitched his thumbs in his waistband. For in the instant he sucked in his stomach and lifted his chest to get his thumbs under his belt, he looked strong and powerful and that bare expanse of white shirt looked like an invitation, like a sail billowed out, beckoning Melanie on a voyage to faraway, exotic places.

She threw herself on that shirt and Don put his arms around her. To him, the skin of her bare arms felt as soft as the silk scarf he sometimes wore around in the attic. And to her his chest felt the way a clean pillowcase feels to a tired head.

Todd, Tim and the ladies stumbled down the stairs, stunned, having confronted themselves in the attic. Don and Mel stumbled into the kitchen, stunned, having confronted each other in the peonies.

Nobody knew quite what had happened, but everyone knew something had been revealed to them. Then Mel quietly cut another cake and poured coffee for everyone. The group stood against the counters, ringing the room. The light streamed in the kitchen window, striking everyone somehow. It showered Mrs. Mortenson's hair with silver. It polished the frosting on the cake and replaced the coffee in their coffee cups. Melanie passed out pieces of cake and they all took a bite, the sweet taste of almonds lingering in their mouths. Then they all lifted their coffee cups in a toast, seeing their reflections just briefly before they swallowed themselves down, taking communion in the kitchen.

Margi Preus. *I am the co-founder and artistic director of Duluth's Colder by the Lake theater company. Under my direction, this comedy theater company has, since its inception in 1983, produced a series of live radio broadcasts,* A Midsummer Night's Dream, *a collaboration with the Lake Superior Chamber Orchestra, 26 comedy revues, a daily morning radio show, a broadcast quality video, numerous tours, four calling birds, three French hens, two babies, and a lot of stupid props.*

In addition to directing, I also write for the theater—and rewrite, including A Midsummer Night's Dream, A Comedy of Errors, Love's Labor Lost, *and* A Christmas Carol—*and have done so for several theaters.*

My fiction has been published in Stiller's Pond, Minnesota Monthly, Loonfeather, MSS *and other teeny weeny literary journals nobody reads.*

I live in Duluth in a little house overlooking the big lake with my two small sons and one medium-sized husband.

Writing is like collage making—putting bits and pieces of things together—things you've seen, people you've known, photographs that stick in your mind, conversations all jumbled together on a page,

*moved around, cut apart, glued, torn up, re-glued, and finally left
alone, sticky at the edges, not ever quite all smoothed down.*

It is possible I spent too much of my childhood cutting up old National
Geographics, *which explains why I think of writing as*

Near the edge

NO PREDOMINANT GROUP

Sun, wind, earth,

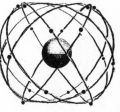

Valid only if postmarked by October 3, 1994

 Resistance to Fading.

and water

Eavesdropping

A way to throw an inkwell at the devil

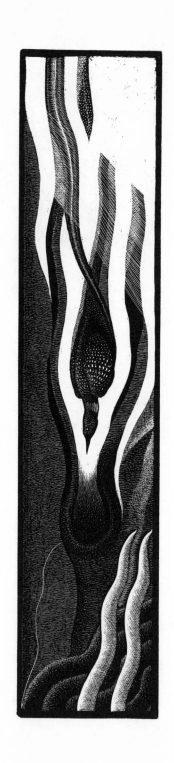